Metropolitan Government and Governance

Theoretical Perspectives, Empirical Analysis, and the Future

G. ROSS STEPHENS

NELSON WIKSTROM

New York • Oxford
Oxford University Press
2000

Oxford University Press

Oxford New York
Athens Auckland Bangkok Bogotá Buenos Aires Calcutta
Cape Town Chennai Dar es Salaam Delhi Florence Hong Kong Istanbul
Karachi Kuala Lumpur Madrid Melbourne Mexico City Mumbai
Nairobi Paris São Paulo Singapore Taipei Tokyo Toronto Warsaw

and associated companies in
Berlin Ibadan

Published by Oxford University Press, Inc.
198 Madison Avenue, New York, New York 10016

Oxford is a registered trademark of Oxford University Press

Library of Congress Cataloging-in-Publication Data

Stephens, G. Ross.
    Metropolitan government and governance : theoretical
perspectives, empirical analysis, and the future / G. Ross
Stephens, Nelson Wikstrom.
        p. cm.
    Includes index.
    ISBN 0-19-511297-0 (cloth : alk. paper)
    ISBN 0-19-511298-9 (pbk. : alk. paper)
    1. Metropolitan government—United States. I. Wikstrom, Nelson.
II. Title.
    JS422 .S74 1999
    320.8'5—dc21   98-36766
                                                        CIP
                                                        Rev.

1 3 5 7 9 8 6 4 2

Printed in the United States of America
on acid-free paper

To Delia and Anita

CONTENTS

Preface *ix*

CHAPTER 1. The Metropolitan Governmental Mosaic *3*

CHAPTER 2. The Logic of Metropolitan Government: Origins and Evolution *29*

CHAPTER 3. The Elusive Quest for Metropolitan Government *51*

CHAPTER 4. Metropolitan Government I: City-County Consolidation *68*

CHAPTER 5. Metropolitan Government II: The Urban County and Limited Regional Structures *88*

CHAPTER 6. Public Choice: An Alternative Perspective *105*

CHAPTER 7. Incremental Change and the Metropolis *122*

CHAPTER 8. Local Government in an Intergovernmental Context *149*

CHAPTER 9. The Future of Metropolitan Government and Governance *166*

Notes *175*

Index *193*

PREFACE

Throughout the twentieth century, political scientists and other scholars of urban and metropolitan areas have maintained a rather steady interest in the nature of governmental organization and structure in metropolitan areas, as evidenced by the voluminous literature on the subject.[1] In this regard, virtually every metropolitan area contains a large number of general-purpose and special-purpose local governmental bodies—on average about 100— including cities, towns, counties, authorities, special districts, and school districts, plus an increasing number of residential community associations. These associations may be appropriately classified as quasi-neighborhood governments, since they provide from a few to a range of services for their residents. Due to this bewildering maze of governments and quasi-public units, scholars have described the governmental structure of metropolitan areas as being either fragmented, fractionated, decentralized, or polycentric in character.

In the first half of the twentieth century, virtually all political scientists agreed with the premise of Paul Studenski's landmark work *The Government of Metropolitan Areas*[2] that the fragmented nature of local government constituted the major political problem of the metropolis and that simple logic dictated that local governments should be consolidated into an areawide metropolitan government. This metropolitan government argument, as it was soon labeled, maintained that a metropolitan government would be more efficient and effective, engage in better comprehensive planning, and deliver better and more uniform public services. Whatever may be the theoretical merits of this position, however, only a handful of metropolitan governments have been established in the United States.

However, in mid-century, a group of scholars, led by Elinor Ostrom and Vincent Ostrom of Indiana University, commenced a concerted intellectual attack on the metropolitan government argument. These scholars argued, in what is identified as the public choice or political-economy perspective, that the fragmented character of the governmental structure in the metropolis is not only defensible, but preferable to that of an areawide metropolitan government, since it stimulates competition between and among local governments and, hence, governmental efficiency, and allows the citizens or consumers of these services within the metropolis to better realize their public policy and service preferences.[3] Of course, the larger consequence of all of this is that, unlike their earlier counterparts, present scholars of metropolitan governmental organization no longer "dance to the tune of the same drummer" concerning what should constitute the nature of governmental organization in the metropolis.

The authors are of the persuasion that, as we move into the twenty-first century, it is imperative for students enrolled in an undergraduate or graduate course in urban government and politics to gain a comprehensive understanding of the nature of local government in the metropolis and its relationship to the larger intergovernmental system, to become fully acquainted with the various theoretical statements concerning metropolitan governmental structure, and to acquire insight into our limited experience with metropolitan government and our far wider experience with various incremental change strategies in the metropolis. We believe that this volume comprehensively responds to these needs.

As professor emeritus, Ross Stephens wishes to thank and acknowledge the support from the faculty and staff of the Political Science Department, its Chair, Dale A. Neuman; the Dean of Arts and Sciences, James R. Durig; the Vice Provost and Executive Dean, Marvin R. Querry, at the University of Missouri–Kansas City, as well as many others, including the University of Missouri Research Board for the support of earlier research. Just as important is the support received from my wife, Delia, in my continuing research and writing efforts with reference to this book and other academic interests. In addition, I wish to acknowledge the complementary support from and interaction with my co-author in terms of comments and sources of information that has been extremely helpful in this endeavor. Considering the problems currently experienced relative to the decline in funding and personnel, the Government Division of the Census Bureau has been extremely helpful in the provision of available information.

Nelson Wikstrom wishes to acknowledge the support of a number of individuals who have played a significant role in his professional development and have stimulated his research and scholarship on the government and politics of metropolitan areas. First, and foremost, I want to extend my sincere thanks to my faculty and staff colleagues of the Department of Political Science and Public Administration at Virginia Commonwealth University for their kind and generous support. I am pleased to acknowledge that it is a department marked by individual diversity, in virtually every sense of the term, and professional civility. Each of my colleagues has profoundly influenced, much more than they individually realize, the manner in which I think and write about government and politics. Second, I wish to acknowledge my profound intellectual debt to my co-author, who first introduced me to the subject of metropolitan government and politics while I was a graduate student at the University of Connecticut and who has continued to encourage and influence my research and scholarly efforts over the years. And, finally, I want to acknowledge the strong support and love that I have received over the years from my wonderful daughters Amy, Sarah, and Jessica. In addition, my individual and group discussions with them have provided me with many valuable and crucial insights concerning government and politics.

Collectively, we wish to extend our appreciation to Victor Jones, professor emeritus of the University of California at Berkeley, who read over the manuscript and offered a number of valuable suggestions. In addition, Nelson Wikstrom wants to acknowledge a special note of appreciation to Victor for graciously sharing his thoughts and notes about metropolitan government and politics with him while visiting at the Institute of Governmental Studies of the University of California at Berkeley during the summer of 1995. My visit with Victor was extremely rewarding, but all too brief. In a similar vein, we wish to thank Vincent Marando of the University of Maryland, who reviewed the manuscript and provided us with a score of insights and suggested substantive changes.

We trust that this volume will constitute a valuable and useful addition to the literature on metropolitan government and politics and prove to be helpful to our professional colleagues and students, and the larger public. As is customary in any work of this nature, we assume responsibility both for the wisdom that we have conveyed and for any errors that we have made.

G. Ross Stephens
University of Missouri–Kansas City

Nelson Wikstrom
Virginia Commonwealth University

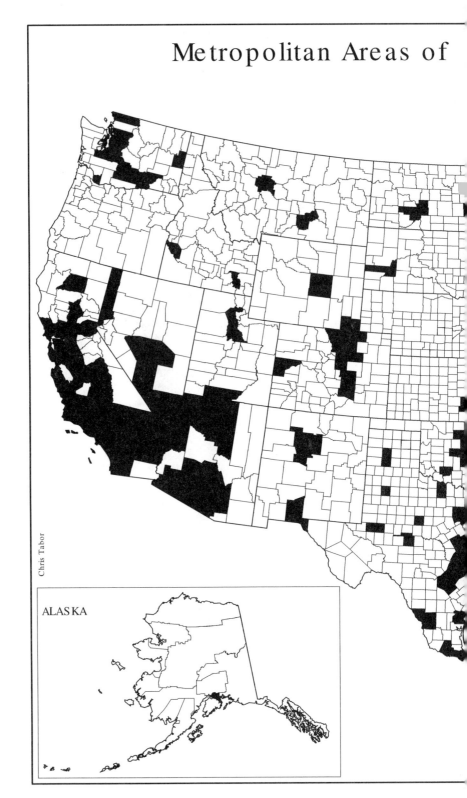

Metropolitan Areas of

Chris Tabor

ALASKA

the United States, 1998

(Maps are not to scale.)

HAWAII

Source: U.S. Bureau of Census

Metropolitan Government and Governance

CHAPTER ONE

The Metropolitan Governmental Mosaic

Will the city disappear or will the whole planet
turn into a vast urban hive?—which would be another
mode of disappearance . . . Is there still a choice
between Necropolis and Utopia?

Lewis Mumford, The City in History, *1961*[1]

At mid-twentieth century, a little over half (56 percent) of the resident population of the United States lived in Census-defined metropolitan areas, but by 1996 the comparable estimated figure was four out of five (80 percent). Metropolitan area population increased from 85 million to 213 million—an increase of 150 percent, partly due to the increase in number of metropolitan areas from 170 to 315 by 1992, and to 329 by 1998, with another 6 in Puerto Rico. For this same period, total resident population increased from 151 million to an estimated 264 million, up 75 percent. All of this growth took place in metropolitan areas, with well over two-thirds (70 percent) in suburban areas and urban fringe areas.[2]

Moreover, counties bordering deep water coastal areas and interstate highways, including circumferential interstates and expressways, seem to define the nation's new *lineal metropolis*. This is particularly true of interstates running through coastal county areas. Coastal county population increased faster than inland or land-locked areas with most of this change occurring in those bordering South Atlantic, Gulf of Mexico, and Pacific coastal regions. Coastal counties, including those bordering the North Atlantic and the Great Lakes, now account for over half of the U.S. population (see Figure 1.1). Excluding coastal areas, which also contain major portions of the interstate highway system, most states experienced population growth only in those counties adjacent to these arterials.

Between 1950 and 1995, the population of the nation increased 73 percent, and that of metropolitan areas (MSAs) increased 165 percent, while non-MSA areas declined by 23 percent. For this same period, coastal county population rose 165 percent, but the increase for the Gulf coast was nearly 200 percent and that for South Atlantic coastal counties slightly exceeded 400 percent. At an increase of 162 percent, Pacific coastal counties rose only slightly faster than that for metropolitan areas generally. Being more developed in 1950, only the Great Lakes and North Atlantic increased at a much slower pace, 32 percent and 39 percent, respectively. By the mid-1990s, coastal counties represented 53 percent of the U.S. population.

Figure 1.1 illustrates the comparative rates of population increase for the nation, its metropolitan and nonmetropolitan areas, and coastal county areas in various regions. According to a 1997 press release by the Census Bureau, a quarter of a million more people left metropolitan areas than moved in during 1995–96. This could well be the part of the

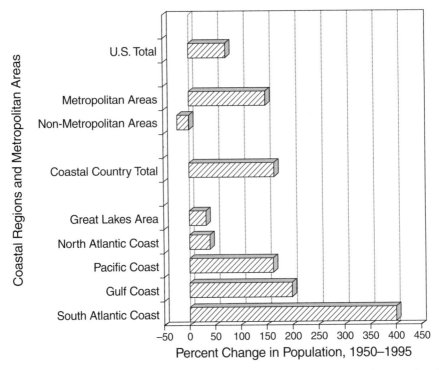

Figure 1.1. Growth of Coastal Counties, Metropolitan, and Non-Metropolitan Areas, 1950–1995. The definition of metropolitan areas and coastal counties has changed somewhat over the years, but the differences are not significant enough to alter the basic trends. *Sources:* U.S. Bureau of the Census, 1950 and 1990 *Census of Population*; 1996 *Consolidated Federal Funds Reports*, vol. 1; 1979 (p. 10) and 1997 (p. 39) *Statistical Abstract of the United States* (Washington, DC: Government Printing Office.)

process whereby county areas are added to existing metropolitan areas. The same thing happened during the 1992–93 period.[3]

Worldwide, urbanization is largely a twentieth-century phenomenon, though urban areas have existed throughout much of recorded history. Urbanization is importantly a function of the systems of transportation, engineering, communication, and technological sophistication, as well as the system of agricultural production and distribution. Contemporary cities and urban areas can be viewed, over time, as the end products of overlapping modes of transportation and communication: from human and animal power through the evolution of water transport; steam power and the railroads; electricity and electric-powered transport; the internal combustion engine in automobiles and aircraft; to the development of telecommunications, personal computers, and the Internet.

Each of these elements left its imprint on patterns of urban development, though some of the high-tech developments have yet to run their course in terms of the ecology of urban areas in the United States and elsewhere. Personal computers and the Internet may well lead to a further dispersal of the population into more remote areas of the planet.

Today, the heavy to almost exclusive use of the personal automobile for transportation in the United States has led not only to extremely high-cost travel for the individual, but to excessively high infrastructure costs for government in order to keep the system functioning. The failure of government to effectively control patterns of land development, combined with the expanded use of the automobile, has caused what some call the "spread city," the scattering of residences, businesses, industries, and other social and economic activities across the countryside into low-density suburbs. This, in turn, has led to other high-cost facilities, such as utilities, as well as escalating the costs of police and fire protection, traffic control, and many other public services. Moreover, vast amounts of good agricultural land are taken out of production annually by urban and suburban expansion, not to mention the urban development of coastal areas and other natural resources.

Cities, suburbs, small towns, and urban regions are a function of their socioeconomic base. Many cities and suburbs are highly specialized. Their economic base may range from serving as a retailing center for an agricultural area to providing retail services to suburban areas or highly technical services and production ("Silicon Valley" in California and Route 128 in the Boston area). Some specialize in various kinds of industry, including the defense industry; medical services (Rochester, Minnesota); government (Washington, D.C. and many state capitals); retirement communities; tourism, entertainment, and/or gambling (Las Vegas, Nevada, and Orlando, Florida); education (as with many state universities and college towns); residential communities of varied socioeconomic status (read: social rank); production of oil, gas, or other extractive activities such as mining; professional services; shipping and trade. A few even stake their economy on a particular religion (Unity Village, Missouri). Individual suburban areas are often very highly specialized relative to residential, commercial, industrial, and recreational activities.

The larger the city, suburb, or urban region, the more likely it is to have a diversified economic base, combining various economic activities. San Antonio, Texas, for example, combines five military bases and tourism, including acting as host to large numbers of conventions. Madison, Wisconsin is the state capital and the location of the University of Wisconsin, while Tallahassee, Florida is similarly situated with Florida State University and the state capital. The Pensacola/Fort Walton Beach/Panama City, Florida coastal area is the center for several military installations as well as tourism, retirement, and associated activities. Larger cities, such as Chicago, New York, and Los Angeles, are even more diversified in terms of economic base. In the United States, metropolitan areas as a percentage of state population are highly associated with gross state product (GSP), which is a state-by-state measure of economic activity.[4]

The Federal System

In the United States, urban regions are layered onto one of the world's most complex federal systems, with a national government, fifty states and several state-like entities, such as Puerto Rico, the U.S. Virgin Islands, Guam, the District of Columbia, and so on; 87,453 local governments as of 1997, with the number increasing over time; and an estimated 180,000 semi-private residential community associations (RCAs)[5] that usually provide a limited number of community-type services. Moreover, states and state-like entities are highly disparate in terms of the manner in which each organizes its system of local government as well as the characteristics of different types of local government. The number of some types of local government has changed radically over the last several decades, particularly for school and special-district governments. Yet there are at least twice as many local governments per unit of population in the United States as in other federal systems. Both nationally and for metropolitan areas, local government is continually improvised.

State/local systems range from the simple to the highly complex, in terms of governmental organization, and from highly centralized to more decentralized, though the trend for the first nine decades of the twentieth century was toward greater state centralization vis-à-vis local government. At the local level, RCAs, sometimes called "homeowners" or "condominium" associations, have, to some undetermined degree, decentralized and privatized local government–type services. At the central government level, change has been less unidirectional. The federal government has shown a long-term trend toward increased centralization, specifically in reaction to major crises like the Great Depression of the 1930s and the two World Wars, but after each crisis is past, it reverts to a lower level of activity—never quite returning to the precrisis level.

These changes and disparities are not always recognized by federal, or even state, government policy makers in the enactment of policies that affect state and local governments. Nor is the average citizen very aware of how these systems operate. In addition, local public institutions are divided into both discrete and layered segments when it comes to how the system affects individuals and groups of citizens. Public policy is similarly fragmented. Confusion abounds. It's fair to say that this situation all too often leads to distrust and disgust with the performance of government(s).

The Census of Governments

For the last four decades, the Governments Division of the Census Bureau has conducted a *Census of Governments* every five years, collecting data on different types of local entities. Local units are classified into five groups—counties, municipalities, townships (including New England towns, which are very different from Midwestern townships), school districts, and special districts (sometimes called special authorities). [Unfortunately, as of 1998, only the 1997 count of the number of local governments, by type and by state, was available from the Census; therefore some of the analysis of local governments only covers the period up through 1992 (see Endnote 2).] This classification is not entirely discrete, as states apply different terms to the same kind of local entity and multiple terms are often applied to the same type of local unit. States often have several gradations for municipalities and sometimes for county and township governments as well. Terminology may vary widely from one state to the next. One survey revealed eighteen different names applied to townships in different states.[6] Using the Census typology, the roles played by the same kind of local unit are highly diverse among the fifty states and often within a particular state. Confusion abounds—not only for citizens, but often among state and federal policy makers.

In fact, the Census classification of local governments ranges from moderately to seriously in error for at least fifteen states in terms of activity levels for different types of local government.[7] The 1992 *Census of Governments* indicated that 35 percent of all local governments listed have zero full-time equivalent (FTE) personnel. In other words, they have no full-time paid employees and their part-time paid employees add up to zero—entities one of the authors labeled "toy governments." This situation exists for only three counties and 2 percent of school districts, but applies to nearly one-fifth of all municipalities,

46 percent of townships (mostly in the Midwest), and 56 percent of special districts, for a total of 29,522 "toy governments." Three-fifths of all local governments with zero FTE employees are special districts (see Table 1.1).

As a result of federal personnel reductions—so-called "downsizing"—the Commerce Department, which conducts all of the various Censuses, lost half its personnel between 1990 and 1996. As a result, many reports are late and many others have been eliminated. In other words, considerably less information is now available, which means that much of the analysis concerning state and local government and metropolitan areas is limited to that from the 1992 and earlier Censuses of Governments.

The 1997 *Census of Governments* lists 87,453 local governments in the fifty states. The number declined from almost 183,000 in 1932 to 78,218 in 1972, then increased to the present figure by 1997. The decline was almost entirely the result of school district consolidation after World War II. The number of school districts declined from 128,548 to the present number of 13,726, down 89 percent. On the other hand, special districts and authorities, mostly single-purpose or dual-purpose entities, declined from over 14,500 in 1932 to about 8,300 in 1942, then increased to 34,683 by 1997. Moderate increases in

Table 1.1

DISPARITY IN RELATIVE ROLES PLAYED BY LOCAL GOVERNMENTS IN THE FIFTY STATES USING THE CENSUS CLASSIFICATION OF LOCAL GOVERNMENTS, 1991[1]

Census Typology of Local Governments	Low State	U.S. Average	High State
Counties	0.0% CT, RI (0.3% VT)[2]	21.9%	74.2% MD
Municipalities	16.2% NV	31.5%	57.4% NY (87.4% DC)
Townships	0.0% 30 states (0.2% MO)[3]	3.2%	52.4% MA
School Districts	0.0% 5 states[4] (0.6% TN)	34.5%	65.7% VT[5]
Special Districts	* HI[6]	8.9%	28.3% NE[7]

[1]This is simply the average of the average percentages of total local for three variables, i.e., own source revenues, direct expenditures, and fulltime equivalent (FTE) employees. This table uses the tabulation of the Governments Division of the Bureau of the Census without alteration (GF/91–5 and GE/91–1).

[2]Counties do not exist as civil governments in Connecticut and Rhode Island and are very inactive in Maine, Massachusetts, and Vermont.

[3]Of the twenty states with civil township governments, those in Missouri are the most inactive.

[4]Alaska, Hawaii, Maryland, North Carolina, and Virginia, plus the District of Columbia. In addition to Tennessee, school districts account for very small percentages of local activity in Connecticut, Massachusetts, and Rhode Island. Most states fall in the range from 25 percent to 40 percent.

[5]Vermont is a rather highly centralized state so local schools are relatively more important. School districts account for between 52 percent and 53 percent of local activity in West Virginia and Montana.

[6]The 16 special districts in Hawaii probably should not be counted as civil governments. Their total own source revenue was 1 cent per capita in FY 1992, with 10 cents from federal, state, and other local governments. The 16 have a total of 2 FTE employees.

[7]Washington State at 27.5 percent runs a close second to Nebraska.

the number of municipalities (+18 percent) and a moderate decline in towns and townships (–17 percent) occurred over the same time period. Some of the increase in incorporated municipalities is the result of the incorporation of Midwestern-style (weak) townships as municipal governments; a small part of the decline in townships is also explained by New England towns choosing to call their units municipalities. The number of county governments has remained virtually the same for the last seven decades, declining less than 1 percent, from 3,062 to 3,043. If recent rates of change continue, there will be well over 88,500 local governments by the year 2000 (see Table 1.2).

State Systems of Local Government

No two states have exactly the same state system of local government (SSLG), but there are some commonalities among the states in the way they organize their local units. There are five reasonably discrete systems of local government with some variation within the last three classifications. Twelve or thirteen states utilize some combination of these basic arrangements, depending on whether New York is classified as a conventional or combined system. Ranking SSLGs from the simple to the complex, centralized states tend to be

Table 1.2
LOCAL GOVERNMENTS IN THE UNITED STATES, 1932 TO 1997[1]

Year	Counties	Municipalities	Towns and Townships	School Districts	Special Districts	Totals
1932	3,062	16,442	19,978	128,548	14,572	182,602
('37)	3,053	16,332	19,183	113,571	9,867	162,006
1942	3,050	16,220	18,919	108,579	8,299	155,067
('47)	3,049	16,360	18,051	95,521	9,302	142,283
1952	3,049	16,778	17,202	56,346	12,319	105,684
1957	3,050	17,215	17,198	50,454	14,424	102,341
1962	3,043	17,997	17,144	34,678	18,823	91,685
1967	3,049	18,048	17,105	21,742	21,264	81,248
1972	3,044	18,517	16,991	15,781	23,885	78,218
1977	3,042	18,862	16,822	15,174	25,962	79,862
1982	3,041	19,076	16,734	14,851	28,078	81,780
1987	3,042	19,200	16,691	14,721	29,532	83,186
1992	3,043	19,279	16,656	14,422	31,555	84,955
1997	3,043	19,372	16,629	13,726	34,683	87,453

[1]Various Census reports for later years sometimes differ slightly from the data reported in earlier Census reports as to the exact number of local governments for a given Census of Governments year. The years shown in parentheses (1937 and 1947) are estimates.
Sources: 1957 through 1992 *Census of Governments*, Vol. 1 and 1997 fax from Governments Division of the Census Bureau, May 1998; W. Brooke Graves, *American Intergovernmental Relations*, New York: Charles Scribner's Sons, 1964), p. 699.

smaller in terms of population, have the simplest systems of local government, and a larger proportion of state and locally elected officials at the state level. The first two types are unique to a single state:[8]

1. *State/County Type.* Hawaii is our simplest and most centralized state/local system with three county governments and one city-county (Honolulu). There are sixteen insignificant special district governments that probably should not be counted as separate local units. The state receives a rating of 82 on a scale of 0 to 100 using Stephens's typology of state centralization for 1992 (with 0 representing a completely localized system and 100 where all governmental activity is at the state level).[9] The state government of Hawaii performs many services directly that are elsewhere delivered and financed by local government, including public education.

The city-county of Honolulu and the three other counties raise and spend comparable per capita amounts of money. In fact, the three other counties raised 8 percent more per capita revenue and spent 11 percent more than Honolulu in FY 1992. Hawaii's sixteen special districts combined raised a grand total of 1.2 cents per capita in own source revenue and spent less than 11 cents. Over 88 percent of the special districts' total revenue came from federal, state, and county governments.

If Puerto Rico were a state, it would be placed in this category. It has 76 municipios, which are area-type units like New England towns and which cover the entire island. The commonwealth is even more centralized than Hawaii.[10]

2. *State/Municipal Type.* Alaska is the lone example of this arrangement and is, along with Delaware, our second most centralized state/local system with a rating of 71 using Stephens's typology. Alaska has 12 county governments, called boroughs; 3 consolidated city-borough governments—Anchorage, Juneau, and Sitka; 146 other municipalities, most very small; and 14 special district governments. Special districts play a very minor role as they constitute only 1.1 percent of local government activity (measured by per capita own source revenue, direct expenditure, and FTE personnel per 10,000 inhabitants). Thirteen of the 14 special districts are for housing. Municipalities exist both inside and outside borough territory.

There are no minor civil subdivisions, but there are eleven unorganized boroughs. Unorganized boroughs are used as Census areas and, where possible, conform to the boundaries of Alaska Native Regional Corporations. There are no independent school districts. Eleven dependent school systems are administered by boroughs, twenty-two by municipalities, and twenty-one by the state government. Nearly three-fifths of the land area of the state has no local civil governments. In these areas, whatever governmental services exist are provided by the state, though a few services such as housing may be delivered by Native Regional Corporations.

3. *Southern System.* In the Southern system, counties and large cities and/or city-counties are the important local governments in terms of raising revenue and delivering local public services. Most, if not all counties in these states should also be classified as municipal corporations, given their levels of activity in terms of the number of services delivered, per capita own source revenue, direct expenditure, and FTE personnel. Public education is almost exclusively provided by county, city-county and/or large city governments, with one exception in Virginia and fourteen "special" school districts in Tennessee. In its purest form the Southern system applies only to four states—Maryland, Virginia, North Carolina, and

Tennessee. There are no minor civil subdivisions and, except for North Carolina,[11] these states make below average use of special districts.

4. *New England Towns.* For the six New England states, both towns (area-type units the Census calls townships) and municipalities are incorporated places. Cities are towns that choose to call themselves cities, but there is no basic difference in jurisdiction between these classifications. There are a few minor exceptions, where there is a borough located within a town. For the three southern New England states, virtually all local services are provided by town governments. There are a few combined school districts, but member towns retain control over appropriations for education and, therefore, school districts probably should not be considered as separate local governments. Vermont and New Hampshire have separately organized coterminous school districts. Maine has both dependent and independent school systems. Maine's independent school systems are coterminous with towns and cities.

5. *Conventional System.* The conventional system exists in twenty-six states and exhibits a variety of different types of local government with both discrete and overlying jurisdiction; that is, counties and municipalities—both usually set out in different classifications relative to the authority they exercise; school districts that are rarely coterminous with other local political boundaries; and special districts. The use of special districts ranges from minor to major. There are a number of subtypes within this classification relating to the existence and use of township governments. Twelve states have township governments, though in Missouri and Nebraska they exist in only 20 percent to 30 percent of the counties. Missouri has road districts in rural counties that basically perform the same service as township governments, maintaining minor roads in rural areas where there are no townships.

Seven states have townships in all or most county areas (Illinois, Indiana, Kansas, Ohio, North Dakota, South Dakota, and Wisconsin). These are traditional Midwestern unincorporated townships that perform only a few services, largely in areas outside municipal boundaries. Township services are often limited to maintaining minor roads and/or providing volunteer fire protection, or, in a few cases, handling some other minor activity. In Wisconsin townships, called towns, have been able to increase the number of services provided by creating coterminous township special districts.

Minnesota, Michigan, and New York have classified townships into two or three categories, one or two of which have authority comparable to villages or third- and fourth-class cities. New York has given municipal corporate authority to county governments.[12] Townships do not exist in fourteen states (Arizona, Arkansas, California, Colorado, Delaware, Idaho, Iowa, Montana, New Mexico, Oklahoma, Oregon, Texas, Washington, and Wyoming).

6. *Combined Systems.* The remaining states combine the features of two of these basic systems. Ten combine the use of separate coterminous, or mostly coterminous, school district governments with the Southern system (Alabama, Florida, Georgia, Kentucky, Louisiana, Mississippi, Nevada, South Carolina, Utah, and West Virginia). Only South Carolina has mostly noncoterminous school districts. New Jersey and Pennsylvania combine a conventional system with that of New England–type towns, where all townships have corporate authority. It is possible to trace the adoption and adaptation of state systems of

local government westward as settlement proceeded from the seventeenth century on, from New England and the old South to the Western states.

From the Political City to the Dependent City

In 1969, Henry J. Schmandt and John Goldbach outlined what they viewed as the major trend of the twentieth century relative to the autonomy and operation of local government. Using "city" as a generic term for local government, they divided the activities of government into two classifications: (1) the distributive system, by which they meant the allocation of resources, and (2) the delivery system, that is, which level(s) of government delivers public services. Each were divided into local and nonlocal (performed by higher levels of government). They pointed out that authority and autonomy are present for both the distributive and delivery functions.[13]

The "political city" existed during the first three decades of the twentieth century, with local governments performing both functions, allocating most of whatever resources were available and delivering most public services. From the early 1930s on, state and federal governments assumed greater responsibility for the distribution of resources, but most services were still delivered locally. This process later progressed toward two newer types of local entities. The "administrative city" still delivered most public services while extralocal governments were much more involved in the control and allocation of resources.

The other type that evolved Schmandt and Goldbach labeled the "contract city," where locally elected officials established tax rates and decided which services would be provided, but contracted with one or more other local governments for the collection of revenues and the delivery of public services, e.g., Lakewood, CA. The final step in this sequence is the "dependent city," where both distributive and delivery functions are largely performed by extralocal governments. In 1969, local government had not reached the culmination of this progression, the dependent city.

The number of contract cities has increased over time, but Schmandt and Goldbach did not envision two developments that have taken place over the last three or four decades. One is the increased contracting out of public services to other local governments. More important, in recent years, local governments increasingly are contracting with private firms for the delivery of public services. One stimulus to privatization is that neither the contractor nor the local government need provide fringe benefits or pension plans for the personnel hired by private contractors.

The other development is the massive increase in privately funded local organizations, residential community associations (RCAs), often referred to as homeowners or condominium associations, that provide some services to limited local areas, usually middle- or upper-middle–class residential areas. Compulsory fees and charges are levied against homeowners. The U.S. Advisory Commission on Intergovernmental Relations (ACIR) estimated the number of RCAs in 1989 at 130,000, up from somewhere between 1,000 and 4,000 in 1960. Assuming a comparable rate of increase through the present day, there were over 180,000 such entities by the mid-1990s.

According to ACIR, RCAs range in size from fewer than ten residents up to as many as 68,000. Seven out of ten are located in the western and southern states. Services often include building and maintaining private streets as well as building and subdivision controls and occupancy regulations. In other instances they may also include security patrols, trash and garbage collection, animal control, as well as street lighting, recreational services such as club houses, swimming pools, and tennis courts, and maintenance of other common areas. These private governing entities normally contract with private contractors and/or local governments for all of the services they provide. In many cases it is difficult or impossible to change the basic charter by which these entities operate because of the extraordinary majorities required to enact change. They are aimed at maintaining property values and a certain lifestyle. These private governing bodies further complicate the local governmental mosaic as well as local intergovernmental relations.[14]

The relative role played by traditional local governments has steadily been eroded over the course of the twentieth century, not only by the creation of RCAs, but also by the incursions of larger governments. Using own source revenue as a measure of distributive authority and direct expenditures to gauge service delivery, local governments have gone a long way toward what Schmandt and Goldbach labeled the dependent city. In 1913, local governments accounted for over three-fifths of all own source revenue. By FY 1992, the local role had dropped to less than one-fifth. In terms of service delivery, local government declined from nearly two-thirds to one-fourth over the same time span. Considering only domestic public services and revenues allocated to domestic activity, the distributive function dropped from nearly three-fourths to less than one-fourth; domestic service delivery declined from almost four-fifths to one-third (see Figure 1.2 and Table 1.3).

Related to these developments, state/local systems have become far more centralized over the course of the twentieth century. At the turn of the century, states were the least active level of government, and local governments the most active. Excepting World War I, local government dominated until the Great Depression. States more than doubled their relative position between 1927 and 1942, leveled off for a decade, then continued to increase at a reduced pace for the three and one-half decades between 1952 and 1987, dropped slightly, then increased somewhat into the mid-1990s.[15]

Figure 1.3 illustrates the changes in the relative roles of federal, state, and local governments over the course of the twentieth century, using measures that reflect government personnel, services delivered, and financial responsibility for public services. The figure reveals the dominant role the federal government played during the two World Wars. It also shows the general decline in the federal position since the end of World War II; the relatively stable position of local governments since that time; and the increased level of state government activity. It should be pointed out that government expenditures as a percentage of gross national product (GNP) were only 8 percent at the turn of the twentieth century. They increased to 52 percent during World War II, with 48 percent federal, and by the mid- to late 1990s stood at 40 percent, with roughly 20 percent federal and 20 percent state and local. Figure 1.3 illustrates the rise and fall in the relative importance of the three levels of government over the course of the twentieth century.

With the perceived federal budget crisis and attempts to balance the budget in the mid- to late 1990s, there is a very real question as to future trends in terms of the roles played by federal, state, and local governments. As the government in Washington, D.C. downsizes and shifts more responsibility to subnational governments, analysts must determine if the twentieth-century trends relative to centralization at the state level will continue or if

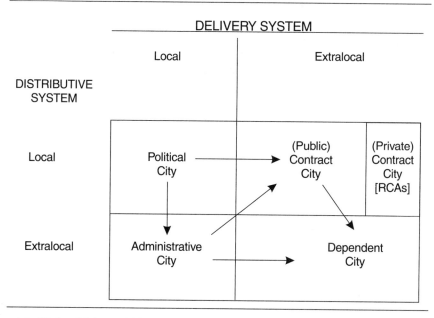

Figure 1.2. Updated Schmandt/Goldbach Conceptual Model. This sketch updates the Schmandt/Goldbach model from the 1960s to the 1990s so that it includes changes in local and extralocal activity and includes the massive increase in the use of residential community associations (RCAs), more commonly called homeowners or condominium associations, to deliver services that were once associated with local government.

states will download more of the federal shift in responsibility on local government. Some downloading has already taken place. Depending on the measure used, some twenty-nine to thirty-five states have below average revenue capacity according to ACIR.[16] For poorer state and local governments, downloading responsibility will undoubtedly mean cutbacks in state and local public services.

The central government role has expanded over the course of the century in terms of domestic activity, partly in response to the Great Depression and increased social services through the 1990s. Radical changes in the federal position relative to other levels occurred during the two World Wars. In terms of relative role, at least, states responded earlier than the central government to the problems caused by the Great Depression.

In absolute terms, as a percentage of gross national product, all levels have become more pervasive since the turn of the twentieth century, but the rates of change are highly variable. Overall, as a proportion of the total economy, government today is five times larger than it was at the beginning of the twentieth century. Averaging own source revenues and direct expenditures, the central government's proportion of GNP is 7.6 times greater than its 1902 proportion, while states are 11 times higher than the earlier figure. Local governments have increased only 1.8 times, though they started the century with a larger base.

Table 1.3
CHANGE IN THE LOCAL ROLE VIS-À-VIS LARGER GOVERNMENTS, 1913–1992[1]

	Distributive System (Own Source Revenue)				Delivery System (Direct Expenditure)			
	1913	1938	1972	1992	1913	1938	1972	1992
Total Government								
Federal	26.4%	35.4%	40.8%	55.4%	24.3%	40.5%	52.3%	54.9%
State	13.1%	29.0%	31.3%	25.5%	10.0%	18.4%	18.1%	19.6%
Extralocal	39.5%	64.4%	72.1%	80.9%	34.3%	58.9%	70.4%	74.5%
Local	60.5%	35.6%	27.9%	19.1%	65.7%	41.1%	29.6%	25.5%
Domestic Activities								
Federal	9.6%	26.4%	40.8%	47.1%	8.7%	32.7%	39.6%	41.7%
State	16.1%	33.1%	31.3%	30.2%	12.0%	20.8%	23.0%	25.4%
Extralocal	25.7%	59.5%	72.1%	77.3%	20.7%	53.5%	62.6%	67.1%
Local	74.3%	40.5%	27.9%	22.7%	79.3%	46.5%	37.4%	32.9%

[1]Illustrative materials for the years 1913, 1938, 1972, and 1992 are shown to indicate the changed role of local government in the American federal system. The years shown are to mitigate the effects of foreign war and at the same time show the progression of the distributive and service delivery system in the United States from local to higher levels of government. Own source revenue illustrates the distributive authority of government; direct expenditure is a measure of the service delivery system.
Sources: U.S. Bureau of the Census, *Historical Statistics of the United States: Colonial Times to 1957*, 1961; 1982 *Census of Governments*, "Historical Statistics on Governmental Finances and Employment," GC82(6)-4, 1985; 1992 *Census of Governments*, "Compendium of Government Finances," GC92(4)-5, 1997, (Washington, DC: Government Printing Office).

The Metropolis

> A metropolis is not an assemblage of
> individuals so much as a collection of
> communities in which individuals are
> assembled.
>
> —*Thomas H. Reed, 1934*[17]

The 1920 Census marked the first time a majority of the U.S. population (51 percent) resided in urban areas, but not until the 1930s did metropolitan area residents become a majority of the population. Urban, for this purpose, is defined as incorporated cities, villages, boroughs, and, in certain states, towns. In 1790, there were only twenty-four places with more than 2,500 residents and only 5 percent of the population lived in urban areas. By 1950, the urban population had increased to 64 percent, with the 1990 proportion at 75 percent. There were changes in the definition of *urban* after 1950 to include unincorporated

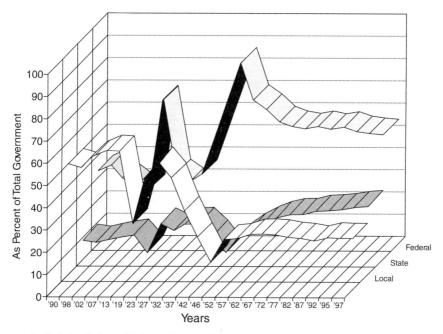

Years

Figure 1.3. Relative Roles of Federal, State, and Local Governments, 1890 to 1997. This graph uses Stephens's typology of state centralization (based on three subindices measuring services delivered, financial responsibility, and personnel adjusted for interlevel differences in inputs of personnel versus cash and capital) and a comparable index of federal versus state and local activity, measured the same way for the average state. Data for this graph are much less complete prior to 1902.

urbanized areas around larger cities and to exclude rural territory within the boundaries of incorporated municipalities.[18] By the year 2000, the percentage is expected to increase to 76 percent, assuming the continuation of past trends and the incorporation of another 120 municipal governments.

Any discussion of the government and governance of metropolitan areas must face the problem of how such entities are defined. The term "metropolis" originally meant "mother city" or principal center of activity. For the purposes of this exposition of metropolitan government and governance, the definition of metropolis is, of necessity, the one that the federal government uses to collect data on the nation's urban regions. Without going into all the problems this definition causes, most but not all who dwell in metropolitan areas live in the urbanized portions of these areas. Using the government's definition is essentially a pragmatic decision.

The definition of what is called a metropolitan area, more recently referred to as "metropolitan statistical area" (MSA), has changed somewhat over time. It is basically: (1) a county or counties with a core incorporated place of at least 50,000 population; or (2) an urbanized area of at least 50,000 population and a total of 100,000 residents (75,000 in New England). In addition to the county or counties containing the core city or urbanized area, MSAs may include outlying counties that meet specified characteristics such as commuting to work, population density, and percent urban. As of 1990, there were 245 MSAs, 16 New

England county metropolitan areas (NECMAs), and 54 primary metropolitan statistical areas (PMSAs), as designated by the U.S. Office of Management and Budget (OMB), for a total of 315 metropolitan areas, not counting consolidated metropolitan areas (CMSAs), defined below.

These definitions of what constitutes a metropolitan area can, at times, be quite confusing, as the Census also defines larger areas as primary metropolitan statistical areas and aggregates adjacent primary metropolitan statistical areas (PMSAs) and New England county metropolitan areas (NECMAs) into consolidated metropolitan statistical areas. In 1983 the designation of standard metropolitan statistical area (SMSA) was replaced by four terms. MSAs and NECMAs are described above. Consolidated metropolitan statistical areas (CMSAs) combine and define twenty-one of the largest metropolitan regions (seventeen outside of New England, three in New England, and one in Puerto Rico). The seventeen CMSAs are subdivided into fifty-four primary metropolitan statistical areas (PMSAs) and several NECMAs. For metropolitan complexes of 1 million or more inhabitants, these separate component areas (PMSAs) are defined if specific criteria are met. Local opinion must support the recognition of a PMSA. For the 1990 census, there were nineteen MSAs of 1 million or more for which no component PMSAs were established. Stated differently, CMSAs consolidate PMSAs and/or NECMAs into even larger urban regions. To further complicate the data, OMB has added counties and towns to some of the metropolitan areas since 1990.

In order to better separate urban from rural areas, the Census also defines "urbanized areas" (UAs). These are essentially unincorporated areas (outside of municipal corporations) with a density of 1,000 inhabitants per square mile or other urban-type land use that is within one and one-half road miles of the urban core (of 50,000 or more residents).[19] Unfortunately most of the socioeconomic data currently reported by the Census is for central cities and/or central counties as opposed to the remainder of the metropolitan area.

Nevertheless, the 315 metropolitan areas (MSAs, NECMAs, and PMSAs) identified in the 1990 Census are the basic units used to define the metropolis in the United States and the focus of these discussions of metropolitan government and governance. By 1998 there were 329 metropolitan areas, plus six in Puerto Rico, including NECMAs, PMSAs, and MSAs that are a portion of CMSAs.[20] MSAs, NECMAs, and PMSAs, as a totality, will be referred to as metropolitan areas or MSAs in this chapter. Again, as a working definition, "suburban" refers to all the parts of a metropolitan area outside the central city or central cities.

Ninety-nine percent of the 153 million increase in population between 1930 and the estimate for the year 2000 has occurred in the nation's metropolitan areas, variously defined. The remaining net 1 percent increase, about 1.4 million, probably took place in coastal counties outside metropolitan areas. The only region that has experienced growth in non-metropolitan areas since 1960 is the Mountain states (Arizona, Colorado, Idaho, Montana, Nevada, New Mexico, Utah, and Wyoming). By the year 2000, three-fourths (77 percent) of this increase in metropolitan area residents—118 million—will have taken place in suburban portions of these regions. Much of the growth of central cities, particularly during the last four or five decades, took place in smaller urban regions, while population in most older, larger core cities declined. The year 2000 estimate for suburban areas represents a sixfold increase over 1930, from under 23 million to over 140 million residents.

Coastal counties, containing many of the nation's metropolitan areas, added over 93 million out of a total increase of 153 million additional residents, thus comprising 61 percent of total added inhabitants.[21] Partly due to changes in definition, population outside metropolitan areas has been somewhat variable. Nonmetropolitan areas increased from 58 million to 66 million between 1930 and 1960, dropped to 51 million in 1990, and is projected to be a little under 57 million by the year 2000.

As of 1996, 211 million (79.9 percent) of the 264 million resident population of the United States dwelled in the nation's metropolitan areas with, 77.5 million in central cities (29.4 percent) and 133.5 million (50.5 percent) in suburban and outlying areas. Only one-fifth of the resident population (54 million, 20.1 percent) lived outside these urban regions.[22] In both 1991–92 and 1995–96, 250,000 to 300,000 more people left MSAs than moved in. This may be part of the process whereby additional counties are added to MSAs or it may mean that the newer forms of electronic communication are allowing more people to live farther from the urbanized areas.

The governing of metropolitan areas is further complicated by the fact that at least 34 MSAs and PMSAs cross state and/or international boundaries. Twenty MSAs, one PMSA, and one CMSA cross the boundary of two states. Three MSAs, two PMSAs, and three CMSAs cross the boundaries of three states, while one CMSA involves four states. The Washington, D.C. MSA straddles two states and the District. In addition, there are two instances where the urbanized area crosses the international boundary between the United States and Canada (Detroit–Ann Arbor, Michigan/Windsor, Ontario; and Buffalo–Niagara Falls, New York/Niagara Falls–St. Catharines, Ontario). In another five cases the urbanized area crosses the Mexican border (El Paso, Texas/Ciudad Juarez; Laredo, Texas/Nuevo Laredo; McCallen-Edinburg-Mission, Texas/Reynosa; Brownsville-Harlingen, Texas/Matamoros; and San Diego, California/Tijuana). As of 1990, 28 percent of the U.S. resident population and one-third of the metropolitan population lived in the 34 areas that were complicated by state or international boundaries.

Population and Representation

In 1990, minority population, particularly African American and Hispanic, was concentrated in central cities. There was an extremely high association between minority population and the population of central cities in each state (the simple correlation coefficient is +.94, which explains over 80 percent of the variation). The manner in which population is scattered among the fifty states and distributed between central cities, metropolitan areas outside central cities (which are predominantly suburban), and nonmetropolitan areas, distorts representation in the U.S. Senate. Suburban and nonmetropolitan areas are overrepresented, central cities underrepresented, given the proportions of state residents that constitute a majority or a plurality in each of the fifty states. Twenty-six states with less than 18 percent of U.S. population have fifty-two members of the U.S. Senate. The nine largest states, with 52 percent of the population, have 18 percent of Senate membership.

If it is assumed that population distribution relates to that sector that is most influential in terms of representation in state and national legislatures, then, the fact that central cities, with 29 percent of the population nationally, have a majority of residents in only two states (Texas and Arizona) and a plurality in another two (Alaska and New York) is important to the character of representation in the U.S. Senate and Senate leadership, which is also dominated by small states. Given this distribution, it is inevitable that central cities and minorities would be underrepresented in the Senate—and they are, both in terms of representation and Senate leadership. Suburban areas represent a majority of the population in eleven states and a plurality in another seventeen. Nonmetropolitan areas have majorities in five states and pluralities in another thirteen.[23]

This pattern of population distribution among the fifty states is important to decennial redistricting of both state legislatures and the Congress. Given that (1) state legislatures are ultimately responsible for redistricting their own seats, plus those in the U.S. House of Representatives; (2) some type of *gerrymandering*[24] is a nearly universal phenomenon; and (3) the single-member-district-plurality system is universal, it is almost certain that central cities, as well as minorities, will be seriously underrepresented in both state legislatures and the lower house of Congress. This situation translates into a decided lack of concern for the problems faced by the nation's core cities and ethnic minorities. In other words, the structure of the federal system distorts the manner in which urban residents are represented at higher levels of government. This situation can be critical from a public policy perspective.

The Governmental Mosaic

As seen by many, the "metropolitan problem" is the political fragmentation that exists in most MSAs, where there are from a few dozen to hundreds of discrete and overlaying political jurisdictions of municipalities, townships, counties, school districts, and special authorities. It is a rare case where a single local government has jurisdiction over the entire MSA for a range of local government services. Politics and services are divided into fragments; local units have jurisdiction that is usually quite limited both geographically and functionally. There is often multiple responsibility for the provision of a single service; in other instances, no local unit is responsible for a given activity. Revenue sources are similarly divided, with both rich and poor local governments. Residents may receive services and pay taxes and other charges to a dozen local governments. It is difficult to see where these monies are going and who is responsible for the provision of public services. This situation is complicated by the varied division of services between state and local governments from one state to the next. This is one reason that, over the course of the twentieth century, many have advocated the creation of a metropolitan government in many of the larger MSAs.

Between 1952 and 1992, the number of local governments in metropolitan areas doubled from 16,630 to 33,004 (see Table 1.4), partly due to a rise in the number of metropolitan areas. More importantly, it is the result of the increase in the geographic spread of MSAs, NECMAs, and PMSAs, with the inclusion of 740 counties, up from 267 in 1952, and the very large increase in the number of special district governments. Special districts increased 156 percent nationally, but for metropolitan areas the number escalated 412 percent, from 2,661 to 13,614. The number of municipalities in metropolitan areas increased from 3,252 to 7,590, while the number of towns and townships more than doubled. Only school districts declined, from 8,106 to 5,993, the result of a 74 percent decline nationwide, as the consequence of school district consolidation during the first part of this period.

Table 1.4

LOCAL GOVERNMENTS IN METROPOLITAN AREAS, 1952 AND 1992

Units	1952	1992	% Change
50 State Total	105,694	84,955	−20%
Counties	3,049	3,043	− *
Municipalities	16,778	19,279	+15%
Towns, townships	17,202	16,656	−3%
School districts	56,346	14,422	−74%
Special districts	12,319	31,555	+156%
Metropolitan Area Total	16,630	33,004	+98%
Counties	267	740	+177%
Municipalities	3,252	7,590	+133%
Towns, townships	2,344	5,067	+116%
School districts	8,106	5,993	−26%
Special districts	2,661	13,614	+412%
Average Metropolitan Area	99	104	+5%
Counties	2	2	+ —
Municipalities	19	24	+26%
Towns, townships	14	16	+14%
School districts	48	19	−60%
Special districts	16	43	+169%
No. of Metropolitan Areas	170	315	+85%
Outside Metropolitan Areas	89,014	51,951	−52%
Counties	2,782	2,303	−17%
Municipalities	13,526	11,689	−14%
Towns, townships	14,458	11,589	−20%
School districts	48,240	8,429	−83%
Special districts	9,658	17,961	+86%

*At −0.2%, this is an item too small to be shown in these terms.
Sources: U.S. Bureau of the Census, *1957 Census of Governments* "Governments in the United States," and *1992 Census of Governments*, "Government Organization," vol. 1, no. 1. (Washington, DC: Government Printing Office, 1957 and 1994).

Outside MSAs, special districts were the only unit to increase in number, from 9,568 to 17,941, up 86 percent. The massive increase in the number of special districts is partly due to their use to solve service deficiencies and financial problems in both metropolitan and nonmetropolitan areas. In many states, districts are relatively easy to establish and flexible as to the territory they serve. Some even cross state boundaries. Special districts tend to be located in more decentralized states and states where the state and other types of local government are less active in providing public services.

For 1992, nearly all the differences among the fifty states in terms of special district activity—93 percent—were explained by two variables, and both relationships are negative: (1) percent of local direct expenditures by other, nonspecial district local governments and (2) state centralization (Stephens Index, 1974 and 1992). Exactly the same relationship was found using 1987 data.[25] The use of special-district governments increases with a lesser degree of state level activity and a lower level of activity on the part of other local governments. Use is defined by an index of district activity composed of three subindices that measure per capita direct spending and own source revenue, plus full-time equivalent personnel per 10,000 residents with the average state having an index rating of 100.0. The range in district activity is from 0.03 (Hawaii) to 455.3 (Nebraska). The District of Columbia, which is not included in the average, is rated at 643.8. The number of special districts in each state is significantly related to metropolitan area as a percent of state population.[26] These data indicate that special districts are used to fill the service gaps left by other local units and the state government.

The 1,800 Census-defined "large" special districts are predominantly located in metropolitan areas. Though they account for less than 6 percent of all districts, they constitute 87 percent of all district revenues; 88 percent of expenditures; and 91 percent of gross debt incurred by these entities. Large is defined as those units with revenues or expenditures of more than $5 million and/or gross debt of $20 million or more for FY 1992.[27] Large districts' percentage of district expenditures in each state is negatively associated with state centralization, while the sheer number of large districts in each state is positively related to the state's special district activity index rating.[28]

Nationally, the relative role for each (Census) type of local government has changed considerably over the 1952 to 1992 time span. ("Role" is again defined as an activity index measuring per capita own revenue and direct expenditures, plus FTE personnel per unit of population.) Only school districts showed moderate change, with an increase of 4.5 percent. Municipalities declined by one-fourth even though the number of municipal corporations rose by 15 percent. With a 3 percent drop in the number of towns and towships, their relative role decreased 13.6 percent. The role of county governments rose 36.2 percent, while that for special districts increased 92.4 percent, with a rise of 156 percent in their number.

For the overwhelming majority of metropolitan areas, jurisdiction of local governments is layered vertically in terms of functions and divided horizontally relative to discrete geographic areas. The number of local governments in metropolitan areas ranges from what is, for all practical purposes, one local government in a few places like Honolulu to well over 1,000 in some of the consolidated metropolitan statistical areas (CMSAs) like New York (1,716) and Chicago (1,510). Cook County (Chicago) alone has 532 local units. Even a mid-sized MSA like Kansas City, Missouri–Kansas City, Kansas, with an estimated 1997 population of 1,799,000, has 446 local governments, with two-thirds on the Missouri side of the state line.

The average area, if such an entity exists, with a population of about 635,000, consists of 104 local governments—two counties, twenty-four municipalities, sixteen townships, nineteen school districts, forty-three special districts, plus an uncounted number of RCAs. Over the course of the century, this confusion of governments has led many scholars and others to look for ways to rationalize the way we govern our metropolitan areas (see, for example, Studenski, 1930, and Jones, 1942).[29] Yet many, perhaps a majority, of the citizens of these vertically and spacially demarcated communities seem most concerned with the concept of place as a method of maintaining a particular lifestyle.[30]

The Public Bureaucracy

Federal, state, and local government employment increased from 11.6 million to 19.0 million full-time equivalent (FTE) workers over the four-plus decades between 1952 and 1995, up 64 percent, not including the half-million elected officials, many of whom are part-time. Nationally, this represents a 2 percent decline in public employment per unit of population. In fact, private non-agricultural employment increased at a considerably faster rate than public employment. Over this period there was a rather massive shift in public employment tallies from federal to state and local.

Substantial misinformation passes for fact concerning the public bureaucracy in the United States. Statements by many conservatives, pundits, and others are far too simplistic. They are fond of denigrating bureaucrats and decrying the uncontrolled growth of bureaucracy, particularly the federal bureaucracy. Writing in 1933, Charles A. Beard and William Beard describe the same kind of bureaucrat bashing witnessed in the 1980s and 1990s:[31]

> Among the latest deliriums is that of waging war on the bureaucracy, full of noise and promise. Some of our very best people are doing it, usually without discrimination, for discrimination takes the edge off propaganda. (*Scribner's Magazine*, April 1933)

With certain provisos concerning defense and nondefense agency personnel, all of the growth of the public bureaucracy over the last forty-plus years occurred at the state and local levels of government. Nevertheless, the changes between levels of government and the emphasis on defense-related expenditures in our federal system are highly significant. Many who look at the changes in public personnel fail to (1) include the largest federal bureaucracy, the military; (2) allocate military and civilian personnel between defense and nondefense activities; or (3) consider the displacement of federal civil servants through the use of defense procurement contracts.[31]

Counting both civilian and military FTE employees, the number of federal employees has declined by 28 percent between 1952 and 1995. FTE employment declined from 7.1 million to 5.1 million over this forty-three-year period. Civilian agency employment increased 47 percent, but per unit of population declined by 12 percent; military agencies dropped 44 percent in total FTE and by nearly two-thirds per 10,000 population. Counting all the agencies and parts of agencies involved in defense activities, these data indicate that 65 percent of all FTE employees are in defense-related activities; only a bit more than one-third are involved with domestic services, with the latter scheduled for further reduction.

In actual fact, however, FTE employment by military agencies did not decline this much over this time span for two reasons. The years selected for this analysis start with our involvement in the Korean War and end in a year of relative peace after the so-called "Cold War." Military agency employment has always responded to hot and cold wars.

From 1950 to 1952, defense procurement contracts amounted to barely 20 percent of defense expenditures; by the 1990–1996 period, military-related procurement contracts for all the agencies involved in defense amounted to an average of 51 percent. For this same period, 1990–1996, defense procurement contracts averaged slightly over 55 percent of Defense Department direct expenditures. Defense procurement contracts employed hundreds of thousands—perhaps more than a million—civilians. In any case, the 75 percent constant dollar increase in defense procurement contracts over this period seems to offset the 44 percent decline in civil service and military personnel. Defense-related procurement contracts still represent the world's largest pork barrel.

The federal increase in nondefense personnel is due to increases in social services, but the decline per unit of population mostly occurred between 1992 and 1995. In fact, there is a very real problem concerning the ability of the central government to provide even the more limited package of domestic services with federal downsizing. The responsibility for some formerly federal social services is being shifted from Washington to the state and local governments, and there is a serious question concerning the ability of poorer subnational governments to absorb these changes—particularly states with below average revenue capacity, older larger central cities, and the more rural parts of the nation.

The calculable increases in public personnel occurred at the state and local levels of government. States increased their FTE workers from less than 1.1 million to nearly 4 million between 1952 and 1995, up 273 percent for a 123 percent increase per unit of population. Local government FTE employees grew from less than 3.5 million in 1952 to over 10 million by 1995—up 189 percent, for a rise of 73 percent per 10,000 inhabitants (see Table 1.5).

Growth at the state and local levels of government is hardly surprising. The nation has become much more urban and even more suburban over this forty-three-year period. Population in metropolitan areas grew from 85 million to 206 million, with over 70 percent of this increase in expanding suburban areas. The 142 percent increase in population residing in central cities and suburban areas requires additional services—services delivered by state and local governments.

Another reason for increases in state and local personnel is the increase in federal grants to state and local governments. These subventions escalated from less than $2.6 billion to more than $253 billion between 1952 and 1997. This represents an increase of nearly 1000 percent in constant dollars adjusted for inflation. Along with the money came strictures concerning the use of qualified personnel.

Between 1957 and 1992, there was an increase of 80 percent in the number of local employees per 10,000 inhabitants in metropolitan areas. Using "county area aggregate" data, central county areas increased employment by 49 percent compared to 155 percent in suburban county areas. Personnel in counties located outside metropolitan areas grew even faster at 195 percent. Given the limitations of these data, and the lack of data for central city versus the rest of the metropolitan area, there is reason to believe that suburban personnel grew at a much faster rate than county area data indicate.[33]

The enormous increase in nonmetropolitan local employment is partly due to a decline in population and the fact that federal grants to state and local governments are much less discriminating in terms of the activity levels of state and local governments in different states. States vary considerably in their respective roles vis-à-vis their local governments. The same can be said concerning federal aid to different types of local units when federal aid is compared to state grants. State grants seem to go to more active local governments. Federal General Revenue Sharing grants went to some 11,000 local governments with zero

Table 1.5

GROWTH AND DECLINE OF THE NUMBER OF FULL-TIME
EQUIVALENT (FTE) PUBLIC EMPLOYEES, 1952 TO 1995

Level of Government	FTE Employees (in 000)		Percentage Change
	1952	1995[1]	
FEDERAL Government	7,076	5,059	−28.0
Defense Agencies[2]	5,860	3,269	−44.2%
Non-defense Agencies	1,216	1,790	+47.2%
STATE Governments	1,060	3,951	+272.7%
LOCAL Governments	3,461	10,016	+189.4%
TOTALS	11,597	19,026	+64.1%

	FTE Employees per 10,000 Residents		Percentage Change
	1952	1995[1]	
FEDERAL Government	449.1	192.0	−57.2%
Defense Agencies[2]	371.9	124.1	−66.6%
Non-Defense Agencies	77.2	67.9	−12.0%
STATE Governments	67.3	150.0	+122.9%
LOCAL Governments	219.7	380.2	+73.1%
TOTALS	736.1	722.2	−1.9%
U.S. Resident Population (000)	157,553	263,434	+67.2%

[1]Data for the 1992 to 1995 period obtained from the Census internet site (www.census.gov) and from the
Statistical Abstract of the United States (Washington, DC: Government Printing Office, 1997).
[2]Includes the Department of Defense, the Coast Guard, active duty military personnel, an FTE estimate for
the military reserves, and the parts of the Energy Department and NASA devoted to military activities.
Sources: U.S. Bureau of the Census, *1992 Census of Governments*, "Compendium of Public Employment," vol. 3,
no. 2 (Washington, DC: Government Printing Office, 1994); *Statistical Abstract of the United States* (Washington,
DC: Government Printing Office, 1953 and 1997); and the Census site on the Internet (www.census.gov).

FTE employees, which are disproportionately located in nonmetropolitan areas.[34] During
FY 1992, as has been the case historically, the federal government gave over twice as much
money as state subventions did to special districts. In part, this reflects federal aid to and
stimulus in the creation of housing districts, as well as those related to agriculture and natural
resources. Special districts received less than 2 percent of state grants to local governments
in FY 1992.

One factor relating to the rather large increase in state government activity is that,
over the past four decades, most states have gone through something of a metamorphosis
by reorganizing their administrative, judicial, legislative, and representative structures—the
latter at federal behest so people, not cows or acres, were used in drawing legislative districts.

States have updated and broadened their revenue systems and assumed more financial and service responsibility compared to local units.

While there has been much less reform at the local level, both state and local governments have greatly improved and professionalized their personnel. Some of this change has been the result of federal mandates at the state level, and federal and state mandates at the local level. Partly because of these developments, for states and, to a lesser degree for large local governments, change has meant some parroting of federal administrative organization with the creation of "little HUDs," "little DOTs," and "little EPAs."[35]

Metropolitan Governments, Councils of Governments, and Assorted Other Local Entities

Historically, the normal method for city expansion has been annexation. But with the rapid increase of urbanization and suburbanization; the incorporation of suburban areas as separate governmental entities; and the spread of population to encompass outlying, already incorporated municipalities, annexation ceased to be an option in most large urban areas, with a few exceptions. Outside of New England and some Southern states, state legislatures have abandoned special legislation (legislation that applies to only one local unit of government), including the practice of passing state statutes that annex territory to a specific city. In most states annexation became a procedure requiring approval of voters in the area to be annexed. In some cases annexation has remained an effective tool for city expansion where states allowed home-rule cities to set their own unilateral procedure for acquiring new territory, as is still the case in Texas, and was the case in Missouri until the early 1970s. In Virginia, annexation is by court decision, but this has not prevented the spread of metropolitan areas to outlying counties. Currently, as a result of state legislation, there is a moratorium on annexation in Virginia. Throughout the twentieth century, it has become more and more difficult for most cities to expand using this approach because of suburban opposition.

The "rationalization" of local government in most metropolitan areas has been frustrated by continuing rapid urbanization and suburbanization and/or the failure of metropolitan governmental reforms to achieve acceptance by existing local governments, states, public officials and bureaucracies, and citizens, where the citizens are given the opportunity to be a part of such decisions. In the few cases that metropolitan government has been implemented through city-county consolidation, city-county separation, or some other arrangement, population generally has spilled over the boundaries of the new entity within a few decades, tempering whatever achievements resulted from this process. Examples include all of those listed in the following paragraph, plus Baton Rouge and Denver. Most recent major restructuring has occurred in Southern states or in Alaska with their simpler systems of local government.

City-county consolidation or city-county separation has a long history. At least five cases antedate the twentieth century: Boston (1821), Philadelphia (1854), New Orleans (1874), St. Louis (1876), and New York (1898), though New York involved a consolidation of five counties that became the present-day city of New York. Excepting St. Louis, all of the nineteenth-century reforms were imposed by state legislatures. Between the turn of the century and the end of World War II, there was considerable interest in city-county consolidation, but no adoptions.

In 1876 the city of St. Louis expanded its territory, separated from St. Louis County, and became a city-county. This option was included in the new Missouri constitution adopted in 1875. By the turn of the twentieth century, the urban population had spilled over into St. Louis County (outside the city-county of St. Louis). The MSA now covers ten counties on both sides of the state line.

In the case of St. Louis, as with a number of other metropolitan areas, there have been numerous attempts at metropolitan reform since the nineteenth century. The only successes have been a few special districts, largely but not entirely limited to the city of St. Louis and St. Louis county. These include a zoological park and museum, a convention center and sports complex authority, and a sewer district. In addition, there is a bistate development district—similar to the Port Authority of New York and New Jersey—for transportation services, created by the state legislatures of Missouri and Illinois. St. Louis County, outside the city-county of St. Louis, has become a de facto suburban metropolitan entity by providing countywide services and contracting with a number of the eighty-eight, mostly small, suburban municipalities for the provision of selected public services.

Starting with the city-county consolidation of Baton Rouge and East Baton Rouge Parish in 1947, interest in metropolitan reform continued through the 1960s and, in a few areas, beyond that decade. Most of those that were successful occurred in small to medium-size Southern metropolitan areas. After an unsuccessful attempt in 1958, the Nashville–Davidson County consolidation took place in 1962. Other successes, including different kinds of reform, occurred in Atlanta's annexation and reordering of city and county services (1952), Miami's comprehensive county plan (1957), the Jacksonville consolidation (1967), and Indianapolis's Unigov (1969). In 1997, as a result of severe financial problems, the city of Miami considered disincorporation, which could have meant Dade County would have become responsible for the services now performed by the city. This move failed to receive voter approval. Augusta and Richmond County, Georgia voted to consolidate in 1995 after four failed attempts at consolidation. In the first attempt at merger, the city of Kansas City, Kansas and Wyandotte County voted to consolidate on April 1, 1997.[36] Over the last four decades more limited forms of governmental restructuring have succeeded through the use of single and multipurpose special-district governments, particularly in metropolitan areas.

During the last half of the twentieth century, most attempts at metropolitan govern-mental reform failed for a variety of reasons. Even attempts by the federal government to foster regional planning and councils of elected officials—such as councils of governments (COGs) in metropolitan areas—failed to stimulate major metropolitan governmental re-form. COGs are associations of elected public officials from most and/or from the major local governments within an urban or metropolitan area. Their purpose is to establish consensus concerning area needs and actions to solve local and interlocal problems. COGs are voluntary associations that represent governments, but are not themselves governments.[37] Require-ments for metropolitan planning and/or COGs as a precondition for receiving money from selected federal grant programs, and the interaction of local officials in metropolitan planning agencies and COGs, may have stimulated greater formal and informal interlocal cooperation, but major restructuring has not resulted from these efforts.

Some Reasons for the Failure of Metropolitan Reform

Community leaders, political scientists, economists, business leaders, and others sometimes consider themselves "philosopher kings" as they confront the fragmented maze of governments in our metropolitan areas, often referred to as the "metropolitan problem." In 1962, Scott Greer noted in *The Emerging City*:

> The image of the city as a sovereign state, a military power, an integrated and powerful governmental unit, has eroded with the increasing scale of the carrying society. But what remains is not a vacuum to be neglected in our concern with the nation-state. It is a vast interconnected system of organizations operating in an inherited physical landscape and sharing in many respects a common fate . . . The metropolitan community is without moral or legal father, without obedient estates, without simple questions of right or wrong. It is, in this sense, large-scale society in miniature.[38]

Though the central government in Washington is in the throes of retrenchment, over the last several decades both state and federal governments have increased their respective responsibility in both funding and/or delivering public services. Both higher levels are far more important as a proportion of the total economy and, even with federal "downsizing," play a much larger role than in earlier periods not only relative to financing and delivering public services, but also in regulating both subnational governments and the economy. Not only have states accepted more responsibility, they are no longer the backwater of American politics.

Other factors are involved as well. While states increased their relative and absolute roles compared to local governments between 1952 and the 1990s, not all local units declined in this respect. Serving a larger area than most municipalities, county governments increased their activity in terms of local governance over the last four decades both relative to other local units and in absolute terms as a proportion of the economy. This is particularly evident in urban areas. Special districts also accounted for a larger share of local activity by the 1990s. Both county and special district governments, along with federal and state subsidies and services, have been utilized to solve some of the more pressing service problems faced by metropolitan areas. These solutions are largely ad hoc. The fragmented system of local organization remains, but the system does work at some level of effectiveness, if not efficiency. Government services have not collapsed as they did in the Toronto area in the late 1940s.

Massive increases in the number and role of special districts is in some major proportion, at least, a response to urban problems. While voters often reject extensive governmental reform, they have been much more amenable to the solution of specific problems by the creation of special districts serving both limited and more extended geographic areas. This is particularly true for what Oliver Williams called "system-maintaining services," that is, the services necessary for the functioning of the metropolitan area as a whole. These include major transportation facilities, pollution control, water and sewerage systems, and, in some cases, flood control (where this is a problem) and fire protection (where there are major risks of conflagration). These services are often provided and/or financed (with regulations) by state and/or federal agencies as well as the enhanced role of special districts and county governments. What Williams calls "lifestyle" services are much less amenable to integration—services such as land use, building and subdivision controls, zoning, schools, and, at times, police and fire protection.[39]

Local as well as metropolitan governance is continually improvised. The need for major restructuring of local and metropolitan government has been mitigated by a variety of developments, including the effective, if not efficient, provision of system-maintaining services; county, state, and federal assumption of greater responsibility; and the extensive use of special districts to fill in the service gaps left by other local and larger governments.

The Following Chapters

Chapter 2, "The Logic of Metropolitan Government," focuses on the theoretical and pragmatic origins of metropolitan governmental reform, which argues for the elimination of political and governmental fragmentation of metropolitan areas and the substitution of a more "rational" political structure. The consolidationist perspective, or one-government strategy, is traced from its origins in the nineteenth century down to the two-tier, or federative, approach of the latter half of the twentieth century. Attention is given to the policies of federal and state governments as they relate to this issue along with various private and community activists.

Chapter 3, "The Elusive Quest for Metropolitan Government," discusses the factors that affect the success and failure of metropolitan governmental reorganization attempts. The difficulty of changing the structure of local government is affected by the underlying cultural norms, which have been written into the legal/constitutional system. The chapter uses a recent (1997) successful city-county consolidation to explain some fourteen factors that are often critical to the success or failure—mostly failure—of local reorganization movements.

Chapters 4 and 5 are, in a sense, one package. Chapter 4, "Metropolitan Government I: City-County Consolidation," outlines the reorganization of local government in five metropolitan areas where reforms were adopted, as well as the expectations of those who supported and opposed these reforms. The case studies include Baton Rouge, Nashville, Jacksonville, Miami, and Indianapolis. Chapter 5, "Metropolitan Government II: The Urban County and Limited Regional Structures," focuses on the establishment and experience of the federative, two-tier governmental structure in Miami–Dade County, Florida, and the limited areawide governmental structures in the Minneapolis, Minnesota and Portland, Oregon regions.

Chapter 6, "Public Choice: An Alternative Perspective," outlines the origin and evolution of the public choice perspective that defends the fragmented or polycentric character of the existing fragmented political and governmental structure of the metropolis. This chapter assesses the impact of this perspective on the current debates concerning governmental organization and governance of the metropolis.

Chapter 7, "Incremental Change and the Metropolis," documents the changes that have taken place in local government over the course of the twentieth century, with emphasis on the period since the 1950s. Local governments in metropolitan areas and elsewhere are in the process of continual adaptation, continual incremental change. At least seventeen different approaches or strategies are utilized to provide needed services to the residents of the nation's metropolitan areas, ranging from informal and formal cooperation to city-county consolidation and two-tier and three-tier structural entities.

Chapter 8, "Local Government in an Intergovernmental Context," places local and metropolitan governments in the federal system and discusses the manner in which federal and state governments affect, influence, and sometimes control what takes place at the local level of government. The proper placement of decision making, revenue collection, and service delivery authority between federal, state, and local governments is a difficult question even without the contemporary situation where urban regions have evolved with relatively little adaptation of the exceptionally complex pre-existing federal structure.

Chapter 9, "The Future of Metropolitan Government and Governance," sums up the findings of the earlier chapters and advances the authors' estimate of the prospects for governing the nation's 300-plus metropolitan areas in terms of both the public choice and the metropolitan government perspectives. It examines the role the states and the national government can and probably should play relative to the service needs of our urban areas.

CHAPTER TWO

The Logic of Metropolitan Government: Origins and Evolution

Throughout the twentieth century, the concept of metropolitan government or metropolitan political integration has constituted the research focus of countless numbers of scholars of urban affairs—largely political scientists and sociologists, but also economists, geographers, and planners—and has been the goal of a large number of reform efforts, mostly unsuccessful, to reconstitute the governmental structure of the metropolis. Literally dozens of volumes and hundreds of articles have been written on various aspects of the topic.[1] Thomas H. Reed, a longstanding scholar of urban government and politics and a prominent supporter of metropolitan government, wrote in 1949: "On no domestic topic has more been said, except possibly the weather, and on very few has less been done."[2]

There are two basic versions of metropolitan government. The first variant calls for the establishment of one general-purpose government for the entire metropolitan area, and the abolishment of all prior existing cities, towns, and special districts. Under this arrangement, the metropolitan government provides all local services to the citizenry. Although this version of metropolitan government, referred to as the one-community, one-government or unitary-in-design approach, was popular among scholars during the first part of the twentieth century, virtually no support for this version of metropolitan government is presently found in the scholarly community.

By contrast, most present-day scholars of urban affairs predisposed toward metropolitan governmental reform endorse a federative, two-tier type of metropolitan governmental structure—the second variant of metropolitan government. Under this arrangement, a refurbished county government or an entirely new governmental unit usually serves as a general-purpose metropolitan government, providing for the citizenry regionally oriented "system-maintenance"[3] services, such as water, sewers, and mass transportation. In contrast to the one-community, one-government or unitary version of metropolitan government, the latter version retains existing cities and towns, which continue to be responsible for delivering local "lifestyle"[4] services, most prominently elementary and secondary public education.

Over the years a number of reform strategies have been adopted in the quest to establish a metropolitan government. These strategies include: annexation, the merger of municipalities, city-county consolidation, city-county separation, and the establishment of a comprehensive urban county. No attempt has been made in any metropolitan area to establish an entirely new, singular, areawide, general-purpose metropolitan government. Annexation involves the core city incorporating adjacent urbanized suburban territory and providing the newly incorporated area with city services. The merger of municipalities approach involves the creation of an entirely new municipality through the merger of two

29

or more existing cities or towns. City-county consolidation involves the merger of the core city government with that of the county. City-county separation—designed to make the boundaries of the core city better conform with those of the true urban metropolitan area—separates the city from the surrounding county. And, finally, the comprehensive urban-county approach requires the strengthening of the fiscal, managerial, and service capacity of the county government, enabling it to function as the general-purpose metropolitan government for the region. In this arrangement, cities and towns continue to provide locally oriented services.

This chapter is concerned with the pragmatic, historical, and intellectual origins and evolution of the metropolitan reform government argument and its contribution to the present debate concerning what should be the nature of metropolitan governance. Initially, the discussion focuses on the implementation of metropolitan government during the nineteenth century through the reform strategies of annexation, merger of municipalities, city-county consolidation, and city-county separation. Attention is then directed to the broad intellectual origins, evolution, and refinement of the concept of metropolitan government during the twentieth century, as evidenced in the writings of scholars of urban affairs. Following this discussion, attention is given to the widespread efforts to restructure the government of metropolitan areas in the 1960s, usually ending in failure (although some successes were registered in the Indianapolis, Jacksonville, and Nashville metropolitan areas, adding to earlier successes in Baton Rouge and Miami), the relative lack of scholarly interest in the topic between 1970 and 1990, and the resurgence of scholarly interest in metropolitan government and governance commencing in the early part of the 1990s. The concluding discussion advances the contributions of the metropolitan government argument to the present-day debate concerning what should constitute the proper governance structure of the metropolis.

The Pragmatic and Historical Origins of Metropolitan Government

In a pragmatic and historical sense, metropolitan government originated as the result of the annexation, merger of municipalities, city-county consolidation, and city-county separation experiences of cities during the nineteenth century.[5] These experiences of local government reorganization were based on the premise that the central city should constitute the sole governing unit and be the general service provider for the entire metropolitan area. Throughout the nineteenth century, cities—most notably, Baltimore, Boston, Chicago, Detroit, New York, Philadelphia, Pittsburgh, and St. Louis—significantly expanded their geographical boundaries through a series of successful annexation efforts, usually authorized by special legislation. In addition, present-day New York city resulted from the merger of New York and Brooklyn, Queens, and Richmond counties in 1898. Also, metropolitan government came into being in a number of metropolitan areas because of either city-county consolidation or city-county separation. The former took place in Philadelphia (1854) and New Orleans (1874). In a reversal of direction, metropolitan government was realized as a result of city-county separation in Baltimore (1851), San Francisco (1856), St. Louis (1876), and Denver (1903).

In retrospect, it is clear that these early examples of metropolitan government provided future scholars of urban affairs with pragmatic and working models for thinking about and structuring the most effective, efficient, and responsive way for organizing the governmental structure of the metropolis. After reviewing the experiences of these governments, a number of prominent scholars became outright advocates of metropolitan government and provided through their stream of writings, commencing in the first several decades of the twentieth century, a constant nourishing of scholarly legitimacy.

The Intellectual Origins and Evolution of the Metropolitan Government Concept

The broad intellectual underpinnings of the metropolitan government concept may be traced back to the principles set forth by municipal reform advocates, during the period from 1880 to 1920, in their quest to render local government more accountable and democratic, and less corrupt. Intellectually, the reformers were indebted, in particular, to the writings of Woodrow Wilson, Frank J. Goodnow, and Frederick W. Taylor.

Wilson emphasized in his writings the virtue of efficiency in government, the dichotomy between administration and politics, and the need to conduct public administration in a businesslike fashion. Pervading his scholarly contributions was the belief that the problems of government could be corrected by appropriate structural change. In his work *Congressional Government*, published in 1885, Wilson argued that "efficiency is the only just foundation for confidence in a public officer under republican institutions no less than under monarchs."[6] In his seminal article "The Study of Administration," Wilson noted: "It is the object of administrative study to discover, first, what government can properly and successfully do, and, secondly, how it can do these proper things with the utmost possible efficiency and at the least possible cost either of money or energy. On both these points there is obviously much need of light among us; and only careful study can supply that light."[7]

Wilson repeatedly emphasized the distinction, both in a theoretical and a practical sense, between administration and politics: "[A]dministration lies outside the proper sphere of politics. Administrative questions are not political questions. Although politics sets the task for administration, it should not be suffered to manipulate its offices."[8] He further emphasized the businesslike character of public administration: "The field of administration is a field of business. It is removed from the hurry and strife of politics; it at most points stands apart even from the debatable ground of constitutional study."[9]

The writings of Frank. J. Goodnow, a leading scholar of municipal government and politics, and Frederick W. Taylor, who sought to make work routines more efficient, served to augment the principles advocated by Wilson. Throughout his text *Politics and Administration*, published in 1900, Goodnow strongly emphasized the distinction between administration and politics.[10] In addition, municipal reformers were strongly influenced by the principles of scientific management advocated by Taylor and by his insistence that there was "one best way" to accomplish every task.[11]

In summary, metropolitan governmental reformers extrapolated from the writings of Wilson, Goodnow, and Taylor the following normative principles concerning metropolitan governmental organization. First, each major urban area should be governed by a single government; second, the electorate in each major urban area should be called upon to elect only the most important policy-making officials, constituting relatively few in number; third, separation of powers should be eliminated from the internal structure of a single metropolitan government; fourth, the function of administration should be separated from that of politics, and the work of administration should be carried out by well-trained and adequately compensated public servants; and, finally, local governmental structure should be organized in an integrated command structure in accordance with the hierarchical principle, with authority tapering upward and culminating in a single chief executive.

In addition, the rapid development of metropolitan areas at the turn of the twentieth century attracted the scholarly attention of social scientists, intent upon better comprehending this new urban phenomenon and providing it with a precise definition and proper governmental organization. Ernest W. Burgess, a highly respected scholar of urban affairs at the University of Chicago, advanced in 1925 an early preliminary definition of a metropolitan area:

> In Europe and America the tendency of the great city to expand has been recognized in the term "the metropolitan area of the city," which far overruns its political limits, and in the case of New York and Chicago, even state lines. The metropolitan area may be taken to include urban territory that is physically contiguous, but it is coming to be defined by that facility of transportation that enables a businessman to live in a suburb of Chicago and to work in the loop, and his wife to shop at Marshall Field's and attend grand opera in the Auditorium.[12]

President Herbert Hoover's Research Committee on Social Trends, in its report *Recent Social Trends in the United States* (1932)[13] provided the first major assessment of the demographic, economic, and social aspects of the metropolitan community. Roderick D. McKenzie, commenting on this *Report,* noted that the metropolitan form of the American city could be traced back to the turn of the twentieth century and would serve as the prevailing form of American urban settlement in the future.[14]

By the early 1930s social scientists were in agreement that a metropolitan area might be described as an integrated economic and social unit with a large population base, encompassing a significant expanse of geographical territory. Subsequently, in later years, scholars sought to move beyond this general definition and advanced various "hard" statistical measures designed to more precisely define the metropolis. These measures included: newspaper circulation,[15] commuting,[16] and various business and trade areas.[17] Reflective of this mode of thought and weaving these various measures into their definition, Amos H. Hawley and Basil G. Zimmer defined, in the early 1960s, a metropolitan area as composed of a "total population, together with the area it occupies, which carries on its daily life through a common system of relationships administered from a central city."[18]

The argument that a single general-purpose government, providing all local public services, should govern a metropolitan area slowly yet steadily evolved in scholarly writings throughout the first part of the twentieth century. Initially, the concept of metropolitan government, based on the efficiency and effectiveness principles of the scientific management movement,[19] was advanced by reformers in a rather simplistic fashion; however, with the passage of time, the concept and its supporting rationale became more sophisticated and theoretically based.

The National Municipal League, especially through its publication the *National Municipal Review* (currently the *National Civic Review*), proved to be (and continues to be) an early and persistent advocate of the reform perspective. The origins of the National Municipal

League may be traced back to a national conference entitled "National Conference for Good City Government," which convened in Philadelphia in January 1884. At this conference, participants representing twenty-one cities in thirteen states, after the conclusion of a series of progressive, reform-oriented speeches denouncing the widespread "evils" of local government and politics, set upon a course of action designed to "clean up" city government and politics. For this purpose, the delegates established a permanent executive committee which, in turn, founded the National Municipal League in 1895.[20]

Over the course of the years, reform advocates—largely scholars of urban affairs—contributed articles to the *National Municipal Review* articulating the virtues of metropolitan government and condemning the multiplicity of governments found in the typical metropolitan region. John Nolen, in the first issue of the *Review*, published in 1912, proposed a "metropolitan planning board" for the Boston metropolitan area, which would serve to mitigate the service problems resulting from the multiplicity of local governments:

> Nowhere else in the world does there exist a political situation parallel to that of Metropolitan Boston. Here are thirty-eight towns and cities as intimately related in everything that concerns daily life as the wards of an American city, but with no power or means, barring water supply, sewerage disposal, and parks, of controlling, constructing, or improving public works or of taking public action that is for the metropolitan district as a whole.[21]

In a more general and lasting sense, Nolen's criticism of the multiplicity of local governments in the Boston area, and the adverse consequences resulting from this condition, eventually became a central part of the reform argument.

Not long after the publication of Nolen's article, additional reform advocates contributed articles to the *Review*. In 1917, George Hooker, primarily concerned with the virtue of comprehensive city planning, urged in the *Review* the establishment of a special metropolitan district for the Cleveland region; further, in a more sweeping fashion, he argued that Cleveland should be allowed to extend its territorial jurisdiction in order to conform its boundaries with the entire metropolitan region.[22] In a *Review* article published the following year, in 1918, George C. Sikes proposed a metropolitan government for the San Francisco area: "It seems to me, however, that the municipalities around the San Francisco Bay constitute one natural metropolitan community and that the policy of the city and county consolidation calls for the merger under one government of all the Bay cities."[23]

Although Nolen, Hooker, and Sikes in their *National Municipal Review* contributions advocated some sort of metropolitan or regional government, none provided a comprehensive argument on its behalf. However, this deficiency was soon overcome with the publication of Chester C. Maxey's extended contribution, "The Political Integration of Metropolitan Communities,"[24] constituting the entire August 1922 issue of the *Review*. Maxey's article represents the first systematic reform statement on behalf of metropolitan government, including an extended discussion of the various problems associated with governmental fragmentation in the metropolis.

Chester Maxey, *The Political Integration of Metropolitan Communities*

Maxey began his contribution by taking note of the discrepancy between the governmental and nongovernmental boundaries of the metropolitan area:

> The city as a political entity is not identical with the metropolitan community as a social and economic fact; and so, like a house divided against itself, the metropolitan district finds itself obliged to struggle for civic achievement amid the conflicts, dissensions, and divergences of its several component jurisdictions.[25]

He argued that "[P]olitical development seldom keeps pace with social and economic facts and that the fractionalization of local governmental authority serves as an obstacle . . . gravely impeding all progress and comprehensive undertakings."[26] From Maxey's perspective, the usual political disunity of the metropolis was "absurd and anomalous" and should be replaced by the implementation of greater governmental centralization, which was "indispensable to every metropolitan community that aspires to attain its maximum development as a center of industrial, commercial, and social activity."[27] On this score, he buttressed his argument by making historical reference to the local governmental reorganizations that had taken place in the nineteenth century in New York (1898), Philadelphia (1854), New Orleans (1874), Baltimore (1851), St. Louis (1876), and San Francisco (1856).[28]

Maxey asserted that greater political integration would result in the following benefits:

> One gain about which there can be little doubt is the amelioration of civic conditions subsequent to the political unification of metropolitan communities. Elaborate public improvements, better articulation of thoroughfares, extended and improved public utility services, more comprehensive and careful city planning, more adequate educational and eleemosynary institutions, and better governmental services—these are reported as invariable results of political unification.[29]

Maxey elaborated on the past political difficulties associated with achieving metropolitan political integration. These difficulties included: first, political integration invariably required the passage of authorizing state legislation and/or the adoption of a state constitutional amendment; second, gradual consolidation through incremental stages of annexation by the core city had not proven successful; and, finally, plans to bring about metropolitan political integration usually encountered a considerable amount of citizen resistance. However, on this last point he added: "[P]opular consent to unification has seldom been deemed indispensable."[30]

Maxey's extensive contribution, although it involved little rigorous theorizing, is a well-crafted early statement in support of the reform argument. His essay served to reinforce the virtue of the "one community-one government" perspective and to underscore the various problems stemming from fragmented governmental structure in the metropolis.

Early Additional Writings on Behalf of Metropolitan Government

Following Maxey's contribution, several scholars of urban politics lent further support to the reform argument. Thomas H. Reed in his *National Municipal Review* contribution in 1925 strongly advocated the disestablishment of special districts—but not cities or towns—and the creation of metropolitan governments responsible for planning and zoning, mass transportation, traffic, highway construction and maintenance, water supply and drainage, and certain police, health, and charitable activities. Reed suggested that the members of the metropolitan government council should be directly elected by the citizenry, utilizing a proportional representation electoral system.[31] Writing in the *American Political Science Review* the following year, Shelby M. Harrison concurred with Reed's listing of metropolitan governmental responsibilities.[32] In a more specific sense, Rowland A. Egger, in an article published in the *American Political Science Review* in 1929, praised the Pittsburgh area city-county consolidation effort as the "event of the year" in local government.[33]

In sum, the contributions of Nolen, Hooker, Sikes, and Maxey, along with those of Reed, Harrison, and Egger, provided further legitimacy to the reform perspective that the metropolitan area is a single economic and social community, which should be governed and functionally provided for by a single areawide government. In essence, then, according to these early scholars, *the fundamental problem of the metropolis* was the decentralized or fractionated nature of local government. This perspective was advanced in the municipal government textbooks of the era, authored by William Anderson,[34] A. Chester Hanford,[35] Joseph Wright,[36] William Bennett Munro[37] and, of course, Maxey[38] and Reed.[39] This reform point of view was adopted by the city planners of the time, along with a variety of municipal research bureaus. However, not until the publication of Paul Studenski's work, *The Government of Metropolitan Areas in the United States*,[40] published in 1930, did a scholar undertake a synthesis of the literature and provide a general treatment of the reform perspective.

Paul Studenski, *The Government of Metropolitan Areas in the United States*

Paul Studenski's work *The Government of Metropolitan Areas in the United States* is the first comprehensive undertaking concerning the government of metropolitan areas. It was sponsored by the National Municipal League and, to a significant degree, was the product of the League's Committee on Metropolitan Government, established in 1924, of which Studenski was a member. In the committee's foreword to Studenski's work it noted the purpose of the book:

> The Report on the Government of Metropolitan Areas is the first comprehensive study of its kind to be published in the United States. The Committee puts it forward with much diffidence, realizing that the last word remains to be said. It is believed, however, that the factual data regarding the widely-varying efforts to solve regional government will be of value.[41]

At the outset of his work, Studenski repeated the central reform theme that the central city along with its surrounding suburbs constitutes a single economic and social metropolitan community, which is artificially politically divided into cities, special districts, and counties. The resultant governmental complexity he attributed to obsolete state laws concerning the organization of local government and the delegation of incorporation and annexation decisions to local initiative, devoid of the guidance of any "superior authority" or comprehensive plan to control urban growth. Therefore, according to Studenski, the result was:

> The political organization of metropolitan areas may be best described as no organization at all, but a mere conglomeration of political divisions of various kinds, established at various times, and not bound together in any way.[42]

According to Studenski, the basic problem of the metropolis, reflecting the view of his earlier like-minded reform predecessors, was the fragmentation of governmental structure, along with the negative consequences associated with this condition:

> Whatever the reasons for the great number of political divisions, they do not provide an ideal political organization for metropolitan regions. They tend to divert the attention of the inhabitants from the fact that they are members of one large community and lead them to act as members of separate units. They result in great variation in municipal regulations in force in different sections of the metropolitan area, and in the standards of the services maintained, in sectional treatment of problems which are essentially metropolitan, in radical inequalities in the tax resources of the several political divisions, and in jurisdictional conflicts. The political subdivisions are jealous of each other and proceed in virtual independence. . . . It is difficult under these conditions to bring about concerted action throughout the metropolitan area. Consequently it is often well-nigh impossible to solve effectively municipal problems common to all.[43]

Studenski's observations concerning the myriad array of problems resulting from governmental fragmentation in the metropolis became a central and longstanding part of the reform argument.

In order to overcome the problem of fragmented local government, Studenski advocated the establishment of a metropolitan government, providing for the needs of the citizens and responsible for the following functions:

> The social and economic problems which concern the various municipal divisions of a metropolitan area are largely the same for all. They are the usual problems of urban life, somewhat magnified by the fact that they arise out of conditions which exist throughout the entire metropolitan area and not merely in a particular locality. In general, they relate to water supply, sewerage, drainage, construction and maintenance of streets, transportation, police, fire protection, public health, disposal of garbage and other wastes, parks, playgrounds, schools, libraries, hospitals, and the like.[44]

Acting on the premise that a large number of services should be delivered to the citizenry through a regional approach, Studenski reviewed a variety of incremental and more drastic strategies designed to integrate the government of the metropolis. He took note of voluntary cooperation between local governments, most prominently involving the use of intermunicipal arrangements for the construction of bridges and sewers, and the sale of water by central cities to suburban communities. Studenski stressed the limited effectiveness of the voluntary approach because of the general inability of governmental units to negotiate mutually satisfactory agreements with each other and their basic lack of desire to engage in cooperative endeavors. Further, he viewed intergovernmental arrangements of dubious value because of the inherent inequalities of the relationship between the seller and buyer: "Sooner or later they place the city which sells the services in an equivocal position with respect to the communities served. One part of the metropolitan region becomes too dependent upon the efficiency and good will of another. The relationship of buyer and seller is not one which necessarily promotes accord."[45] Studenski concluded in regard to intermunicipal arrangements: "Intermunicipal cooperation . . . has not succeeded in unifying the government of a metropolitan area sufficiently to make possible the comprehensive and effective solving of the problems of the area. . . . In a word, the scheme is of limited application. It does not afford a basis of real, democratic, comprehensive, and permanent organization of the metropolitan community."[46]

Studenski directed his attention to various examples of more drastic forms of metropolitan political integration. In his sweeping review, he noted that past greater metropolitan political integration had been achieved by central city annexation, municipal consolidation, city-county separation, city-county consolidation, the financial and management enhancement of the urban county, and the establishment in 1898 of the borough system of New York. He painstakingly defined each reform strategy, provided examples, and commented on their merits and limitations. Studenski underscored the limited utility of the annexation and municipal consolidation strategies and noted in regard to several past examples of city-county consolidation and city-county separation that only in the instance of city-county consolidation in the Philadelphia area did a true metropolitan government result: "The unification of city and county government under the schemes described, may be said to have been executed on a fully metropolitan scope only in the case of Philadelphia, where the consolidated city and county embraced practically the entire metropolitan territory."[47] And, further, in a general sense, he advanced his lack of enthusiasm for both the alternatives of city-county separation and city-county consolidation; the former, he advanced, would increase the costs and complicate the structure of local government, while in regard to the latter Studenski noted: "City-county consolidation can hardly be expected to offer a solution to the difficulties confronting most of the metropolitan regions today. All that can be hoped of it is that it will eliminate one source of confusion—the duplication of city and county governments within the central city. . . . But the obstacles that stand in the way of city-county consolidation are so great, as attested by the failures of all efforts made during the past twenty years, that prudence should suggest other lines of attack."[48] He dismissed New York's experience as peculiar to the area, without any real applicability to other metropolitan areas.

Studenski devoted an extended amount of discussion to the urban county serving as a metropolitan government. He described the urban county alternative as an effort "to adapt the county government to the service of metropolitan needs by broadening its scope and remodeling its structure."[49] As an example of the enhanced urban county approach, he utilized the example of Los Angeles County, which adopted a home rule charter in 1913, and by 1920 was delivering many citylike services. Although his overall assessment of the urban county serving as a metropolitan government was pessimistic, Studenski did register some small measure of hope: "This does not mean, however, that the county cannot evolve into a truly metropolitan government."[50]

In a more theoretical sense, Studenski elaborated on the concept of the "federated city" as a politically viable way of achieving greater political integration in the metropolis. He described the federated city as a structural arrangement whereby "the constituent municipalities are not completely merged but continue to exist as separate entities exercising a degree of local control within their boundaries."[51] In contrast to the other drastic strategies designed to promote political integration, Studenski was optimistic about the future applicability of the concept of the federated city: "We may expect considerable experimentation in the near future with various plans for federated or dual metropolitan government."[52] He argued that the establishment of a federative metropolitan government must be predicated upon the following conditions: first, an acknowledgment that the basic integration of authority at the metropolitan level would allow for the automatic expansion of metropolitan boundaries to new suburban developments; second, constituent units could be regrouped or rearranged as conditions may require; and, finally, there would take place over time a progressive integration of government into a homogeneous social unit.[53]

Toward the end of his work, Studenski set forth an exhaustive evaluation of special metropolitan authorities, governments established usually to provide a single service that could not be delivered by existing local governments. He noted that special metropolitan authorities were usually involved in the provision of water and sewer services, and port development. Although aware of their political feasibility and practical utility, Studenski stressed the limitations of the special metropolitan authority device: "Special metropolitan authorities have distinct limitations. They are essentially a makeshift. They do not offer a conclusive answer to the problem of integration of government of metropolitan areas."[54]

In his brief concluding chapter, Studenski reiterated the following: first, there is no single remedy or answer for the metropolitan problem of fragmented government; second, the different types of organizational responses to the problem of fragmented government are not mutually exclusive—indeed, he argued, for example, that in some areas the alternatives of a federated governmental structure might well be used in conjunction with the strategy of core city annexation; third, public leaders need to focus on a comprehensive response to governmental fragmentation, rather than on individual projects; fourth, political leaders should recognize that the political interests of the region are greater than the sum of the interests of local governments and that "[P]roperly conceived home rule does not confer a right to perpetual existence as a separate political entity when common interests demand that the smaller locality be absorbed into a larger political community. . . . The state and even the nation as a whole are concerned in the proper governmental organization and development of the great metropolitan regions."[55] Studenski added to these conclusions the customary plea for additional scholarship on the governmental structure of metropolitan areas.

For three reasons, Studenski's work constitutes a major benchmark in the study of the government of metropolitan areas. First, he systematically set forth a discussion of metropolitan governmental organization, incorporating and reinforcing the value judgments of earlier reform scholars, such as Maxey and Reed, supporting the need for political integration in the metropolis. These value judgements included: (1) the metropolitan area is a single economic and social community, but is arbitrarily divided into numerous governmental units; (2) the aggregate public needs of the metropolitan area cannot adequately be met by the collective action of existing local governments, characterized by deterioration and chaos; and (3) in the final analysis, the public welfare of the entire metropolitan area can only be sufficiently addressed by the establishment of a metropolitanwide integrated governmental structure.

Second, Studenski's work, building on yet extending beyond the contributions of early reform scholars, continued a pattern of metropolitan governmental analysis that was universally adhered to by scholars for the next thirty years. His belief that the fundamental problem of the metropolis was the decentralized or fragmented nature of local government was adopted as a central working premise by a generation of scholars of urban government and politics.

And, finally, *The Government of Metropolitan Areas in the United States*, along with other reform-oriented materials, served as a catalyst for metropolitan governmental reform efforts in a score of metropolitan areas during the period from 1930 to 1970. Studenski's work, therefore, not only represented a central contribution to the scholarly literature but also significantly framed for a generation the larger attentive public debate concerning what should be the appropriate structure of metropolitan governmental organization.

Metropolitan Government: Additional Contributions of the 1930s

Following the publication of *The Government of Metropolitan Areas in the United States,* scholars provided further support to the reform perspective that the fundamental problem of the metropolis was the fragmented nature of local government, which could only be remedied by governmental integration. Charles E. Merriam, Spencer D. Parratt, and Albert Lepawsky, in their study of local government in the Chicago region, published in 1933, noted that the 1,600 local governments "may all swing harmoniously through their orbits, time in accord with all the others, without clash or loss [but this possibility was] wholly unlikely, and that jealousy, neglect, and inertia will cause widespread inefficiency in the performance of duties vital to the safety, health, and welfare of the community."[56] They added: "One of the most serious problems presented by the number of independent governments in Chicago, in Cook County, and in the Region is the difficulty of obtaining any adequate degree of central control over so large a number of different bodies. It is practically impossible for the Regional judgement or Regional will to be brought to bear upon the Regional government."[57] Nevertheless, Merriam, Parratt, and Lepawsky concluded that the social and economic trends of the region suggested that, "Time seems to be on the side of the Greater City, its unification and organization; time and the trend of the social and economic conditions which are the material out of which political forces and forms are developed."[58] In 1934, William Anderson proposed, as part of his plan to make sense out of the bewildering array of local governments in the metropolis, the elimination of all special districts and city-county consolidation in areas with a central city of at least 25,000 residents.[59]

In addition, McKenzie's seminal work *The Metropolitan Community,*[60] cited previously, which underscores the notion that the metropolitan region is a single economic and social community, spurred on further scholarly impetus concerning the need for metropolitan government. This reform perspective was further advanced by the National Resources Committee's report, *Our Cities: Their Role in the National Economy,* published in 1937, in which the committee declared that the government of metropolitan areas is a "bewildering maze of duplication, confusion, and competition. . . . If an orderly development and higher level of life for the people of the imposing supercities are to be attained, some measures calculated to endow them with the capacity to act collectively as a political unit are indispensable."[61]

In sum, by the close of the 1930s a widespread consensus prevailed among scholars of metropolitan governmental organization that the fundamental problem of the metropolis was the fragmentation of local governmental structure, resulting in lack of a metropolitanwide political perspective, conflicts between local governments, and severe service problems. The only remedy for this condition involved the establishment of a metropolitan government. This perspective was given full force, a few years later, in Victor Jones's classic work, *Metropolitan Government.*[62]

Victor Jones, *Metropolitan Government*

Victor Jones's landmark work *Metropolitan Government* was published in 1942, although it was originally completed in 1939 as his doctoral dissertation, under the direction of Charles E. Merriam at the University of Chicago. Jones stressed the by now well-developed theme that the central city and suburbs constituted a single economic and social community, but were artificially divided into a multiplicity of governmental units. This fragmentation ensured competitive behavior between local governments, an inability to solve regional problems, an uneven distribution of tax resources, a lack of citizen control of local government, and the unequal distribution of services, especially pertaining to mass transit, sewerage and garbage, water supply, public health, law enforcement, and firefighting.

In response to what Jones decried as the "disintegrated local government in metropolitan areas,"[63] he set forth a variety of reform alternatives designed to achieve varying degrees of metropolitan political integration. The first set of alternatives he labeled as requiring no structural change, followed by a group of alternatives necessitating fundamental structural change. Alternatives requiring no structural change included: extraterritorial jurisdiction for the central city, the provision of central city services to suburban units through intergovernmental agreements, the creation of metropolitan special districts, the transfer of local governmental functions to the state, and the enlargement of the federal governmental administrative and policy role in metropolitan areas.[64]

Jones stressed that the first set of alternatives was fundamentally flawed, providing little real or permanent relief for the fundamental problem of fragmented local government. He perceived these alternatives as either "stopgaps, as complements to a more comprehensive scheme of integration, or as expedient stepping-stones to a comprehensive unit of local government for the entire metropolitan area."[65] He emphatically rejected the premise that political accommodations among local governments would result in their mutual advantage. For instance, Jones noted that bestowing upon the central city extraterritorial powers made for "jurisdictional conflicts, bickering, and hard feelings [rather than cooperation] . . . All such conflicts make the task of effecting comprehensive reorganization more difficult."[66]

Similarly, Jones—like Studenski—did not favor intergovernmental contracts and special districts. He argued that the provision of central city services to the suburbs through intergovernmental contracts tended to foster discord and in the long run served to preclude more meaningful metropolitan governmental reorganization. Of metropolitan special districts, he wrote, "Instead of simplifying local government, their existence confuses the citizens and voters and makes it more difficult to secure responsible local government in large urban communities."[67]

Convinced that incremental change was insufficient, Jones argued that any meaningful permanent solution to the metropolitan problem of fragmented government required the employment of more drastic structural changes, involving: (1) annexation; (2) municipal consolidation; (3) city-county consolidation; (4) city-county separation; (5) the merger of special authorities with either the city or county; (6) the reorganized urban county; (7) the establishment of a federated government; or (8) the institution of the city-state. Jones dismissed, because of their inherent political infeasibility, the alternatives of annexation, municipal consolidation, and the institution of the city-state. In contrast, he underscored his support for a reorganized urban county, city-county consolidation, or a federated government, arguing that the "end-products will differ only in small details. Each will be a giant municipality."[68]

Jones devoted a considerable amount of discussion to the potential role of the states and the federal government as agents of metropolitan governmental reform. He argued that because of the unitary constitutional relationship of the states to their local governments, states possess plenary powers over the structure and functions of local government. In view of this relationship, Jones advanced that states should more aggressively use their powers by assuming outright the duties of metropolitan governments or exercising close administrative supervision over the activities of local governments.[69]

Drawing on the general experience of New Deal programs, Jones set forth a number of strategies through which the federal government could impact on the nature and possible reform of metropolitan governmental structure. These strategies included: first, demonstration and experimentation, as exemplified by the establishment of metropolitan-wide governments such as the National Capital Park and Planning Commission; second, conducting research, surveys, and statistical reporting; third, disseminating data gathered on a metropolitan basis; and, fourth, utilizing grant-in-aids, contractual relationships, policy regulations, and credit controls as reform pressure strategies.[70]

Toward the conclusion of his work, Jones stressed, to a much greater degree than earlier reform writers, that "the politics of integration are the most significant aspects of the problem."[71] Groups most central to the politics of metropolitan reform, he noted, included business leaders, organized labor, and politicians. Jones took particular note of the usual suburban resistance to governmental reform: "Most of the suburban opposition to integration with the central city seems to be expressed by suburban politicians and suburban publishers, some of whom are subsidized by interests opposed to integration. But it would be a mistake to assume that, on the whole, their constituents do not share their attitude."[72]

Taking direct aim at the political opposition to reform, Jones urged that political leaders bent on governmental organizational change should devote particular attention to the strategy and tactics of reform implementation. Campaigns for metropolitan government, he argued, should be organized in such a manner that, first, details are carefully executed by technicians; second, proposals are systematically and persistently sold to the public and politicians; third, propaganda techniques are carefully devised to counteract the "symbol-reinforcing" propaganda of the opponents; and, fourth, appropriate action is taken on a statewide basis and a lobby is established at the state capitol to offset opposition suburban interests and their allies.[73]

For the most part reiterating his earlier analysis set forth in *Metropolitan Government*, Jones, in 1953, contributed an extended essay to Coleman Woodbury's edited volume, *The Future of Cities and Urban Redevelopment*,[74] in which he emphasized the reform argument that metropolitan government would facilitate the development of metropolitanwide civic leadership, particularly in regard to planning, urban development and redevelopment, and service activities:

> The realization of the objectives of urban development and redevelopment depends upon the kind of local government we have in metropolitan areas—its quality and its competence to plan and to govern. . . . Only a government with community-wide jurisdiction can plan and provide the services, physical facilities, guidance, and controls necessary to relate functional plans with areal plans. None of the metropolitan areas has such a government today.[75]

Jones, drawing on his own analysis and synthesizing the contributions of earlier reform advocates, succinctly set forth the tenets of the metropolitan government argument: first, the most fundamental problem of the metropolis is the fragmented, fractionated, or decentralized structure of local government, consisting of the multiplicity of general and single purpose governments; second, the decentralized governmental structure ensures service inefficiencies, ineffectiveness, and inadequacies; third, the multiplicity of local governmental units renders it difficult to ensure democratic control and accountability; fourth, the decentralized nature of government ensures a significant disparity of financial resources among local governments; fifth, lacking in most instances the appropriate structure, socioeconomic problems cannot be addressed or responded to on a necessary regional basis; and, finally, the decentralized local governmental structure does not facilitate the development of metropolitanwide political leadership.

Several additional caveats should be registered about Jones's work, *Metropolitan Government*. To a much greater degree than his earlier, like-minded reform colleagues, Jones took careful and wide account of the political obstacles hindering metropolitan reform, along with suggesting the most effective way of dealing with these obstacles, and the potential role of the states and the federal government in reshaping the governmental structure of the metropolis. In addition, by incorporating into *Metropolitan Government* the experiences of local government in the metropolitan areas of London, Paris, Berlin, and Hamburg, he introduced a measure of comparative analysis into the discussion of metropolitan governmental structure.

Luther Halsey Gulick, *The Metropolitan Problem and American Ideas*

Following the contributions of Jones, a number of scholars, most prominently John C. Bollens,[76] Betty Tableman,[77] and Robert C. Wood,[78] provided in the 1950s further scholarly support for metropolitan government. However, the singular intellectual dominance of the reform perspective was best symbolized when Luther Halsey Gulick, recognized among scholars as the Dean of American Public Administration, delivered the William W. Cook series of lectures at the University of Michigan in 1960. These lectures provided the foundation for his work, *The Metropolitan Problem and American Ideas.*[79]

Gulick, in his sweeping review of metropolitan area problems, summarized his analysis in a final chapter, titled "Action Program." He noted that metropolitan areas are confronted with the following three problems: first, inadequate services in parts of the region; second, the absence of a comprehensive metropolitan community program for general development; and, third, the lack of regionwide democratic machinery for teamwork, for thinking about and dealing with the common problems of the metropolitan area. Elaborating on the third point, Gulick advanced:

> [W]ithout such machinery, the people who live in the metropolitan areas cannot rise up, develop plans for action, debate proposals, iron out acceptable compromises, and then agree to join hands and take action. Without such teamwork machinery, there is no constituency, no sense of common purpose, no "metropolitan community" in a political sense, and, what is all-important, no "metropolitan leadership."[80]

Gulick emphasized that reformers in the past who have sought political integration in metropolitan areas have placed too much confidence in local political entities and an assortment of other leaders in seeking to realize their goals. Elaborating on this point, he noted: "We sought to consolidate mature political entities by their own volition when we should have known that this is contrary to the laws of political biology. We relied on local initiative when we should have known that such initiative is effectively disqualified outside its own established community."[81] And, in a parallel sense, Gulick further advanced: "We relied on 'home rule' when we should have known that the general system of local government and the determination of constituency limitations are not a local function, but a state responsibility."[82]

Gulick's analysis played down the central importance of the core city and emphasized the primary importance and the new reality of "spread" economic, governmental, and social development throughout the entire metropolis. He noted:

> We are not dealing with a "city" at all. We are dealing with people, industries, shops, offices, community institutions, recreations, methods of transport and easy communication, and a maze of urban services, both public and private, which focus on many centers, one of which may be called "the central city"—though it has no set or static peripheral limits other than an ocean or lake perhaps—and involve kaleidoscopic patterns of movement for people and ideas and goods in production.[83]

Gulick emphasized—indeed it constituted the core of his argument—that the needs and problems of metropolitan areas, including those relating to governmental structure, could only adequately be addressed through the involvement of all three levels, or "extensions" as he phrased it, of the American government: "[I]t is clear that *all "extensions" of American government must take a hand in dealing with our rising metropolitan problems*"[84] [emphasis that of the author]. In this regard, he noted the increasing role of the federal government in metropolitan areas, especially in terms of interstate highways, urban renewal, railroads and commuters, airports, slum clearance and housing, crime syndicates, interstate pollution, and the allocation of major water supplies, and advanced: "What we now need from the federal government is an honest recognition that there is nothing to be ashamed of when the national government does something for urban populations to help solve their nation-wide problems."[85] In regard to the states, Gulick was no less emphatic: "[T]he state holds a key position in determining how a metropolitan area shall proceed to find the way out of its explosive dilemmas."[86] He argued that the states could play a major role in alleviating the problems of the metropolis by establishing a department or office of local governmental affairs; removing constitutional barriers that hindered the establishment of metropolitan governmental experiments; providing expanded education, highways, health and hospital, law enforcement, and recreation programs; and encouraging local intergovernmental cooperation, regional planning, and boundary adjustments. Finally, recognizing the continuing importance of the local sector in regard to metropolitan governmental reform, Gulick noted: "[S]urely nothing can be done without the vigorous and effective action of local governments and local political constituencies and their responsible political, business, and community leaders."[87]

Gulick made it clear that while some services could continue to be provided by existing local governments, delivered through a contract with another governmental unit, or transferred to a county, special district, the state, or even the federal government, he strongly favored, with perhaps the exception of metropolitan areas situated in very small states, the establishment of federated governmental structures in metropolitan areas:

I take the position that there is a political and administrative job to be done which can be handled best, not by the state, but by a new and broader local governmental structure which will deal with the overall activities of an area, without necessarily assuming responsibility for more intimate local services and controls, namely those which concern the local community only.[88]

In terms of a federated metropolitan governmental structure, Gulick envisioned that existing local governments would continue their functional responsibility for the "local" aspects of law and order; fire and health protection; local streets and street maintenance, street lighting, and traffic control; the various utilities—water, sewerage, waste disposal, and mass transportation—institutions; parks and recreation; welfare; education; building-code enforcement; tax and land-title administration; and the maintenance of courts. He noted, however: "Where any of these activities or services cannot be handled effectively by the existing local governmental structure because of the new pattern of settlement, these activities must be reassigned in whole or part."[89] Gulick suggested that aspects of local functions most likely to be reassigned, because of technological or political considerations, would include law enforcement, air pollution, water supply, and sewerage.

Toward the conclusion of his work, Gulick strongly reiterated the intergovernmental nature of the metropolitan governmental problem, by emphasizing that metropolitan governmental reorganization required the assertive and meaningful involvement of the federal, state, and local levels of government. He noted: "Thus the only sensible way we can deal with the metropolitan problem is to agree that the responsibility for action now falls on all three 'extensions'—on the federal government, on the state government, and on the local governments and their people."[90]

Metropolitan Government and Governance: The Enduring Legacy

Gulick's work, *The Metropolitan Problem and American Ideas*, bestowed additional legitimacy on the reform perspective, having a long-term theoretical and practical impact. Indeed, during the 1960s and up to the mid-1970s, the vast majority of scholars of metropolitan governmental organization concurred with the reform argument (with the exception of a nascent minority public choice faction, largely centered at Indiana University). This dominant mainstream position was reflected as late as 1974 in the National Research Council's publication, *Toward an Understanding of Metropolitan America*, prepared by an eminent group of scholars. Among other insights, the publication noted: "The present system of local government fails to answer the needs of a clearly metropolitan society. Fragmented and overlapping government in metropolitan areas (1) aggravates the mismatch between resources and social needs, (2) makes the solution of metropolitan social problems more difficult, and (3) inhibits efficient administration of services."[91]

During the middle portion of the twentieth century, national and regional organizations promoted the virtues of metropolitan governmental reform and regionalism. The Ford Foundation funded major metropolitan interdisciplinary research projects in Cleveland, Dayton, Milwaukee, and St. Louis, providing the groundwork for metropolitan government proposals. The prestigious Committee for Economic Development (CED), a group largely composed of national corporate executives, in its 1966 report, *Modernizing Local*

Government, recommended a massive consolidation of local governments in metropolitan areas and noted:

> The bewildering multiplicity of small, piecemeal, duplicative, overlapping local jurisdictions cannot cope with the staggering difficulties encountered in managing modern urban affairs. The fiscal effects of duplicative suburban separatism create great difficulty in provision of costly central city services benefiting the whole urbanized area. If local governments are to function effectively in metropolitan areas, they must have sufficient size and authority to plan, administer, and provide significant financial support for solutions to area-wide problems.[92]

CED, after undertaking a subsequent study of governmental organization in the metropolis, in its 1970 report *Reshaping Government in Metropolitan Areas*, modified its position by endorsing a federative governmental structure for metropolitan areas: "To gain the advantages of both centralization and decentralization, we recommend as an ultimate solution a governmental system of two levels. Some functions should be assigned in their entirety to the area-wide government, others to the local level, but most will be assigned in part to each level."[93]

The U.S. Advisory Commission on Intergovernmental Relations (ACIR), a federal advisory body on intergovernmental relations, now defunct, conducted a massive study of metropolitan governmental organization and regionalism in the early 1970s. Similar to the reports of the CED, the final two-part recommendation of the ACIR report—*Regional Decision Making: New Strategies for Substate Districts*[94]—strongly reflected the tenets of the metropolitan reform argument, especially in regard to the virtues of governmental effectiveness, efficiency, and accountability. In the short run, the ACIR recommended the establishment in each metropolitan area of a multipurpose regional council (UMJO) capable of linking areawide planning with program implementation and coordinating the activities of special districts. The ACIR envisioned the specific functions of the UMJO as areawide planning, interlocal communications, research, and technical assistance, and serving as the authoritative umbrella policy review agency for the region. In the second part of its recommendation, directed toward the more distant future, the ACIR underscored that the establishment of UMJOs did not preclude the eventual necessity of reshaping metropolitan governmental structure and reassigning governmental functions.

During the same time frame, the argument for metropolitan government and regionalism was promoted by a variety of regional organizations. In this regard, the Metropolitan Fund of the Detroit area constituted one of the most ambitious and well-funded organizations. Dedicated to improving the overall quality of life in the region, the Metropolitan Fund was directed by an eighty-five-member Board of Trustees, composed of leaders drawn from a wide variety of civic, educational, governmental, business, industrial, and labor groups. The Metropolitan Fund, funded by a variety of private and public sources, conducted research on metropolitan needs and aspirations and developed various responsive policies and action programs. It disseminated its findings to the public through the publication of reports and the usage of print and electronic media. And, finally, the Metropolitan Fund assembled a leadership cadre charged with the responsibility of implementing its various action programs.

The Metropolitan Fund's research program resulted in many publications including an anthology edited by Kent Mathewson, *The Regionalist Papers*. The first edition of *The*

Regionalist Papers[95] was released in 1974, followed by a revised edition in 1978.[96] The first part of the volume consists of a series of papers, each authored by a prominent scholar or group of scholars, centering on the experience of metropolitan regionalism throughout the United States. This is followed by a second section focusing on the need to reorganize the governmental structure of the Detroit region, rendering it more responsive, efficient, and equitable to all citizens of the area. In its two-part recommendation, the Metropolitan Fund first called for a reconstituted and strengthened Southeast Michigan Council of Governments, to be followed by the establishment of a more permanent system of regional governance for the region.

The Politics of Metropolitan Governmental Reorganization at Mid-century

During the middle portion of the twentieth century, the metropolitan governmental perspective not only proved to be persuasive among scholars but also served as a catalyst for a flurry of metropolitan governmental reform efforts. In seeking to realize their goal of a regionwide government, reformers resorted to the strategies of annexation, city-county consolidation, and the establishment of the comprehensive urban county.

In the period from 1950 to 1970, a large number of Southern and Western cities significantly enlarged their territorial boundaries through annexation.[97] For example, Oklahoma City increased its geographical expanse from 50 to 630 square miles; during the same period, neighboring Tulsa gained in territory from 27 to 172 square miles. Atlanta increased its territorial limits from 37 to 132 square miles. In a similar fashion, the Texas cities of Dallas, El Paso, Fort Worth, Houston, and San Antonio witnessed a considerable enlargement of their corporate limits. Kansas City, Missouri, which increased its geographical expanse by a strategy of unilateral annexation from less than 85 square miles in 1950 to 316 square miles by 1960, was the only major city situated outside of the South or West that was able to significantly expand its boundaries through annexation.

Several major circumstances account for the success of Southern and Western cities in annexing adjacent territory, as opposed to cities located in the East and Midwest. First, Eastern and Midwestern cities, like Boston and Milwaukee, respectively, are surrounded by incorporated suburban jurisdictions impervious to annexation, whereas cities in the South and West, at the time, were encircled by unincorporated territory, readily susceptible to annexation. Second, favorable annexation laws in the South and West, as opposed to their more stringent counterparts in the other regions, facilitated the annexation goals of Southern and Western cities.

Between 1950 and 1970, reform attempts to achieve city-county consolidation, usually lavishly financed and staffed by the business community and various foundations, were undertaken in numerous metropolitan areas. For the most part, these attempts met with defeat (sometimes more than once) in regions including Cleveland, St. Louis, and Dayton, Ohio, as well as in a score of smaller metropolitan areas. Suburban voters generally played a key role in defeating these consolidation efforts. By contrast, due to unique political circumstances and service inadequacies, city-county consolidation efforts were successful in Baton Rouge (1947), Nashville (1962), Jacksonville (1967), and Indianapolis (1969). In a similar fashion, a metropolitan government based on the comprehensive urban-county approach was established in the Miami region in 1957.[98]

Although attempts to establish metropolitan governments generally met with defeat during this period, a council of governments—designed to promote metropolitan regionalism and cooperation between local governments—was established in practically every metropolitan area because of local, state, and federal support.[99] Also particularly noteworthy was the establishment in 1969 of the Twin Cities Metropolitan Council of the Minneapolis–St. Paul region and the Portland (Oregon) Metropolitan Services District in 1970. These bodies, unlike the usual council of governments, enjoyed limited service and policy review powers.[100]

Resurgence of Interest: Metropolitan Government and Governance in the 1990s

In large part due to the paltry success of reform advocates in the 1950–1970 period, relatively few scholars of urban affairs focused their research efforts on the government of metropolitan areas during the era from 1970 to 1990. However, in the limited scholarship produced, scholars of urban affairs increasingly resorted to the term "metropolitan governance," rather than "metropolitan government," because of its more inclusive structural and process description. This change in terminology was largely due to the writings of public choice scholars. For example, as Vincent Ostrom, Robert Bish, and Elinor Ostrom convincingly registered: "We need to recognize, then, that local government in a democratic society cannot be confined to what transpires in particular corporate entities or agencies identified as units of government. This is why it may be more useful to refer to governance structures than governments. We can appreciate that something viewed as a process of government (governance) requires a much larger unit of discourse than do units of governments as such."[101]

After a hiatus of concern, scholars of urban affairs exhibited a renewed interest in the topic of metropolitan government and governance in the 1990s. This development was initially triggered by the publication of David Rusk's volume, *Cities Without Suburbs*.[102] Rusk, noting with alarm the increasing incidence of economic, racial, and social segregation in the metropolis, with the poor and other disadvantaged citizens disproportionately confined to core cities, argued that central cities, in order to remain viable, must be able to expand their territorial boundaries through an aggressive policy of annexing suburban areas. The failure of core cities to expand their borders, according to Rusk, will ensure their continued economic decline. Citing the adverse effects of fragmented local government in the metropolis, Rusk wrote: "[A] metro area in which local government is highly fragmented is usually incapable of adopting broad, integrating strategies. Conversely, a metro area in which key planning and zoning powers are concentrated under a dominant local government has the potential to implement policies to promote greater racial and economic integration if that government has the courage and vision to do so."[103]

Advocating the concept of metropolitan government through a somewhat different line of reasoning, Neal R. Pierce advanced in his work *Citistates: How Urban America Can Prosper in a Competitive World* that the global economy has become and will increasingly be marked by economic competition between the metropolitan areas of the world, which he labels "citistates."[104] Citistates of the United States, according to Pierce, confront three main barriers in their quest to compete with their counterparts elsewhere around the world. These barriers are: the wide socioeconomic disparity between core cities and suburbs and among suburbs; physical sprawl and its negative environmental and social consequences; and, finally, the hesitancy of Americans to create effective systems of coordinated governance for their citistates:

> The third great disability of American citistates is their common lack of coherent governance —either formal or informal. The result is that fundamentally *public* decisions, on every question from air quality to transportation to solid waste disposal to assuring a competent work force for the future, are reached in piecemeal, often haphazard fashion, or worse still, are never made at all.[105]

Pierce added: "The problem, of course, is that virtually no problem of the modern citistate— be it strategic economic planning, environmental protection, education and work force preparedness, transportation, parks, recreation, urban growth management—can be handled entirely on a municipality-by-municipality basis. . . . The government fragmentation problem is well-nigh universal in American communities large and small."[106]

Anthony Downs's work *New Visions for Metropolitan America*[107] and Henry G. Cisneros in his edited anthology *Interwoven Destinies: Cities and the Nation*[108] each argue that we must develop among the citizenry and leadership segments of metropolitan areas a stronger metropolitanwide perspective, along with a more coherent regional governing process, although not necessarily a metropolitan government, in order to ensure the rational future development of our metropolitan areas and the alleviation of severe socioeconomic problems. In this regard, William R. Dodge, in his work *Regional Excellence: Governing Together to Compete Globally and Flourish Locally*, provides political leaders with a well-developed set of strategies designed to promote regional governance.[109]

Although the above volumes differ in substance, details, and extent of recommendations, Rusk, Pierce, Downs, and Cisneros concur that we need to institute a more coherent process and system of regional governance in our metropolitan areas. In achieving this goal, they are in agreement that initiatives by local public and private leaders must be accompanied by aggressive federal and state action and policies.

The Reform Argument: Summary and Evaluation

In summary, the principal elements of the reform argument are: (1) the *fundamental* problem of the metropolis is the decentralized, or fragmented, character of local government, with its multiple number of local governments; (2) the fragmented nature of local government results in inefficiency and ineffectiveness; (3) due to the disparity of wealth among communities, local public services are marked by inequality and lack of equity; (4) services that should be provided on a metropolitanwide basis are delivered by a multitude of local governments; (5) there is a lack of metropolitanwide political leadership, sensitive to the well-being and interests of the entire region, responsive to socioeconomic problems, and planning for the future; and (6) therefore, there should be established in every large urban region a metropolitanwide governmental structure.

The extensive writings of reform advocates have provided us with a number of insights to be considered in the present debate concerning metropolitan governance. First, although it may be argued that reform advocates placed an undue emphasis on the premise that the fundamental problem of the metropolis is of a structural nature, it remains incumbent upon us to devise a system of metropolitan governance that will reduce the vast disparity of resources available to local governments. Only if this is accomplished can we ensure a minimally satisfactory level of services, such as public education and social welfare, for all the citizens of the region.

Second, virtually all scholars of urban affairs, including those of the public-choice school, agree with reform advocates that some services—such as mass transportation, sewerage, and water, due to their basic operating character and the benefits derived from economies of scale—should be delivered on a regional basis. We need to address, therefore, and arrive at a general consensus concerning which services should be delivered on a regional basis and the appropriate delivery mechanism for these services.

Third, reform advocates have consistently called for the development of political leaders who are motivated by a metropolitanwide, or regional, policy vision. This requirement is undoubtedly of greater currency today than in the past, given the regional character of many urban problems and the competitive nature of the global economy. We need to develop a metropolitan system of governance that will allow political leaders to rise above parochial community loyalties and demands, and to act and devise a policy vision on behalf of the best interests of the entire region.

Forth and finally, metropolitan government advocates have repeatedly reminded us that developing and establishing an appropriate system of metropolitan governance requires an intergovernmental response from the federal, state, and local levels of government. We need to think anew and more forcefully address ourselves to the issue of what roles each of these sectors of government should play in terms of structuring metropolitan governance and whether a popular plebiscite and approval should be required when establishing new systems of governance.

On the other hand, the reform argument may be taken to task on a number of grounds. First, even a cursory inquiry reveals that urban governmental organization and relationships are far less chaotic than reformers have led us to believe. Studies substantiate that through the process Charles Lindblom has labeled "coordination through mutual adjustment"[110] and the employment of horizontal oral agreements and formal contracts, there is far more cooperation between governments in the metropolis and more rationality in local policy making than we have commonly acknowledged. Vincent Ostrom, Charles M. Tiebout, and Robert Warren certainly uncovered and documented this in the Los Angeles area at the beginning of the 1960s.[111] Likewise, H. Paul Friesema found a rather elaborate and deliberate system of informal and formal cooperation between local governments in the Quad-City metropolitan area of Illinois and Iowa.[112] Further, regional councils, such as the Association of Bay Area Governments (San Francisco), the Southeast Michigan Council of Governments (Detroit), and the Metropolitan Washington Council of Governments (Washington, D.C.) facilitate communication and cooperation between local urban governmental entities and introduce a regional perspective into local policy making.[113] It is simply not accurate to portray metropolitan governmental organization as chaotic and composed of noninteracting local political units.

Second, advocates of metropolitan government have stressed that only by establishing areawide structures can there be any possibility of ensuring roughly equal levels of services throughout the metropolitan area because of the disparity of internally generated fiscal resources. This argument, however, fails to recognize that not all individuals want the same pattern of services. Robert L. Bish reminds us that individuals dwelling in urban areas often entertain differing public service priorities. As he notes, "Some individuals prefer to use their economic resources to attain larger private yards rather than public parks, some want more police protection, fire protection, or cleaner streets."[114]

Third, in contrast to the reform argument, studies do not uniformly support the contention that fragmented government enhances the per capita costs of local public services or seriously impairs the effectiveness of service delivery. In their exhaustive study, Brett Hawkins and Thomas R. Dye found no relationship between the extent of fragmented urban government and the costs or quality of municipal services.[115] Similarly, Alan Campbell and Seymour Sacks discerned no consistent relationship between measures of governmental fragmentation and per capita municipal expenditures.[116] And Werner Z. Hirsch reasoned, on the basis of the relevant empirical studies he reviewed, that economies of scale are not uniformly found in the public sector.[117]

Fourth, although reform advocates assert that the consolidation of local governments into an inclusive metropolitan structure will bring about a more viable and responsive political process, there is little empirical evidence to support this claim. For example, no data reveal that citizen participation in the local political system, as measured by voter turnout, is any greater in those few areas that have a metropolitan government. Ironically, a major argument against metropolitan government concerns democratic preference. Popular referenda and survey data substantiate that the majority of the metropolitan citizenry opposes metropolitan government.[118] Vincent Marando reminds us that for every successful city-county consolidation attempt, there have been three rejections.[119]

Fifth and finally, it is prudent to suggest that the adoption of metropolitan government would further alienate the urban citizenry from local government and the political process. As Milton Kotler and others have advanced, political alienation is one of the major problems found in the metropolis.[120] Reflective of this, numerous scholars of the urban political process have called not for metropolitan government, but for the decentralization of service delivery systems and policy making.[121]

In conclusion, reform advocates—strongly influenced by the principles of the scientific management movement, incorporating the ideas of Wilson and Taylor—have played a major role in shaping the continuing debate on metropolitan governance. Indeed, the reform argument and its advocacy of metropolitan government remained virtually unchallenged until the rise of the public choice alternative in the 1960s. The most significant contribution of the reform advocates is their insistence that we need to be mindful of the requirements of regionalism in reference to metropolitan governance. In contrast, the most deficient element of the reform advocates was their frequent failure to provide empirical evidence for the principles they advanced, placing too much emphasis on governmental structure, and neglecting the process of the government and the politics of the metropolis.

CHAPTER THREE

The Elusive Quest for Metropolitan Government

Writing in 1962, sociologist Scott Greer noted:

The difficulties of changing metropolitan governmental structure may usefully be divided into three levels. These are (1) the underlying cultural norms of Americans concerning local government, (2) the resulting legal-constitutional structures, and (3) the political-governmental system built upon them.[1]

Greer went on to say that the need for metropolitan governmental reform had been mitigated through the use of "two subterfuges that have been widely adopted: the special district and outside subsidy." Though there have been other developments that also serve to alleviate the need for metropolitan governmental reform, these two are among the more important.

Concepts of local autonomy, "grass roots" government, and distrust of those who exercise power derive from the ideas of Thomas Jefferson and so-called Jacksonian democracy, where the governmental system is subjected to a veto by the voters, people support the concept that "the government that governs least, governs best," and so on. When these tenets are translated into legal provisions of constitutions and statutes, the result is a limited and highly decentralized—vertically and horizontally—system of government that is, to a considerable degree, incapable of transcending the numerous political boundaries and functional jurisdictions that have evolved over the last two centuries. Political leaders are elected and bureaucracies evolve in conformity with these minor jurisdictions. Divided into minuscule segments, voters are required to approve both major and minor policy changes for very local issues as well as those that transcend these principalities.

In 1958, Robert C. Wood defined suburbia as an ideology, "a faith in communities of limited size and belief in the condition of intimacy." For Wood, the old values explain more about the people and politics of suburbia than any other interpretation and indicate why our large urban complexes are structured the way they are. "The ancient symbol of the 'republic in miniature' persists and the suburb is its contemporary expression."[2]

Two decades later, John C. Bollens and Henry J. Schmandt observed:

The governmental pattern that has evolved at the local level has managed to maintain itself without submitting to major surgery. Few incumbent officeholders or others who benefit from the existing arrangements are willing to gamble on possible gains that a reorganized structure might bring them. . . . Defenders of the *status quo* hold a strategic weapon. Unlike the reformers who have no ready-made machine for mobilizing support, they have access to political cadres and mass based organizations that serve as reference points for voters.[3]

This is an advantage that is hard to overcome in the absence of critical community problems that cannot be alleviated by more modest change or subsidy by state and federal governments. Stated differently, of the half-million elected officials serving close to 87,500 local governments, only a handful serve a metropolitan constituency, and most of these are associated with units having limited jurisdiction. Virtually no political actor gains from a major alteration of the metropolitan political structure. A few may profit from something like county reorganization, county assumption of areawide or supplementary services, or in a very few instances, city-county consolidation. While some type of county structural reorganization and adaptation and/or county assumption of urban-type services is fairly common in urban areas, city-county consolidation is largely limited to smaller urban areas or areas where the ecology of local government is relatively simple compared to average or large metropolitan counties or metropolitan areas. Consolidation also requires that local leaders pay close attention to how the changes affect existing political actors and bureaucracies.

For a number of states and many local governments, the translation of cultural norms into public policy means government by referendum when it comes to tax issues and the alteration of the structure of local government. Commonly, both minor and major changes in local arrangements and policies must be submitted to the voters for their approval—anything from a bond issue to increases in the property tax, the adoption of sales or earnings taxes, county provision of supplementary services to unincorporated areas, the assumption of an areawide service, or a large-scale restructuring such as city-county consolidation.

Voter approval requirements are sometimes so extreme as to prevent any change. Dating back to the 1930s in Ohio, for example, property taxes above a certain level (the ten mill constitutional property tax limit) must be approved by the voters. Even when approved, they apply for only a limited period—usually between three and ten years—then must be resubmitted to the voters for continuation. This has caused some very real problems for school districts.[4] Until the 1960s, in order for a county to become an areawide service provider, the change required the approval of a majority of the voters both inside and outside the boundaries of the largest city, countywide, and in a majority of the political subdivisions (cities, villages, and townships). One of the authors once calculated that 1.5 percent of the voters, properly distributed, could defeat such a proposal in Montgomery County (Dayton), Ohio.[5] Major or even moderate reforms are seldom successful unless the voting requirement is approval by a single areawide or countywide majority. Gauged by the experience of St. Louis and a number of other attempts at restructuring, simply dividing the vote between the central city and areas outside the central city usually results in the defeat of a proposal for major changes of the local governmental system.[6]

Vincent L. Marando and Carl R. Whitely documented voter rejection of city-county consolidation 68 percent of the time—nineteen out of twenty-eight proposals—during the period between 1945 and 1971.[7] In two of the rejected cases, voters overall approved city-county consolidation (Richmond–Henrico County, Virginia, at 54.0 percent, and Roanoke–Roanoke County, Virginia, at 66.4 percent), but the change required separate majorities by voters in the major city and voters outside the major city. This ratio of support has not improved over time. Marando and Whitely note that average voter support for the creation of a consolidation charter commission is 73 percent but approval of the proposals developed by charter commissions average only 47 percent. Where such data are available, voter turnout is low and typically 44 percent higher in county areas outside the city. City-county consolidation is not a grass-roots movement and the benefits of change are often both abstract and long range. Campaigns for the acceptance of this reform utilize the mass media, but they are seldom supported by organizations with a significant political base such as local political parties and local bureaucracies. As Marando and Whitely point out, consolidation referenda are affected by a sometimes unique mix of social, political, and economic factors.

Evidence from the Metropolitan St. Louis Survey of the 1950s and a study of the St. Louis situation by the U.S. Advisory Commission on Intergovernmental Relations (ACIR) indicated that a majority of residents supported some change in local government, but between one-fourth and one-third of the residents favored major restructuring of local government, whereas a similar proportion wanted to maintain the status quo. The remainder were amenable to more modest reform. But when a proposal for major change was voted on, both those favoring more modest efforts and those endorsing the status quo voted against the proposal; conversely, when more modest changes were posited, those for major change and those supporting the status quo voted against change. The city of St. Louis separated from St. Louis County in 1876, but the population had started to spill over the boundary by 1900. Since the 1920s, there have been several attempts at restructuring. All but a few iniatives have failed, partly because of the two-majorities requirement—that is, inside and outside the central city—though some proposals have failed in both areas.

The one reasonably major city-county unit that was approved by large majorities of voters in both the city of St. Louis and St. Louis County in 1954 is the Metropolitan St. Louis Sewer District—at the time, you could smell the problem in both city and suburbs. Other agencies have been created by action of the state legislature. The Bi-State Metropolitan District was originally modeled after the Port Authority of New York and New Jersey. It was created by the legislatures of Missouri and Illinois, and currently operates the Bi-State Transit System and Parks Airport on the Illinois side of the Missouri River. Five other rather minor "cultural" districts have also been created by the Missouri Legislature for St. Louis and the county.[8] As in other cities, voter approval is usually obtained for the integration of "system-maintenance" services. In recent years, voters have also been approving some integration of "cultural" activities. In 1997, voters in four counties on both sides of the state line in Kansas City approved the levy of a small sales tax to support the renovation of Union Station. Moreover, in recent years, state legislatures have sometimes imposed minor reforms without requiring voter approval.

Kansas City, Kansas–Wyandotte County: A Case Study of City-County Consolidation

The ecology of local government is an important factor relative to major alteration of the structure of government in a county or metropolitan area. The term "ecology of local government" refers to the size and pattern of local governments in a county or metropolitan area. Reform is more likely where there are only two—usually no more than three— significant local goverments at the time consolidation is submitted to the voters. School districts and minor entities, such as special districts, are usually left out of successful reorganization plans. Having too many local jurisdictions appears to thwart any major local restructuring. The most recent city-county consolidation, that of Kansas City, Kansas and Wyandotte County (1997), is instructive in this respect. Kansas City, Kansas, should not be confused with the much larger Kansas City on the Missouri side of the state line.

Wyandotte is also a county area that had experienced a significant decline in resident population (18 percent) between 1970 and 1996[9] as well as a comparable erosion of its economic base. Over 90 percent of the 153,000 1996 Wyandotte County residents lived in the central city at the time of adoption. The other two municipalities in the county— Bonner Springs and Edwardsville—had a combined population of about 11,000. Before consolidation, there were one township, five school districts, and one large and eight small special districts. The large special district—the Kansas City, Kansas Board of Public Utilities—provided water and electricity services to the central city, Edwardsville, and other areas outside the boundaries of the central city. Including the county, there were only nineteen local governments prior to consolidation, compared to an average of forty-five for metropolitan counties nationally.

The process of creating the new consolidated government took some three-and-a-half years' effort on the part of local leaders, the governor, and the state legislature—an extremely short time for this type of reform. The movement for reform was started by two local businessmen, Kevin Kelly and Mike Jacobi, who had no prior political experience. They argued that, through consolidation, Wyandotte County could reverse the trend toward high taxes, chronic population loss, pork-barrel politics, and a tarnished public image. The move was supported by Kansas City, Kansas mayors Joe Steineger and his successor Carol Marinovich, and the Kansas City city council. Mayor Marinovich ran for re-election supporting city-county consolidation. The proposal was supported by Governor Bill Graves, a moderate Republican, who appointed a Consolidation Study Commission, which reported favorably to the state legislature. A majority of Wyandotte County's twelve-member state legislative delegation either supported these recommendations or supported the right of the voters to approve or reject this reform. Enabling legislation was then passed by the state legislature and the proposal was subsequently approved by a three to two majority of the voters on April 1, 1997.

Prior to this change, Wyandotte County government was an old-style, patronage-oriented entity with long-time Democratic party control. The central city went though a reorganization in 1983, replacing the three-member commission form of city government with a mayor-council–city administrator system. This earlier reorganization was successful in improving city government and may have been a factor in shaping voter attitudes toward change. Given the fact that over 90 percent of the county residents lived in the central city, Marinovich represented an almost countywide constituency. Moreover, by providing that the city and county bureaucracies would be integrated and personnel reductions would take place only through attrition, bureaucratic opposition to the reform was greatly reduced.

After consolidation, which took place on October 1, 1997, there were still seventeen units of local government in Wyandotte County. The schools, the two small municipalities, and the special districts were left out of the reorganization, though residents of the two outlying small municipalities were given the right to vote for the mayor/chief executive and members of the new legislative body, called a board of commissioners. Only the city, the county, and the one remaining township were included in the consolidation. The new eleven-member city-county commission consists of the elected mayor/chief executive, two at-large commissioners, and eight commissioners elected by districts. The mayor/chief executive votes only in the case of a tie. The newly elected executive, Carol Marinovich,

Table 3.1

KANSAS CITY, KANSAS–WYANDOTTE COUNTY CONSOLIDATION PLAN

Executive Branch	
Elected Officials	*Appointed Officials*
Mayor (also serves as chief executive and presides over county legislature; votes in case of a tie; veto can be overridden by vote of seven commissioners)	County Administrator (appointed by Mayor with consent of county commissioners) Department Heads (appointed by county administrator)

Legislative Branch	
Elected Officials	*Appointed Officials*
8 Commissioners (elected by district) 2 Commissioners (elected at-large countywide) Mayor (acts as presiding officer, chief executive)	Mayor *pro tem* (acts in absence of the Mayor)

Judicial Branch	
Elected Officials	*Appointed Officials*
District Judges	(appointed by Administrative Judge with approval of the Board of Commissioners) Legislative Auditor Ethics Commission Municipal Judges

Source: Kansas City Star, January 7, 1997, p. A-11

former mayor of Kansas City, Kansas, has the authority to appoint a county administrator with commission approval. The administrator, in turn, appoints department heads. The mayor/chief executive has a veto over measures passed by the city-county legislature. It takes a vote of seven members of the legislative body to override a mayoral veto.[10] (See Table 3.1.)

The variables critical to the success of the Kansas City, Kansas city-county consolidation are seldom present in other urban counties; as a result, most attempts at reorganization fail. A large number of interrelated factors are involved in every attempt at major structural reform. For Wyandotte County, nearly all these factors seemed to point toward a successful city-county consolidation. Most successful reorganizations are usually unique to a specific county area. At least fourteen factors or local situations are important to the success or failure of city-county consolidation. They are in many cases important relative to other major metropolitan reforms and are sometimes applicable to less radical change. The listed items are not in any particular order of importance, as that will vary with the type of proposed change and the area where the reorganization is proposed. They are:

1. *Size of County Area.* Success in achieving city-county consolidation appears to be related to the population size of the city and county. Using the data presented by Vincent L. Marando and Carl Whiteley (1972), the critical size appears to be about 200,000 residents at the time the proposal is put forth for voter approval. Below that figure, about half the attempts at city-county consolidation succeed; above it, only about one in four proposals are adopted by the voters.[11] This is probably related to the ecology of local government (see factor 4 below), as counties with over 200,000 residents usually have more competing interests and a more complex structure of local government. Moreover, for larger county areas, the state is more likely to require a double-majority approval—that is, majority approval in central city and in the area outside the central city. Counties with larger numbers of residents are also likely to have a bigger proportion of residents living in suburban areas and are therefore less likely to approve proposed change. All the recent (since 1971) successful city county-consolidations that the authors are able to document had less than 200,000 residents at the time the consolidation took place. At 153,000, the Kansas City–Wyandotte County reform fits this pattern, as do the other recent consolidations of the city of Athens and Muscogee County, Georgia (1991), with a population of 179,000, and the earlier consolidation of three cities and their boroughs (counties) in Alaska—Anchorage (1975 population 161,000), Sitka (1990 population 8,588), and Juneau (1990 population 26,761). Earlier consolidations in Suffolk–Nansemond County, Virginia and Lexington–Fayette County, Kentucky also occurred in county areas of moderate size.[12]

2. *Ethnic Division between City and County Areas.* In principal cities where African Americans are in the majority, or are a very significant minority and have the expectation of gaining control of the city government, they quite consistently oppose changes that would place them in a minority in the reorganized government. Combining the city and county (suburban) electorate often means that African-American residents in the central city will, in effect, become a distinct minority in the new government and therefore unable to exercise much influence. Although the minority population of Wyandotte County was the largest in the metropolitan area at 28 percent—with 26 percent African American in 1990—they did not oppose this change because the system of representation in the reorganized consolidated city-county government gave them essentially the same number of minority commissioners as they had council members under the city government and more than they had before the change relative to the old county government.

The "white flight" to suburban areas in Kansas City, Kansas did take place, but it was somewhat different from that in other urban areas. Most whites who left Kansas City, Kansas, moved across the county line into Johnson County to the south. Johnson County is the wealthiest county in the metropolitan area, with a reputation for the best public schools. It is nearly 97 percent white, with only 1.5 percent African-American residents.

Relative to city-county consolidation, African Americans are concerned about an equitable system of representation; that they not be "layered under" politically by whites and suburbanites; and that the new system create a program for developing human resources and eliminating the dependency of the poor. In addition, they are concerned about political development of the African-American minority and access to jobs.[13] Needless to say, most proposals for city-county unification do not address all of these concerns.

3. *Type of Representation.* Another consideration relating to ethnic and other divisions within the reorganized government is the system of representation for electing public

officials. This may be quite important to the success or failure of a consolidation proposal. Minority groups often prefer the single-member district system because this ensures them positions on the newly created governing body of a consolidated government. At-large elections tend to give the dominant party, ethnic group, faction, or interest group most or all of the seats on the proposed legislative body and, in some cases, this has been a critical issue leading to failure of a referendum. If too many, or all, of the legislative positions are elected at-large, then it may well lead to defeat of the proposed consolidation. At-large election was definitely a factor in the failure of a proposed new charter for the city of St. Louis in 1957. The Kansas City–Wyandotte County consolidation elected eight members of the commission by district and two from the county at-large, which, in this instance, gave proportionate representation to both the African-American community and the remaining suburban municipalities. All seven of the former Kansas City city council members were elected to the new governing body, as was the former mayor of one of the two suburban municipalities.

The adoption of a home-rule charter for Jackson County (Kansas City), Missouri is instructive with regard to the system of representation chosen for the proposed reorganization. The charter was approved in 1972 and went into effect in 1973 after two prior attempts to adopt a charter failed (1949 and 1958). It provided for an elected executive and a fifteen-member county legislature, four elected at-large and eleven by district. The districts were carefully drawn to give proportionate minority representation. At a later date, the at-large districts were eliminated, reducing the number of legislators to the eleven elected by district. The charter was proposed at a time when a number of separately elected county officials were reaching retirement age. The charter eliminated all other elected officials except the judges and the prosecuting attorney.

4. *The Ecology of Local Government.* The size and pattern of local governments in a county can be a critical element for passage of a proposal for city-county consolidation. Too many local units normally means more elected officials concerned with maintaining their bailiwicks and status in the community. It also means multiple bureaucracies concerned about their status after the consolidation takes place. Recent successful city-county consolidations involved situations where there were only two or three major local units to be integrated. For Kansas City, Kansas, only the central city, the county, and the one remaining minor township government were included. The other major unit, the Board of Public Utilities, was excluded, as were other minor local units. Throughout the Kansas reorganization process, the greatest opposition came from the suburban municipalities, where there was concern that they would be saddled with the debt of Kansas City, Kansas. In the case of the Alaskan consolidations (Anchorage, Juneau, and Sitka), only the city and county—and perhaps a minor unit, such as the housing authority—were involved. In Alaska, there are no school districts and thirteen of the fourteen special districts in the state are housing authorities. As will be shown in Chapter 4, the reforms in Baton Rouge, Louisiana, Jacksonville, Florida, Indianapolis, Indiana, and Nashville, Tennessee excluded small outlying municipalities and other minor local units.

Not only are the pattern and size of local government important, but the distribution and characteristics of the population are of equal importance. These characteristics concern socioeconomic status and ethnic identity. Wyandotte County had less than two-fifths of the average number of local governments for metropolitan counties nationally, sixteen of the nineteen being rather minor entities.

5. *Elected Officials.* Wyandotte County area contained 118 elected officials, compared to a national average of 288 for counties located in metropolitan areas. The only elected officials eliminated in Wyandotte County were the county commissioners, administrative county officials (county attorney, register of deeds, sheriff, surveyor, and treasurer), and the township clerk, treasurer, and trustees. Members of the central city council could expect to be elected to the new county commission and the mayor could expect to be elected county mayor/chief executive. Suburban, school, and special-district elected officials remained in office. Some twenty-two elected official positions were eliminated, but only a dozen officials were left without positions in local government. In effect, 93 percent of locally elected officials were either excluded from the reorganized city-county or could expect to be elected to positions in the new government.

6. *Suburban Municipalities.* In Wyandotte County, and other consolidations discussed in later chapters, residents of small outlying suburban municipalities have the right to vote for the new county legislature. In the case of Wyandotte, it also appears that the new legislative districts were structured in a manner that would ensure that someone from the outlying suburban municipalities would be elected. This, too, may have been an element in the passage of this reform. Including small outlying suburban municipalities appears to be a pattern for successful city-county reform.

7. *Central City Dominance.* In 1997, before the consolidation, Kansas City, Kansas covered more than 70 percent of the land area of Wyandotte County and over 90 percent of Wyandotte County residents lived in the central city. This gave Mayor Marinovich an almost countywide constituency. This situation is unusual and is not often replicated in other counties where city-county consolidation is proposed. Moreover, the city itself went through a major structural reform in the 1980s, supplanting a three-member commission form of city government with a mayor-council–city administrator system. This may have helped pave the way for a similar restructuring at the county level, as the voters had some experience with a major restructuring of city government. According to the 1992 *Census of Governments*, the large special district, already serving most of the county with water and electricity, accounted for over 28 percent of local expenditures. Considering only the remaining services, the central city and its school district provided 77 percent of local services (50 percent city and 27 percent school district), with the county government spending only 13 percent. The remaining suburban municipalities, plus school and special districts, accounted for only 10 percent. It is somewhat unusual for the central city to dominate the county area to this extent. The dominance of the central city made the county government almost superfluous.

8. *Bureaucracies and Patronage.* It is quite common for suburban and county bureaucracies to oppose major reform of local government. This is not only true for full-time personnel, but often also applies to part-time and volunteer workers, particularly in the case of volunteer and part-time employees of fire departments and police forces. Volunteer fire departments in outlying areas often take on the characteristics of a somewhat exclusive club. In some cases, even full-time employees are concerned that they will lose their jobs if they are subjected to the personnel requirements of larger city or county governments.

Prior to this change, Wyandotte County was an old-style, patronage-oriented government with long-term Democratic party control. It was criticized as highly inefficient, ineffective, and corrupt. Nevertheless, the reform proposal assured both city and county government personnel that their jobs would be maintained, and that reductions would take place only through attrition. This certainly helped reduce bureaucratic opposition to this change.

In the case of Wyandotte County, Democratic party voters were in the majority in both the city and county governments. Because suburban areas made up less than 10 percent of the residents of Wyandotte County, the more common split between Democrats in the central city and Republicans in the suburban municipalities did not characterize this urban county. The division of population between the central city and outlying areas is important to the success or failure of city-county consolidation movements, as in many cases the core city tends to be Democratic and the suburban areas Republican. And, as Marando and Whitely point out, the turnout of suburban voters tends to be higher than that of the central city residents when the election concerns city-county consolidation. Consolidation can threaten the roles played by political parties in either the core city or suburban areas, or both.

For many county and metropolitan areas (MSAs), the political party division between the central city and its suburban areas is an important consideration. As Robert Wood noted in 1958, "Neither city Democrats nor suburban Republicans are likely to relish exchanging their comfortable local majorities in those parts of the metropolitan area over which they preside for a situation in which a tight two-party fight is almost guaranteed."[14] Whether this situation has changed over the last four decades as the suburban areas increased their size relative to the rest of the metropolitan area is problematic. Suburban areas now encompass three-fifths of the MSA population, which may mean they will find only the integration of system-maintaining services acceptable under certain conditions.

9. *Cadres of Voters*. Bollens and Schmandt made the point that existing local governments have access to cadres of voters in mass-based organizations such as political parties and local government bureaucracies. This is true. But in the case of Kansas City and Wyandotte County, the Democratic party was most important for all of the large local units—the city, the county, and the utility district. The utility district was unaffected and city employees could expect to transition to similar or more important positions in the new government. The county bureaucracy made up no more than 15 percent of all local full-time equivalent (FTE) employees and about one-third of those in the central city. County employee opposition was blunted by the assurance that reductions in personnel would take place only through attrition. Where there is a more equal division between the city and county personnel of the local governments to be integrated, or a more equal political party division, these can be important factors relative to the success or failure of city-county reform.

10. *Crisis Situations*. Successful consolidation of a city and county often involves a crisis situation, in terms of finances, services, or the local economy. In the case of Wyandotte County, it was the local economy that in turn affected both finances and the need for public services. The county experienced an 18 percent decline in population between 1970 and 1996 and a comparable erosion of the local economy. With manufacturing employment accounting for 28.1 percent of jobs, Wyandotte County was the most dependent on this sector of any county in the metropolitan area. The average for the rest of the MSA was

just 17.3 percent. The unemployment rate was the highest in the metropolitan area and was 72 percent higher than the average of the MSA; the percentage of the population on welfare was the highest in the MSA; and it was the only county in the MSA with a declining population. It was 14 percent below average in service employment and 29 percent below average for personal income, compared to the other nine MSA counties. Partly due to a declining population, but also because of a need for higher levels of public services given its economic situation, the Wyandotte County area was 40 percent above the Kansas City MSA average in the number of local government FTE employees per unit of population.

11. *Leadership*. This situation and the perceived inefficiency and ineffectiveness of county government led two community leaders, Kevin Kelly and Mike Jacobi, to propose consolidation of the city with Wyandotte County. Kelly is a successful small business owner and Jacobi a retired U.S. Army officer and the owner of a realty company. In 1994, Kelly volunteered to become an unpaid county administrator and was turned down. He then spent $20,000 running for the county commission and was defeated, but his campaign brought the issue of county reform to the attention of local politicians and the voters. Kelly and Jacobi kept the issue going and late in 1994, then–Mayor Joe Steineger called a meeting of elected officials from Kansas City, Bonner Springs, and Edwardsville. They appointed a task force on city-county consolidation, which Kelly headed. (It is very unusual to have officials of suburban municipalities agree to support such a move.) Late in 1995, the task force recommended that the city and county merge with an eleven-member governing body and a mayor–chief executive with veto power. Early in 1996, State Senator Bill Wisdom introduced a bill authorizing an election date, but the bill stalled and was supplanted by a compromise that established a Governor's Consolidation Study Commission. The state study commission recommended essentially the same proposal as had the local group. Mayor Marinovich, elected in 1995, strongly supported the consolidation. When it came time to pass enabling legislation, all members of the Wyandotte County–Kansas City legislative delegation either supported the proposal or the right of voters to pass on the issue.[15]

12. *Single or Dual Majorities*. City-county consolidation or, for that matter, most areawide or countywide restructuring, is much more likely to pass if only a single areawide majority approval is required. When the vote is divided between the central city and the rest of the area, it is more likely to fail. In 1970 a consolidation of Roanoke City–Roanoke County, Virginia received approval by two-thirds of the voters and failed because separate majorities were required inside the city and in the county. The Kansas City proposal required only countywide approval. Several attempts at reorganization of the city of St. Louis and St. Louis County have failed because dual majorities are required. Such a reform in Ohio is virtually impossible because multiple majorities are required—in the principal city, outside the city, and in a majority of the political subdivisions (cities, villages, and townships). Several factors come into play in determining voter approval, including the pattern and distribution of population, and the pattern and distribution of local governments, political parties, wealth and taxable resources, and so on.

13. *System-Maintaining and Lifestyle Services*. The situation with the Kansas City–Wyandotte consolidation did not involve any "hot button" lifestyle issues. Lifestyle issues such as education, zoning and subdivision control, and sometimes police and fire pro-

tection, were not issues in this campaign. Suburban municipalities, school districts, and special-district governments were not included in the proposed changes. Police protection, sometimes considered a lifestyle service, was already handled primarily by the central city and the county governments. Given the crime rate, police may have been viewed as a system-maintaining service that needed to be integrated. Also, because of the economic situation, the reorganization may have been viewed as a system-maintaining move that could improve the local economy, which was in the interest of all parts of the county area. Suburban areas often agree to changes that involve system-maintaining services, but tend to reject those that threaten the lifestyle of their respective areas.

System-maintaining services such as water and sewers, pollution control, and major transportation systems are integrated in most metropolitan areas by a number of devices: interlocal agreements and contracts, county assumption of services, large special districts, state government assumption of services, or state and federal subsidies. In areas with a high risk of conflagration, fire protection is often considered a system-maintaining service. Where there is a very high crime rate throughout the area, police may be in this category.

14. *General and Urban Services Taxing Areas.* Though apparently not an important issue in the Kansas City, Kansas–Wyandotte County consolidation, where the core city had 71 percent of the land area and over 90 percent of the county population, the establishment of general services districts (GSDs) and urban services districts (USDs) has played an important role in gaining acceptance for city-county consolidation measures for several of these reforms. In these cases, at least two property tax rates apply, one for countywide services that are paid by all taxpayers (GSD) and an additional rate for those receiving urban-type services (USD) (see Chapter 4). In a few cases, residents have been guaranteed that urban services would be delivered to them within a year of the imposition of the additional tax, once an area is annexed to the urban services area.

The new city-county government in Wyandotte County is apparently having some early success in terms of economic development, with a recent agreement to develop a \$252 million NASCAR race track.[16] An earlier development of combined dog and horse race tracks went bankrupt after five gambling riverboats opened on the Missouri side of the state line.

Characteristics other than the fourteen listed above may be important to the success or failure of governmental reform in other metropolitan areas. One that might be of considerable importance is the degree to which an individual state is willing and politically able to encourage or even impose some types of reorganization on their urban regions. It is not a question of authority, but one of the state's responsibility for the integration of system-maintaining services, as in the case of Minneapolis–St. Paul (see Chapter 6). In the 1920s, while the city of Milwaukee was constructing a new sewage treatment plant, Wisconsin imposed a city-suburban sewer district, with both taxing authority over and representation from the suburban area, for Milwaukee and adjacent suburban municipalities; in 1929, the state of Connecticut created a multi-purpose special district for Hartford and the surrounding towns, though the legislation required voter approval in each of the towns. The Hartford Metropolitan District Commission was given the authority to provide five or six services, but has largely confined its activity to sewer and water systems.

Virginia's Independent Cities

As of 1998, Virginia had 40 independent cities, which are situated outside of county jurisdiction and provide all governmental services, except for a minimal number of services provided by special districts and authorities. Recently, Virginia enacted legislation allowing independent cities, through what is known as the "reversion process," to surrender their city status and revert to town status within a county, allowing the city to transfer services to the county government. This procedure allows the city and county, through negotiations, to determine which services should be assigned to the county; the application for reversion is then forwarded to the Commission on Local Government for its review and comment. Ultimately, the reversion application must be approved by a three-judge state court. In some ways, reversion is a modified form of city-county consolidation, or at least the transfer of functions to the county government.

Recently, the former city, now town, of South Boston re-entered Halifax county and transferred elementary and secondary public education, along with a number of other services, to the county government. In addition, a citizens group in Charlottesville, Virginia is presently promoting a movement in the city to have Charlottesville surrender its city charter and revert as a town back into Albemarle County.

Attitudes of Citizens and Public Officials

The attitudes of both citizens and public officials concerning local government and public policy vary considerably from city to city and suburb to suburb. Cities and suburbs are highly differentiated in terms of economic base and social structure. The socioeconomic status of elected public officials is often a reflection of the type of community from which they are elected, though they tend to be of slightly higher social rank. Often elected officials, such as members of city councils, are a microcosm of the communities they represent. Stated differently, the elected officials of a working-class community tend to reflect the characteristics of that city or suburb; the same can be said of communities populated largely by professionals, by middle-class residents, or by those of high social rank.[17]

Central cities are highly differentiated in terms of their economic base and social structure; though on average they tend to have a lower socioeconomic status than suburban communities. Even though suburban communities generally have higher levels of income, they too are highly differentiated with industrial, commercial, and residential suburbs, often of different characteristics related to the political, economic, and fiscal viability of the local community.

In discussing the Philadelphia metropolitan area in 1971, Oliver P. Williams, Harold Herman, Charles S. Leibman, and Thomas R. Dye suggested that location of residence is a causal factor in producing differences in opinions concerning governmental activity and/or the choice of residence itself is related to differences in attitudes toward government and political convictions. It might also be proposed that location of place of work is also a factor. Sometimes people select a community in which other residents, usually of similar socioeconomic position and educational level, share their attitudes and concerns. In other instances, after they become residents they adopt similar attitudes.[18]

Others have proposed that the educational level of residents is also a variable to be considered. Developers using RCAs and municipal zoning ordinances, building regulations, and occupancy codes either select or encourage the location of like-minded residents of similar status. Williams and his colleagues stated that conformity may be the result of subtle social mechanisms involving acceptance or withholding of approval by one's neighbors; deviation tends to invite discord. Location is also a function of the ability of individuals and families to afford the location they consider appropriate. Generally speaking, people with higher levels of income and more education appear to be more amenable to change.

Another determinant may well be stage of life. For example, families with young children often select a location that has what they consider to be an appropriate educational system, public or private. Singles and young married couples may look for different amenities and facilities than older people. People beyond their child-rearing years and those at the retirement stage of life both have different needs for housing and different attitudes toward various amenities. All these factors shape attitudes toward government and the need for governmental services.

Change Over Time

As has been pointed out in earlier chapters, major alteration of the local government structure is the exception rather than the rule. This is not to say that there has been no change in the way we govern ourselves at the local or even the state and national levels. Government at all levels is much more pervasive today than in the early part of the twentieth century, but change has been less pronounced at the local level. Despite the relative lack of restructuring, government has grown and adapted to the changed environment over the course of the twentieth century. In 1900, government constituted eight percent of the gross national product (GNP) compared to between 38 percent and 40 percent in the mid-1990s.

Over this same period, using the Census definition, urban residents increased from 30 million to 192 million and from less than 40 percent to over 75 percent of the U.S. population. Residents of metropolitan areas now constitute 80 percent of the population. It is a given that residents of urban areas require more services and more complex infrastructure than those who live in rural areas and small towns. Even given the fragmented nature of local government in rural and metropolitan areas, individual units and types of local government have adapted to this changed environment, as have states and, to some degree, the federal government, despite some retrenchment during the latter part of the 1990s. In fact, there have been rather massive changes in the role states play in our federal system.

One constant in the U.S. federal system is change. Much of this change is the result of increased urbanization and, in particular, increased suburbanization of the population since 1900. Using government finances measured as a percentage of GNP, the federal role in 1997 was 7.6 times that for 1902; states were 11.0 times the earlier figure; while local government was only 1.8 times higher. Disregarding the large increase followed by a decline in the federal role resulting from World War I, for the first three decades of this century, local government was the dominant level in terms of revenues and expenditures; states the least active level. For example, local units accounted for over three-fifths of all government revenue in 1913 (a year less affected by the downsizing of the federal government after the Spanish-American War and increases resulting from World War I) and nearly two-thirds of direct expenditures; states collected only 13 percent and spent 10 percent of the total (see Figure 3.1).

Federal Aid to State and Local Governments

As Scott Greer pointed out, the need for metropolitan government has been mitigated by federal and state subsidies and the creation of special district governments. The special district device is considered at length in Chapter 7. Federal and state subsidy of local government started to be important in the 1930s and intensified after World War II. In part, at least, federal and state aid became important as the country became more urban, with the need for more adequate urban services and major transportation systems both within and between metropolitan areas.

States have always been directly involved with the creation and structuring of local government. In a few of the colonies, local government preceded the adoption of a charter for the colonial government; for the most part, however, colonies and early states created their own local units. Compared to the federal government, states started earlier in the provision of significant amounts of financial support for their political subdivisions. More direct federal involvement in local government is a twentieth-century phenomenon. The

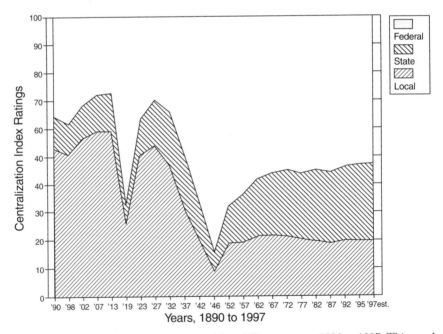

Figure 3.1. Relative Roles of Federal, State, and Local Governments, 1890 to 1997. This graph uses Stephens's typology of state centralization (based on three subindices measuring services delivered, financial responsibility, and personel adjusted for interlevel differences in inputs of personnel versus cash and capital) and a comparable index of federal versus state and local activity measured the same way for the average state. Prior to 1902, data are less reliable, but appear to be close to what is shown above.

most intensive federal involvement was during the period from the mid-1960s to the late 1970s, though federal regulatory authority, initiated through the use of grants-in-aid during that period, still persists. For a more extensive discussion of federal/state, federal/local, and state/local relationships, see Chapter 8.

As has always been the case, much of the change in role of the federal government was in response to real or perceived crises: two world wars, the Great Depression, and the Cold War (see Figure 3.1). Actually, a more detailed, year-by-year exposition of changes in the role of our central government reveals increases and later declines for the Korean and Vietnam conflicts as well. The federal response to the Great Depression was the only major increase in federal activity centered around domestic services. Though erratic, the overall level of federal activity vis-à-vis state and local government has declined since the end of World War II. With stops and starts, there were gradual increases in federal domestic services from the Truman administration through that of President Ford. Beginning with President Carter through the tenure of President Clinton, federal domestic programs have been scaled back.[19] Federal involvement in local government has been largely through the use of grants-in-aid and federal regulatory authority.

With the exception of agencies like the U.S. Postal Service, and possibly the departments of Agriculture and Interior, most federal domestic services are cash intensive. The central government runs programs like Social Security and Medicare; gives grants to states and/or local units to perform or supplement particular services; and underwrites a large number of loan, credit, and insurance programs. Given the fact that over 55 percent of direct expenditures by the Defense Department are in the form of procurement contracts for training, maintenance, equipment, and housekeeping activities, it might be said that a large portion of defense spending is also cash intensive.

Federal aid to state and local government was minuscule during the first two decades of the twentieth century, going primarily for agriculture and natural resources. In the 1920s, grants started to be provided for highways, but it was not until the economic crisis of the Great Depression that federal aid was given more broadly for other domestic services, including those affecting urban areas. With the exception of war years, for the period from the mid-1930s to the early 1960s federal aid constituted between 8 percent and 11 percent of state and local expenditures. It then increased to a peak of over 19 percent by the mid- to late 1970s, with the enactment of a series of block grants and general revenue-sharing grants that went primarily to local government. Over most of the period covered by the data shown in Figure 3.1, 85 percent to 90 percent of federal aid went directly to the states, where it was either spent or passed through to local governments. During the period from the late 1960s to the late 1970s, block grants and revenue sharing gave up to 25 percent directly to local governments for general purposes and a variety of domestic activities. Federal grants have since declined in their relative importance to state and local governments, but particularly for local units. Total federal grants to state and local units have dropped back to about 15 percent of state and local expenditures. Over the last decade, only about 10 percent of these funds were given directly to local governments, bypassing the state government.

In the 1960s, the federal government reorganized consolidating agencies with programs that affect state and local government. Dozens of agencies and programs in the areas of transportation and urban development were reorganized, creating the Department of Transportation (DOT) and the Department of Housing and Urban Development (HUD);

then later the Environmental Protection Agency (EPA). Partly because of grant monies associated with these and other federal programs, the states created their own consolidated agencies of local government, transportation, and environmental protection—little HUDs, little DOTs, and little EPAs.

As Scott Greer pointed out, federal and state subsidies have helped to alleviate some of the more critical financial problems of local government, thus reducing the need for more radical structural reorganization at the local level. State aid to local government has always surpassed federal grants in dollar amounts, even though some portion of state grants is federal aid that is passed through to local units. From the mid-1930s to the early 1960s, local intergovernmental revenue constituted about one-fourth of all local expenditures. With increases in state and federal aid between the late 1960s and the late 1970s, these subventions approached two-fifths of all local expenditures. Largely due to the demise of general revenue sharing and a series of block grants given primarily to local governments, state and federal subsidy of local government has since leveled off at one-third of local expenditures.

Support and Opposition to Reform

The groups that support and oppose the reform of local government are fairly common from one metropolitan area to the next. Differences in outcome are directly related to the political influence exercised by these groups in different urban areas, and the strictures and structure of the system of state and local government in the area considering a major reorganization. In 1962, the U.S. Advisory Commission on Intergovernmental Relations (ACIR) listed the most common groups that support and oppose governmental reorganization in metropolitan areas.

Support generally comes from what are sometimes labeled "good government groups." These include: metropolitan newspapers, radio, and television; central city officials; chambers of commerce; banks; commercial and real estate interests; homeowners; the League of Women Voters; manufacturing interests located in the core city; utilities; and a civic research agency, if one exists, plus a number of academics.[20] Since 1962, with the development of expressways and circumferentials; the dispersal of manufacturing, warehousing, and retailing to the suburbs; and the development of branch banking and the consolidation of banks throughout the region, it is not entirely clear that all of these groups will now support major restructuring. Central city officials and bureaucracies may not always support restructuring if it means a reduction in the influence and/or representation of African Americans, Hispanics, and other minorities in the new government.

Opposition usually comes from suburban and fringe-area local governments and their elected officials and bureaucracies; suburban commercial and business interests; suburban newspapers and throwaways; county employees; volunteer and part-time government employees, particularly volunteer fire departments; and farmers, farm organizations, and rural homeowners.[21] Again, since 1962, it appears that suburban areas, as distinguished from more rural fringe areas, are more amenable to the integration of system-maintaining services. The role played by political parties depends on their patterns of influence and patronage.[22]

Conclusions

The concept of metropolitan government has considerable intellectual appeal, but is difficult to attain given all the variables that influence such a decision and the underlying cultural norms that have been written into the legal-constitutional system, which, in turn, influenced the structure of the systems of state and local government that prevails in the fifty states.

The concept of the "republic in miniature" persists, and as Robert Wood noted in 1958:

> Until these beliefs have been accommodated reform will not come in the metropolitan areas . . . A theory of community and a theory of local government are at odds with the prerequisites of contemporary life and, so far, theory has been the crucial force that preserves the suburb. . . . There is only the stubborn conviction of the majority of suburbanites that it ought to exist, even though it plays havoc with both life and government in our urban age.[23]

Four decades later, similar attitudes seem to prevail, and suburban areas with a majority or a plurality of the population in twenty-eight of the fifty states and half the resident population of the United States are of increasing importance in the halls of state legislatures and Congress.

CHAPTER FOUR

Metropolitan Government I: City-County Consolidation

The concept of metropolitan government, a governmental structure designed to encompass the entire metropolitan area and predicated on the principles of economic efficiency, administrative effectiveness, political accountability, and socioeconomic and political equity, has engendered little citizen support or applied success in large metropolitan areas in the United States.[1] Notwithstanding this widespread citizen sentiment and general lack of implementation experience, several versions of metropolitan government have been established in a handful of large metropolitan areas. As a result of city-county consolidation, metropolitan governments have been organized in the following areas: Baton Rouge–East Baton Rouge Parish, Louisiana (1949), Nashville–Davidson County, Tennessee (1962), Jacksonville–Duval County, Florida (1968), and Indianapolis–Marion County, Indiana (1970). It is of note that with the sole exception of Indianapolis–Marion County, these metropolitan areas are situated in the South, where metropolitan governmental reorganization has been somewhat less difficult to achieve. In part, at least, this is due to less governmental fragmentation and simpler state systems of local government in the South. In addition, a federative, or two-tier, metropolitan government, utilizing the urban-county approach, was established in 1957 in Miami–Dade County, Florida. Although not considered as metropolitan governments, in the Minneapolis–St. Paul, Minnesota, and Portland, Oregon areas, innovative three-tier areawide governmental structures have been established. These possess significant regional policy-review powers and deliver a limited number of services.

The purpose of this chapter is to provide an overview of the general and political circumstances resulting in the city-county consolidations in the Baton Rouge, Nashville, Jacksonville, and Indianapolis areas. This discussion is followed by a review of their structure, service, and policy responsibilities; funding; and an assessment of their experience. In the following chapter, these same concerns are addressed with regard to the Miami–Dade urban county metropolitan, or two-tier, government, and the limited regional governmental structures of Minneapolis–St. Paul and Portland. In addition, Chapter 5 concludes with an overall assessment of the various metropolitan governments and regional structures and their contributions to metropolitan governance.

Baton Rouge–East Baton Rouge Parish

Immediately following the close of World War II, the Baton Rouge metropolitan area witnessed a proliferation of special districts, resulting in increased governmental fragmentation and a lack of comprehensive local governmental control.[2] In addition, water and sewer facilities were inadequate, largely due to population growth that had taken place in the suburbs outside the boundaries of Baton Rouge. The East Baton Rouge Parish government, structured and financed to deliver services for a rural area, was organizationally inept at delivering urban-type services to the burgeoning suburban population.

Responding to these circumstances, the Chamber of Commerce played a major role in placing on the Louisiana ballot in 1946 a constitutional amendment authorizing a city-parish charter commission to draft a county home-rule charter for the Baton Rouge–East Baton Rouge Parish metropolitan area. The amendment was approved by the state voters by a large margin, with 69,894 voting in favor and only 18,886 opposed. Subsequently, in a referendum conducted in 1947, the electorate narrowly approved a charter providing for the semiconsolidation of the governments of the city of Baton Rouge and East Baton Rouge Parish. The passage of the referendum simply required the support of a majority of voters throughout the entire area, rather than a more stringent requirement of separate majority voter support in both the city and the parish. The consolidated city-parish government took office on January 1, 1949.

Structure, Service Delivery, and Funding

The Baton Rouge–East Baton Rouge Parish consolidation plan extended the geographical boundaries of Baton Rouge from five to thirty square miles and involved only a partial consolidation of the city and parish governments. In addition, the plan allowed for the continued existence of two small municipalities, although they were prohibited in the future from annexing any territory. At the outset, the plan provided for an interlocking of the governing bodies of city and parish governments, whereby the seven members of the city council and two other individuals elected from the rural area constituted the parish council. This arrangement was modified in 1985 when a metropolitan council was established as the governing body of the parish. It consists of twelve members, elected from single-member districts on a nonpartisan basis. Members of the Metropolitan Council each serve a four-year term and may be re-elected for two additional terms of office. A mayor-president, elected on a parishwide basis, serves as the chief administrator and is assisted by an appointed chief administrative officer. A president pro-tempore, chosen from the ranks of the Metropolitan Council members, presides over council meetings. The mayor-president, also limited to three terms of office, may not vote in council proceedings, but may veto legislation passed by the council. A veto by the mayor-president may only be overridden by a two-thirds vote of the council. The mayor-president appoints the chief administrative officer, finance director, personnel administrator, public works director, and purchasing director. These individuals serve both the city and the parish. In addition, the mayor-president appoints the police and fire chiefs, who are city officials. The parish council appoints the attorney, clerk, and treasurer, who serve as both city and parish officials. The city and parish equally share the costs associated with the finance department. In sum, there is a considerable amount of personnel and functional integration between the city and parish governments, although each has its own budget and is accountable for its own expenditures.

An innovative aspect of the Baton Rouge–East Baton Rouge Parish plan was the establishment of a variety of service and taxing zones. In this regard, the parish was divided into three zones: urban, rural, and industrial. The boundaries of Baton Rouge were extended to encompass the entire urban area. Services delivered by the city include police and fire protection, garbage and refuse collection and disposal, street lighting, traffic regulation, sewerage, inspection and regulatory services, and the administration and operation of the several airports. City residents pay both municipal and parish real estate taxes.

Bridges, highways, streets, and sidewalks are provided and maintained throughout the region by the public works department, which is financed by parish taxes. Citizens residing in rural areas may receive additional urban-type services through the establishment of special taxing and service districts. Developed areas situated adjacent to the city may be annexed to the urban zone, pending the consent of a majority of the owners of the affected property and the city council. Urban-type services required in industrial areas are provided by the industries at their own expense.

Assessment

At the outset, the Baton Rouge–East Baton Rouge consolidation precipitated a considerable amount of popular hostility, especially among suburban residents who were incorporated into the enlarged city. These citizens had strongly voted against the consolidation plan and were particularly incensed by the fact that their inclusion into the city resulted in their loss of an exemption from local taxation on the first $2000 of their assessed property valuation. Of further concern, they were not immediately provided, as promised by the proponents of the plan, with an enhanced level of municipal services. These citizen concerns led to extended litigation and the defeat of a bond issue in 1950 designed to provide funding for new public improvements. Responding to these developments, the Metropolitan Council levied a 1 percent sales tax throughout the area and, within a period of two years, a higher level of public services was extended to the entire urban area and a capital improvements program was implemented. As a result of these actions, there was an increase in public confidence and an added sense of political legitimacy bestowed on the consolidated government.

The consolidated government has been credited with a variety of accomplishments. William Havard, Jr., a leading scholar and observer of the plan, has written that the consolidated government resulted in a "great improvement in the economy of operations and . . . the orderly development of local government services."[3] In his more extended assessment of the plan, R. Gordon Kean, Jr. credited the consolidated government with a number of achievements, including enhanced fire protection throughout the area, the establishment of comprehensive zoning and subdivision regulations, completion of a major street and drainage system, the establishment of new building codes, the construction of a municipal dock and a new municipal building, renovations and improvements of the courthouse, and a new civil service system for both city and parish employees.[4] On the other hand, the consolidated government has been criticized for several serious shortcomings: The city and parish law enforcement agencies continue to have overlapping jurisdictions; separate civil service systems operate for the fire and police departments; and several offices, which remain independent under the state constitution, are not adequately supervised and controlled by the local government.[5]

Nashville–Davidson County

Similar to the Baton Rouge metropolitan area, the Nashville region—particularly in the suburban areas immediately adjacent to the core city—was plagued in the 1950s by a lack of adequate services.[6] The most serious service deficiency involved an inadequate suburban sewer system. In addition, suburban residents complained about the poor quality or the lack of adequate police and fire protection, refuse services, and public schools. These citizen complaints underscored that the service demands of the region were not being adequately addressed by the city and county governments and the several small suburban governments. Responding to this condition, the Tennessee Taxpayer's Association recommended in 1951 that the service needs of the county could be better and more effectively and economically served by a consolidated unit of local government. This recommendation by the association stimulated the Davidson County delegation to the state legislature to lobby for and ensure the passage of legislation establishing the Community Services Commission for Davidson County and the city of Nashville. The broad responsibility of this commission, funded by the city and the county governments, was to examine and assess the service needs of the region and to set forth a policy response. A year later, the commission released a report, titled *A Future for Nashville*, in which it advanced the following recommendations: (1) public health and welfare services should be provided by the county; (2) the city and the county should be granted "home rule" by the state legislature; (3) electoral districts in the county should be reapportioned to correct for the relative lack of representation of city residents in county government; and (4) large portions of suburban areas should be annexed by the city, ensuring that the citizens of these areas would receive urban-type services. Although the report viewed favorably the consolidation of the city of Nashville and Davidson County, it dismissed this alternative as politically unfeasible.

By and large, the report failed to generate any immediate tangible results; however, it did serve to stimulate the establishment of a joint city-county planning agency, charged with conducting a further assessment of the service problems of the region. It also provided the stimulus for state action facilitating the local governments of the Nashville–Davidson County metropolitan area to develop a plan of action for meeting these service needs. Subsequently, Tennessee voters, in 1953, approved an amendment to the state constitution allowing the state legislature to enact legislation providing for the consolidation of city and county functions, upon the affirmative vote of both a majority of citizens residing in Nashville and residents of the rest of the county outside the boundaries of the city. Several years later, the state legislature passed legislation permitting cities to annex adjacent unincorporated suburban areas without the consent of the residents. In 1956, the Advance Planning and Research Division, an organization established in 1953 by the Nashville and Davidson County planning commissions to conduct long-range research and planning projects, released a report, titled *Plan of Metropolitan Government for Nashville and Davidson County*, in which it strongly endorsed the alternative of annexation as the most appropriate approach for meeting the service needs of the region. In the long run, however, the report urged the establishment of a single metropolitan government as the best way to deal with the inefficiencies associated with the city and county governments. This plan for metropolitan government recommended: (1) the establishment of two service districts within a single government unit consisting of a general services district (GSD) providing general governmental services throughout the county and an urban services district (USD) providing additional governmental services in urban areas; (2) the establishment of two separate tax rates to finance the level of services provided in each district; and (3) the establishment of a single legislative body for the entire county, along with the use of the strong mayor form of government.

The state legislature passed legislation in 1957 providing the legal basis for the consolidation of Nashville and Davidson County. It authorized the establishment of a charter commission responsible for writing a local governmental charter merging the governmental functions of Nashville and Davidson County into a metropolitan government. The commission consisted of ten members, including business leaders, advocates of labor and low-income interests, several prominent African-American political leaders, and a highly respected female attorney. Upon the completion of its work, the commission recommended the creation of a twenty-one-member metropolitan council, with six members elected at-large and the balance elected from single-member districts. The single-member districts were configured to ensure the election of at least two African-Americans to the council.

Reflective of the earlier report—*Plan of Metropolitan Government for Nashville and Davidson County*—the commission recommended that the metropolitan government have a general service tax district (GSD) and an urban services tax district (USD). It urged that suburban areas situated immediately adjacent to the USD be allowed to be annexed to the district upon the passage of a city ordinance. The commission also recommended that the four small incorporated suburban communities in the county be allowed to maintain their independent status.

The campaign on behalf of the metropolitan charter took place during the spring of 1958. The charter was strongly supported by a broad and diverse coalition of political interests, in addition to Charter Commission members. Included in this coalition were the major city newspapers, the city mayor, the most prominent and influential county judge, the Chamber of Commerce, leaders in the business community, labor leaders, the Tennessee Taxpayer's Association, and the League of Women Voters. In contrast, the charter drew strong opposition of private suburban volunteer fire companies, sheriffs, constables, and some city and county business owners, who viewed the proposed metropolitan government as a threat to their interests. Opponents charged that the implementation of the charter would result in bigger government, higher taxes, extended liquor sales, and the monopolization of local political power by the city mayor and his political allies. In a referendum conducted in June 1958, citizens residing in the city voted in favor of the metropolitan government; however, suburban voters in opposition narrowly defeated the metropolitan government charter. Lower-income suburban voters residing on the fringes of the region were especially hostile toward the plan. Concerning the defeat of the proposed metropolitan government, advocates were severely taken to task by pro-merger elements for not waging a more focused, professional, and grass-roots campaign.

Following the defeat of the metropolitan charter, Nashville began to make use of the annexation powers granted to it by the state legislature in 1955. By 1960, Nashville, in several annexation moves, had annexed about fifty square miles of suburbia, containing a population of about 87,000 citizens. Contrary to the promise of the city administration, citizens residing in these areas were annexed without their consent, provoking substantial political resentment toward the mayor. This resentment became more intense when the newly annexed citizens learned that the city was incapable of providing them with urban services in the near future, notwithstanding their payment of increased property taxes.

In March 1961, the state legislature, at the request of the delegation from Davidson County, passed an act establishing a second charter commission for Nashville and Davidson County. City and county voters approved its creation in a referendum conducted in August. Eight of the ten members appointed to the second charter commission had previously served on the prior commission and, hence, it was not surprising that the second charter commission set forth a proposed charter very similar to the one that had been narrowly defeated by the voters. In contrast to the earlier version, however, the second charter proposed a metropolitan council of forty-one members, rather than twenty-one, and a three-term rather than a two-term limit for the mayor.

In the spring of 1962 the campaign began in earnest for the metropolitan government charter. Proponents of the plan included substantially the same political coalition as in 1958, including business leaders, the League of Women Voters, and the Tennessee Taxpayer's Association. However, in this campaign the coalition lost the support of Nashville's mayor and one of the major city newspapers. Proponents of the plan, better organized and more professionally directed than in their previous reform effort, emphasized that a metropolitan government would result in more efficient and economical local government, eliminate city and county service disparities, and initiate areawide long-range planning. They were aided in their campaign by a sense of political resentment among the newly annexed city residents and by the passage of a city council ordinance known as the "green sticker law," requiring citizens throughout the region to obtain an automobile license for utilizing the streets of Nashville.

Political forces that had opposed the 1958 metropolitan government plan reiterated their opposition to the second charter. In addition, as previously noted, this time opponents enjoyed the support of Nashville's mayor and a major city newspaper. They characterized the proposed charter as a utopian scheme and argued that a metropolitan government would fail to achieve its promise of providing better and more rational local government. In a referendum conducted in June 1962, the electorate, by a required separate majority vote in the city and in the county area outside of the city, approved the new charter. The success of the reform proposal reflected the fact that the proponents had waged a highly politicized, professionally organized, grass-roots campaign, and benefited from several key issues. In this regard, David Booth noted that for the voter of the old core city, the issue centered on whether or not to retain Ben West as mayor; a vote for the charter could be interpreted as a vote against the mayor. Concerning the voters in the newly annexed areas, whose attitude on the proposed charter was somewhat framed by the fact that the mayor had broken his pledge guaranteeing their right to vote on whether they wished to be annexed, Booth pointed out that their vote turned on whether they wished, by voting positively, to become, in effect, first-class citizens, or, by voting negatively, to retain their second-class underrepresented status. And, finally, Booth advanced that in regard to the electorate residing outside of the city, the vote was significantly shaped by the following concerns: first, by the realization that their vote against the charter would subject them to annexation at any time, without any guarantee of better services, but that by adopting Metro they would be assured of additional services within one year after any property tax became part of the urban services district; and, second, by voting against the charter, they became more subject to taxation without representation (as in the instance of the "green sticker" tax); by voting for the charter, they acquired the right to participate in the election of six members of the new metropolitan council.[7]

Structure, Service Delivery, and Funding

Nashville's metropolitan government assumed the functional responsibilities of Nashville and Davidson County. The mayor serves a four-year term, and is limited to three terms in office. The mayor is responsible for supervision and administration of the executive departments, agencies, boards, and commissions. The mayor appoints all department heads, subject to the approval of the council. The mayor may veto council ordinances, including line-item budget expenditures; the mayor's veto may be overridden by a two-thirds vote of the council.

The metropolitan government has a two-part legislative organization: the Metropolitan Council and a much smaller urban council. The former consists of forty members, including the president of the council, chosen by the members of the body. Thirty-five of the council members are elected from single-member districts, while the balance are elected on an at-large basis. The president of the council, like other council members, serves a four-year term and also presides over council meetings. The sole function of the three-member urban council is to establish a property tax for the Urban Services District (USD), sufficient to finance the costs of providing services. In practice, however, the larger metropolitan council establishes the property tax rate, which is *pro forma* adopted by the urban council.

The metropolitan government provides for a General Services District (GSD) and an Urban Services District (USD). The General Services District encompasses all of Davidson County and delivers a variety of services, including general government administration, police, courts, jails, health, welfare, schools, mass transit, and parks and recreation. The Urban Services District, which at the outset included only the old city of Nashville, has been expanded to provide an enhanced level of services for all of the urbanized areas of the county. (Under the provisions of the charter, the Urban Services District may be expanded to those areas that need additional services, as long as the metropolitan government is capable of providing these services within one year after the additional USD tax rate is imposed.) The Urban Services District delivers an array of services, including fire protection, water, sanitary sewers, street lighting, street cleaning, refuse collection, and enhanced police protection. To provide financing for these services, all citizens pay a General Services District tax, while citizens residing in the urban areas are assessed an additional tax.

Assessment

Soon after its establishment, Nashville's metropolitan government gained widespread citizen approval and was credited with a number of accomplishments. A survey conducted in 1964 found that about 70 percent of the respondents had a favorable view of the metropolitan government, while the remainder held a measure of dissatisfaction.[8] Citizens in the latter category largely resided in the six incorporated suburbs and the rural areas of the county. Daniel R. Grant, in his comprehensive analysis of the metropolitan government published in 1965, credited it with a variety of achievements, including, first, better local governmental accountability to the citizenry than under the prior system of separate city and county government; second, the realization of considerable economies in local government operations, especially in regard to public schools, sewer services, and the purchase and maintenance of government automobiles; third, a greater equalization of services, both in terms of quantity and quality, throughout the region; fourth, the substantial elimination of city and county fiscal inequities in terms of services and taxes; and, finally, the projection throughout the nation of Nashville's image as a progressive community. In addition, Grant noted that the metropolitan government achieved service improvements without a large increase in property taxes, due to savings realized in government operations and the greater diversification of local governmental revenues, and that African-Americans under the consolidated local government did not experience a diminishing of their political power. On the other hand, Grant acknowledged that overall local governmental spending had increased, primarily due to the rising expectations of the citizenry, and that rural residents were not receiving all the service benefits from the consolidated government that they had anticipated. Further, Grant found only a limited amount of evidence that the creation of the metropolitan government had resulted in a greater professionalization of local governmental personnel.[9]

T. Scott Fillebrown, in his 1969 assessment of the metropolitan government seven years after its establishment, credited it with a series of accomplishments, including, first, suburban residents paying their fair share of costs for countywide services associated with the downtown auditorium, airport, and parks; second, the development and implementation of a unified sewer system; third, an expanded parks and recreation program; fourth, a vigorous downtown urban renewal program; fifth, a consolidated and improved school system; sixth, a regionwide bond structure; seventh, substantial elimination of duplication of services; eighth, greater local governmental administrative and political responsibility; and, finally, a greater sense of identification of suburbanites with the entire region.[10]

However, in a study conducted in 1974, Bruce D. Rogers and C. McCurdy Lipsey found that a sample of suburban citizens who received services from their independent government voiced a greater degree of satisfaction and set forth a higher evaluation of their public services than an equivalent sample of suburban residents provided the same collection of services by the metropolitan government. The only exception to this generalized finding involved fire services. Services surveyed in the study, beside fire services, included police, garbage collection, and street repair.[11]

Three decades after the consolidation of Nashville and Davidson County, Nashville has retained, indeed enhanced, its reputation as a progressive city, serving as a Southeastern sports, cultural, and business center. Nashville is the home of the Nashville Kats of the Arena Football League and in 1998 a new National Hockey League team was established in the city. Over the past decade, Nashville has witnessed a considerable rebirth of its downtown area, with the construction of an arena, a convention center, an office and luxury hotel tower, and a significant number of large residential properties.[12]

Jacksonville–Duval County

Prior to city-county consolidation in 1968, the governmental structures of Jacksonville and Duval County were marked by a large amount of organizational fragmentation. Jacksonville's 1917 charter provided for a city council to serve as a legislative body and a city commission to function as its executive component.[13] The council was comprised of nine members, elected at-large, one of whom was selected by his colleagues to serve as the presiding officer. The commission consisted of five members elected at-large who functioned in an executive capacity and were responsible for various services. Commission meetings were presided over by the mayor, who was elected by the citizens. Other directly elected officers, including the tax assessor, the tax collector, the recorder, and the treasurer, served further to fragment governmental structure, power, decision making, and responsibility for delivery of services. This structure of city government was designed to implement a system of checks and balances, resulting in good and efficient government. However, as Richard Martin, a long-time keen local observer of local politics has written: "In practice, however, the system did not work. Over the years, there was a proliferation of elected and appointed officials and of independent boards. At best, it was a confusing muddled system. At worst, it encouraged its separate entities to work at cross purposes or collaborate for their own ends to the detriment of the public well-being."[14]

The nature of the governmental structure of Duval County contributed to a further degree of local organizational fragmentation and a lack of administrative and political accountability. The county had a traditional governmental structure of five county commissioners, each elected at-large, who functioned as both policy makers and administrators. In addition, the following constitutional officers were directly elected by the voters: sheriff, tax assessor, tax collector, and a score of other officials. In terms of political reality, however, legislative authority resided in the county delegation to the state legislature, which for many years was controlled by a state senator who exercised a great amount of political influence and power. In sum, prior to city-county consolidation, the county government, because of its bewildering structure, lacked the political leadership and authority to effectively meet the service needs of its rapidly growing suburban population.

Prior to consolidation, the operations of the separate city and county governments resulted in a considerable amount of local governmental duplication and inefficiency, along with a lack of political accountability. The city and county governments were unable to successfully cope with a variety of citizen service demands. In addition, city-county cooperation was hindered because of the approvals required by the city council and city commission, the county commission, and the Duval County legislative delegation. Finally, governmental fragmentation in the region was compounded by the independent existence of the small suburban cities of Neptune Beach, Atlantic Beach, Jacksonville Beach, and Baldwin.

The lack of coordinated and effective local government in the region compounded service problems. Jacksonville, which was experiencing a weakening tax base, was plagued by a deteriorating public school system, which eventually resulted in the disaccreditation of all senior high schools in 1964. The city also lacked an adequate sewer system, resulting in raw sewerage being deposited directly in the St. Johns River. Further, the city suffered from a shortage of housing units for the disadvantaged. In a parallel fashion, Duval County, because of a poorly administered tax system and inadequate tax base, was fiscally challenged by a variety of service problems. Like the city, the county lacked an adequate sewerage system, a problem made more severe by its steadily growing population. In addition, county fire and police protection services were haphazard and insufficient.

The effectiveness of local government in the region was further undermined by the dominance of "machine politics" in the city, supported by a political coalition of business and professional leaders, along with a segment of the African-American community. The political machine promoted its parochial interests at the expense of the public interest of the community.

A number of related political developments took place prior to the consolidation of Jacksonville and Duval County. First, Jacksonville, in 1963, seeking to expand its tax base and alleviate its fiscal stress, sought to annex sixty-six square miles of the county, containing 130,000 citizens, but was rebuffed by county voters. A year later, in 1964, a similar effort by the city was again frustrated by the county voters. Second, in 1964, the Southern Association of Colleges and Schools withdrew its accreditation of Jacksonville's high schools. This action resulted in a serious setback of public confidence in the city government and eroded the legitimacy of its political leadership. Third, these developments, in turn, stimulated the establishment of a governmental reform movement seeking city-county consolidation. In line with this, a prominent retired businessman organized a meeting of influential citizens in the community in January 1965. As a result of their deliberations, this group issued a statement, labeled the Yates Manifesto (after the retired businessman who had organized the meeting), that called on the local delegation to the state legislature to seek passage of legislation allowing the citizens of Duval County to vote on consolidating their government with that of Jacksonville. The legislative delegation complied by drafting a successful bill establishing a local government study commission.

The Local Government Study Commission, consisting of fifty members, was composed of numerous business and professional leaders, four African Americans, and five women. Given the political implications of its charge for the African-American community, the commission made a special effort to ensure African-American participation at every stage in its deliberations. A much smaller executive committee, of seventeen members, was given the responsibility of coordinating the study. The commission commenced its work on October 1, 1965, and, after conducting a number of public hearings and meetings focusing on arguments for and against city-county consolidation and reviewing the experience of the metropolitan governments in other regions, released a publication, titled *A Blueprint for Improvement*, recommending the consolidation of Jacksonville and Duval County.

In order to advance its goal of city-county consolidation, the commission created an organization known as Citizens for Better Government. This organization formed a political coalition consisting of representation from the Chamber of Commerce, the Duval County Bar Association, the Duval County Medical Society, the League of Women Voters, the Jacksonville Urban League, the Voters League of Florida, the media, and small business enterprises. The Citizens for Better Government drafted a bill providing for city-county consolidation, which it submitted through the local legislative delegation, to the state legislature. The bill was based on the premise that city-county consolidation would result in more economical, efficient, and responsive local government, better organized and able to confront regional problems.

Opposing the reform efforts of Citizens for Better Government was a coalition labeled Better Government for Duval County, composed of traditional machine politicians, labor leaders, some suburban and African-American political leaders, representatives of several African-American newspapers, and an assortment of extreme right-wing political groups. The members of Better Government for Duval County argued that city-county consolidation would increase the cost of local government and possibly result in the rise of a tyrannical mayor.

The members of the local delegation to the state legislature carefully reviewed the city-county consolidation plan of Citizens for Better Government, along with the opposing arguments advanced by the members of Better Government for Duval County. After a considerable amount of political infighting, negotiation, and compromise, the delegation arrived at a consensus on an amended version of the city-county consolidation plan and successfully lobbied their legislative colleagues to enact legislative authorization for the plan, which was signed by the governor in June 1967.

Citizens for Better Government, upon the passage of the authorizing legislation by the state legislature, began a vigorous campaign on behalf of city-county consolidation. It asserted that consolidation would result in more efficient, responsive, and responsible local government. By contrast, Better Government for Duval County political forces argued that city-county consolidation would reduce the power of the people; some of the more extreme elements suggested that the city-county consolidation plan was a socialist and communist plot. However, the opponents of city-county consolidation eventually lost significant support when a local television station began focusing on an insurance scandal involving a number of highly placed city officials, who were eventually indicted by a grand jury for larceny, perjury, and conspiracy. The political effects of this scandal played a key role in the passage of the consolidation referendum by a vote of 54,493 to 29,768. County voters residing in the urbanized suburban areas adjacent to Jacksonville voted strongly in favor of the plan, while lower-income voters dwelling in the rural areas of the county supported the consolidation proposal by only a slim majority. African Americans, by and large, cast their ballots in favor of the plan; as Lee Sloan and Robert French have advanced: "The fact that black leaders were included in every stage of the consolidation movement in Jacksonville did much to allay their worst fears that the plan was simply a scheme by the white community to dilute the black vote."[15]

Structure, Service Delivery, and Funding

The city-county consolidated government began operations on October 1, 1968. The mayor, who is elected by the voters at-large for a four-year term and may serve two terms, has strong administrative and appointive powers. The mayor may veto appropriations bills and the budgets of the various independent agencies and elected boards. In addition, the mayor appoints, subject to council approval, virtually all department heads and a personnel board. By contrast, constitutional officers elected at-large include the sheriff, the tax assessor, the tax collector, and the supervisor of elections. Independently operated agencies are responsible for operations pertaining to public schools, electricity, port activities (including air and water), public housing, children's services, mass transportation and expressways, downtown development, and sports development. The City Council consists of nineteen members, fourteen elected from single member districts and five elected at-large; each city council member serves a four-year term and may serve two terms. The consolidated government has eliminated the overlapping and duplicating agencies of the former city and county governments. It has established a central support system monitoring the following functions: budgeting, auditing, purchasing, personnel, data processing, communications, and legal and vehicle services.

The consolidated government has a two-tier tax structure, similar to that of Baton Rouge and Nashville. Property taxes are levied by a general services district (GSD) on all property owners, and an urban services district (USD) levies an additional tax on residents residing in urban areas. The general services district encompasses the entire metropolitan area and delivers the following services: police and fire protection, health and welfare, recreation, public works, housing, and urban development. The urban services district includes the former city of Jacksonville and the four small municipalities of Jacksonville Beach, Atlantic Beach, Neptune Beach, and Baldwin. The urban services district provides the following additional services: street lighting, refuse collection and disposal, street cleaning, and debt service. Any portion of the general services district may be incorporated into the urban services district, on the provision that services can be provided within a year.

Soon after its establishment, the city-county consolidated government realized a score of achievements, including a reduction in local taxes.[16] Due partly to its acquisition of a score of privately owned utility operations, the government equalized utility rates throughout the area. Police and fire protection services were unified and upgraded, resulting in better citizen protection and a significant reduction in suburban crime. Many volunteer firemen were replaced by professionally trained, full-time firefighters. In addition, the consolidated government established a comprehensive ambulance rescue system, utilizing ambulances and additional forms of specialized equipment; established a division of consumer affairs; and launched a downtown urban renewal program.

Further, the city-county consolidated government made service improvements in a number of other areas. Septic tanks were eliminated throughout the region and the sewer system was rebuilt. The government cleaned up many neighborhoods with the implementation of a more effective solid waste disposal program, compulsory garbage services for all residents, and expanded weed- and rat-control programs. Recreation programs were expanded and increased, and health services were improved with the construction of a central health center and the establishment of ten neighborhood health centers. In addition, a major street improvement program was undertaken in 1971–72, resulting in the repaving of about seventy miles of roads, the construction of three miles of sidewalks, the completion of 347 drainage improvement projects, and the installation of more than 50,000 streetlights.

Early on, the city-county consolidated government realized additional achievements, including the implementation of a countywide land-use plan and zoning code, facilitating the orderly development of the region. Second, it implemented a new set of building, electrical, mechanical, and sign codes throughout the county. Third, the government projected an image of itself throughout the nation as an area committed to fostering a good business climate and promoting economic growth. As a result of these efforts it was successful in attracting to the region a score of national corporations, resulting in the local investment of millions of dollars. And, finally, race relations took a turn for the better with the election of four African Americans to the consolidated council. African Americans enjoyed better electoral representation than they had in the prior system of separate city and county governments. Reflecting these accomplishments, the consolidated government gained a public acceptance rating of 64 percent in March 1969; this figure increased a year later to 79 percent.[17]

In the 1970s, 1980s, and 1990s, Jacksonville's consolidated government continued to make progress in a number of areas. First, by continuing to promote its reputation as committed to a good business climate and by entering into a series of public-private partnerships, the city attracted many large companies, resulting in extensive downtown economic development. Second, the consolidated government terminated its reliance on property taxes through the imposition of user fees; realized economies and efficiencies in governmental administration and operations; and implemented more aggressive public safety and recycling programs. Third, it constructed a variety of public facilities, including a metropolitan park, a riverwalk, and a convention center. And, finally, the consolidated government implemented a broad program of volunteer citizen participation in government through the creation of advisory committees. Citizen members of these committees assist government officials in identifying community problems and suggest policies that should be adopted to alleviate these problems.[18]

Several scholars have advanced strong criticisms of Jacksonville's consolidated government. First, Bert Swanson has noted that the government failed to significantly reduce the economic, fiscal, and racial disparities in the area. Jacksonville continues to be one of the most racially segregated cities in the United States, with the vast majority of its African-American population residing in the core of the former city, while the suburbs remain overwhelmingly composed of white residents. African Americans reside in areas with the highest rates of crime and continue to have the highest incidence of poverty and female-headed households. In addition, they have the lowest levels of educational attainment, median family income, employment, and skilled jobs. Further, the African-American community perceives that it does not receive its fair share of governmental services.[19] Finally, the plight of African Americans is further magnified by their seeming loss of political power over the years. As Richard Feiock advanced in regard to the Jacksonville experience: "In the short run, access of minorities can be guaranteed by drawing one or more minority districts, but in the long run minority representation is diluted."[20]

Second, the consolidation plan continued local governmental fragmentation in the area and many functional operations still are not under the direct control of the mayor. About 40 percent of the governmental budget is expended by various independent boards, commissions, and authorities, most notably the school board and the Jacksonville Electric Authority. And although constitutional officials such as the sheriff, the tax collector, the tax assessor, and the supervisor of elections are responsible to central budgetary control, their separately elected status serves to limit their accountability. Further compounding the problem of governmental structure and accountability is the continued existence of the four small communities of Jacksonville Beach, Atlantic Beach, Neptune Beach, and Baldwin. These receive services from the urban services district (USD), but deliver their own package of general district services. These communities are reimbursed by the metropolitan government for the cost of providing these services.

Third, the long-term fiscal experience of Jacksonville's consolidated government provides little support for the contention that consolidated local government provides a permanent reduction in per capita taxes and expenditures. In a rigorously conducted investigation, J. Edwin Benton and Darwin Gamble found that per capita taxes and expenditures have increased in Jacksonville since the consolidation of the city and county governments. They wrote: "In examining the short- and long-term impact of consolidation in Jacksonville, one finds that consolidation led to a short-term decrease in per capita expenditures; however, the data indicate that the long-term impact was to *increase* [emphasis that of the authors] the growth rate. Therefore, any decrease in the short-run is overshadowed by the increase in the long-run." As a result of their study, Benton and Gamble concluded that, in reality, the reformers in Jacksonville who sought consolidation were primarily interested in achieving the delivery of more public services, rather than reduction in taxes and expenditures.[21]

Fourth, Swanson noted that positive citizen perception of local political leadership in Jacksonville declined from 50 percent in 1985 to 29 percent in 1993. He noted: "This decline reflects the rise of urban challengers to protect environmentally sensitive lands, neighborhoods, and the black community. . . . Voters have expressed anger over their sense of paying more and getting less, the number of city employees being reduced, residents in the old city being asked to pay for garbage collection for the first time, and the belief that public services are inequitably delivered."[22]

And, significantly, the advent of Jacksonville's metropolitan government has resulted in a transformation of the structure and nature of political power and decision making. As Swanson has keenly noted: "The most integrative force in Jacksonville has come from the informal power system, which has been significantly transformed from a tight, consensual, inner clique that used oligarchic control to impose its orthodox political ideology of a minimum government with low taxes. . . . The new consensual elite has become a 'growth machine' with an operative ideology of progressive conservatism toward an expansive use of governmental authority and public resources to facilitate growth."[23]

Indianapolis–Marion County

Prior to the city-county consolidation of Indianapolis and Marion County on January 1, 1970, popularly known as Unigov, Marion County had a total of approximately sixty local governments.[24] In addition to the county government and the city government of Indianapolis, there were twenty-two cities and towns, nine townships, eleven school districts, and sixteen special-purpose districts responsible for various functional activities. This fractionated governmental structure contributed to the widely held perception by the citizenry that local government was inefficient, ineffective, and unresponsive.

The traditional governmental structure of Marion County, consisting of three county commissioners, a five-member county council, and numerous other elected officials with limited duties and responsibilities, was unable to meet the service needs of the rapidly growing suburban population in the immediate post–World War II period. Reflective of this service inability on the part of the county, was the expansion, just after the war, of the city sewer and sanitation district beyond the municipal boundaries of Indianapolis. This was followed, in 1947, with the expansion of city library services to a county-wide basis, and in 1953 with the establishment of a corporation that constructed and maintained a joint city-county office building in Indianapolis. In 1955, a countywide planning, zoning, and subdivision control commission was established, followed by, in 1961, the organization of several countywide agencies for the provision of airport and park and recreation services. In 1963, the Metropolitan Thoroughfare Authority was established and in 1965, a countywide corporation was created to construct and operate a convention and exhibition center. In addition, studies were conducted regarding the feasibility of consolidating school districts and police services; however, the consolidation of these services was abandoned because of political resistance.

Although the above developments extended some city services beyond Indianapolis to areas of the county, they achieved relatively little in terms of functional integration. Consequently, it was apparent by the beginning of the 1960s that a major political effort was required to bring about some measure of structural and functional integration. This need was further underlined by the fact that the mayor, the city council, and various county officials exercised only partial and sometimes overlapping powers. Responding to this challenge, the Republicans were successful in electing Richard Lugar mayor in 1967, and managed to win a majority of the seats on the city council and a majority of the county offices. The following year, in the 1968 statewide elections, the Republicans elected the governor and secured a majority of seats in both chambers of the state legislature. This succession of Republican electoral victories provided them with a unique position, especially in view of the highly partisan tradition of politics in Indiana, to reorganize local government in the Indianapolis area. This Republican opportunity to reorganize local government was facilitated by the fact that popular approval, as expressed by a referendum, was not required by state law.

Mayor Lugar, influenced by the city-county consolidations in Nashville and Jacksonville and his own early frustrating administrative and policy experiences, began to advocate and campaign for local governmental reorganization. In this effort, he was given advice, assistance, and encouragement by the Greater Indianapolis Progress Committee, composed of business and civic leaders and established by his Democratic predecessor. Toward the end of 1968, Mayor Lugar sponsored a series of meetings regarding governmental reorganization with community and governmental leaders. These leaders inclined toward governmental reform, although representative of various business, professional, political, and governmental interests, had a strong sense of personal camaraderie and a loyalty to the Republican party. As a result of these meetings, the participants reached a general consensus on a model of governmental reorganization. An attorney was given the responsibility of preparing a reorganization bill to be introduced in the forthcoming 1969 session of the state legislature. At this point, the reorganization plan was widely publicized and it quickly drew the support of a number of Democratic leaders, several African-American political leaders, the League of Women Voters, and a score of other community leaders. A group labeled the Mayor's Task Force on Improved Governmental Structure was created to promote political support for the reorganization.

However, some political opposition developed toward the proposed reorganization, involving three segments of the community. First, a score of Democratic activists opposed the reorganization out of partisan self-interest, perceiving that the reorganization of government would provide the Republicans with a significant advantage in city politics. Second, a number of African-American political leaders opposed the reorganization proposal, concerned that it would dilute the political power of their community and effectively preclude, at least in the short term, the election of an African-American mayor. And, third, many suburbanites who had recently departed from the city negatively viewed the plan because it would once again make them city residents. The strength of these forces opposed to reorganization, however, dissipated over time, due to internal divisions.

The Unigov proposal was formally presented to the public on December 19, 1968, and was endorsed by the Chamber of Commerce, the League of Women Voters, and the mass media. Shortly thereafter, Mayor Lugar and the members of the Marion County delegation to the state legislature began a campaign to secure legislative support for the proposal. When the 1969 legislature convened in January, the Unigov bill was referred to and reported out of the Affairs of Marion County Committee, with several technical amendments added by the Senate. After overcoming only a limited amount of opposition, the bill was passed by the state legislature and signed by the governor on March 13, 1969.

The successful city-county consolidation of Indianapolis and Marion County may be credited to a number of factors, including the fact that it did not require the approval of the public as expressed through a referendum. Across the United States, this usual requirement has served to defeat numerous city-county consolidation attempts. Second, Republican victories in the municipal elections of 1967 and in the state elections the following year provided them with a uniquely dominant political position facilitating their reorganization of local government. This was an especially important factor given the highly partisan character of state and local politics in Indiana. And, finally, advocates of Unigov, especially Mayor Lugar, practiced a good deal of political leadership and savvy, as reflected in their willingness to compromise on a number of structural issues in order to achieve their overall goal.

Structure, Service Delivery, and Funding

Unigov resulted in a significant measure of central administrative control to many formerly separate agencies and service districts. They were consolidated into six departments, headed by a director appointed by the mayor. The departments are: Administration, Metropolitan Development, Public Works, Transportation, Public Safety, and Parks and Recreation. Five of the six departments—only the Department of Administration is an exception to this generalization—have boards as part of their organizational structure. Each of the boards, except for the Metropolitan Development Commission, situated in the Department of Metropolitan Development, consists of five members, two appointed by the mayor and two by the council. The fifth member of the board is the director of the department, who also serves as the presiding officer. The boards have a number of review responsibilities involving operating budgets, the disposition of property, the purchase of capital equipment and facilities, and the acquisition of real estate. The Metropolitan Development Commission consists of nine members: four appointed by the mayor, three by the council, and two by the county commissioners. The Metropolitan Development Commission serves as a planning board, zoning board, and redevelopment commission.

The city-county council assumed the legislative functions previously exercised by the prior city council, county council, county commission, and the various boards and commissions of the former independent agencies and service districts. The council consists of twenty-nine members; twenty-five are elected from single-member districts and four are elected at-large. Council members are elected on a partisan basis and serve four-year terms, with no restriction on the number of terms of office they may serve. The council enacts legislation of countywide import and has a variety of specific powers, including approving the budget, levying general and special taxes, appropriating funds for the various departments, confirming the mayor's personnel appointments, and making some of its own appointments. The fiscal review powers of the council include many of the independent agencies and boards and extend to the "constitutional" officers of the consolidated government, whose powers were not altered by the consolidation.

The number of governments in the region is approximately the same as prior to the establishment of Unigov. This is due to the fact that a complete consolidation of Indianapolis and Marion County would have required a constitutional amendment—a long, drawn-out process involving approval by the state legislature in two consecutive sessions—and approval by the voters in a popular referendum. With this in mind and due to time considerations, reform advocates were satisfied with only a partial consolidation of the governments in the area. Hence, the political entities of Indianapolis, Marion County, nine townships, three incorporated cities, and numerous organized towns continue as political bodies. The three cities of Lawrence, Speedway, and Beach Grove, as well as the town of Southport, were exempted from the consolidation because of suburban political resistance. The residents of these municipalities continue to elect their own mayors and councils; they also take part in the elections for the mayor and council of the consolidated city, who represent them in regard to countywide matters. The separately elected county assessor, auditor, clerk, coroner, prosecutor, recorder, sheriff, surveyor, and treasurer continue as constitutional officials and remain responsible for those duties not transferred to the consolidated government. The Marion County Board of Voter Registration and the Marion County Election Board have maintained their separate existence. The Marion County assessor, auditor, and treasurer serve *ex officio* as the Marion County commissioners.

A number of other governmental units also retained their preconsolidationist status. No changes were made in the judicial system or the school districts. In addition, several autonomous agencies continue to operate, although in a number of instances their operating independence was reduced by the mayor's enlarged appointive powers and the council's enhanced fiscal review responsibilities. These agencies include the Capital Improvements Board, the City-County Building Authority, the Health and Hospital Corporation of Marion County, the Indianapolis Airport Authority, the Indianapolis Public Transportation Corporation, and the Indianapolis–Marion County Public Library.

As the preceding underscores, Unigov did not result in a substantial reduction in the number of governmental units in the county, nor did it significantly expand the authority or jurisdiction of many of these governmental units. Unigov did, however, facilitate the goal of immediate and future functional integration to a considerable degree. In regard to the future, the territorial limits of service districts may be expanded, subject to the approval of the voters to be served. Further, municipalities not a part of the original consolidation plan may join Unigov, pending the approval of 51 percent of their electorate.

In the first few years following its enactment, the Unigov Act was modified in the following ways: The mayor's appointment powers were enhanced and the mayor assumed the powers of the former county commissioners; the police personnel system was modified; the redevelopment tax district was expanded; a requirement was enacted that a council member could participate in discussions pertaining to a service agency only if a minimum of 58 percent of the council member's district—a increase in the earlier requirement of 50 percent—was covered by the service agency; and a provision was made for the establishment of a system of community councils, designated "minigovs," involving communities of at least 5,000 residents. Each community was to decide by a referendum whether it wanted to establish a community council. Councils were to receive their authority and funding from the city-county council, and the latter was obligated to consult local councils concerning any planning or zoning actions affecting their communities. Due to a lack of interest among the citizens, however, the "minigov" concept was never fully implemented.

The delivery of public services in Indianapolis–Marion County is significantly more complicated than the Unigov structure would suggest. As William Blomquist and Roger B. Parks have noted: "The continued existence of the county, the school districts, the excluded cities, the included towns, and six of the special-purpose municipal corporations means that the Consolidated City of Indianapolis is far from being the only provider of local public services in Marion County. . . . Some local services are provided by the city-county government and extend over the territory of the pre-Unigov 'old city' of Indianapolis, others extend over the territory of the Consolidated City (i.e., Marion County minus the excluded cities), others extend over areas that correspond with none of the above."[25]

Services provided countywide exclusively by Unigov include planning, zoning, and land-use regulation; street maintenance and traffic flow; emergency communications; public housing; and sanitary sewers, solid-waste collection (in the "old city" by the government, elsewhere under contract by private companies), and solid-waste disposal (by private contractors under the supervision of the government). Additional countywide services include public health and hospitals, mass transportation, and the administration and operation of airport facilities, provided by independent agencies. Unigov has been a leader, especially in the 1990s, among U.S. cities in implementing the principles of competition and privatization with regard to the delivery of services. City departments are regarded as distinct businesses and compete with private companies to provide services. Through competition and privatization, Unigov has saved an estimated $100 million since 1992, reduced by about one-quarter the number of city employees, won wage concessions, and increased the productivity of the work force.[26]

Unigov shares in the delivery of some services, most notably public safety and fire protection, and is not involved in elementary and secondary education. For example, while the consolidated city provides police protection to an area somewhat larger than the "old city," the remainder of county residents receive police services from Marion County. Fire protection is provided by Unigov for most county residents, although this service is provided to some residents by township fire departments. Public schools are operated by the Indianapolis public schools, a separate unit of government, and by eight township school districts, the city of Beach Grove, and the town of Speedway.

As the above pattern of service delivery implies, property tax rates in the consolidated city-county are far from uniform. As Blomquist and Parks underscored: "Not only do Indianapolis residents continue to pay different bundles of taxes depending on where they live in the county, the number of different tax rates in the county has increased since Unigov. This is due to the presence of 61 different taxing units within the county (the county, the cities and towns, the independent municipal corporations, the townships, and the school districts), plus the use by the consolidated city of special service districts and special taxing districts to support different services and capital projects."[27]

Unigov's basic operating fiscal philosophy is based on the premise that the scale of taxation should coincide with the scale of benefit, resulting in two significant effects: First, a large proliferation of different tax rates and taxing units within the county, since each new endeavor tends to be funded through the establishment of a new special service or special taxing district; and, second, property tax rates that are higher in the inner city, since this area receives all countywide services in addition to several traditional municipal services that either are not provided or are provided and financed by other means elsewhere in the county.

Assessment

Soon after its establishment, Unigov was credited with a number of accomplishments, including the unification of administrative control under the mayor and city-county council. This served to eliminate a significant amount of administrative and political disorder associated with the previously dispersed and sometimes overlapping units of government. Unigov's stronger administrative control resulted in economies in government operations, realizing substantial savings in insurance, legal services, purchasing, and trash collection, and increased interest income on government investments.[28]

Second, Unigov in the 1970s was credited with significantly improving the infrastructure and physical services of the region. In the early 1970s, it resurfaced an annual average of 112 miles of roads, compared to only 16 miles per year countywide prior to the consolidation. In the same period, Unigov purchased hundreds of acres of land for recreational purposes, constructed six new swimming pools, and provided supervision for forty-seven additional summer playgrounds. Further, it achieved a 33 percent reduction in the rate of pollution, removed thousands of abandoned cars, and realized a large reduction in the crime rate. And, finally, Unigov carried out, with a large amount of federal funding, a construction program resulting in increased housing units for low-income and elderly residents.[29]

Third, Unigov has been credited with attracting to Indianapolis, through various public-private partnerships, a large amount of business investment, which has spurred economic growth and job opportunities. Over the past three decades, business growth in Indianapolis has continued at a substantial pace, resulting in a new downtown shopping center, various office and hotel facilities, a sports facility, a convention center, and a renovated railroad station. Through its various promotional and economic activities, Indianapolis has earned the distinction of being the amateur sports center of the United States.[30]

It is clear, however, that the establishment of Unigov diminished the political and economic interests of the African-American community. Soon after Unigov came into existence, York Willbern stated: "At the most obvious arithmetical level, it is clear that the black voting strength has been diluted, and most of the black leaders have been and are unhappy about this. . . . If the old city had remained the basic political constituency, the blacks would still have been far from having a majority, but their political leverage, especially within the normally victorious Democratic party, was becoming very considerable."[31] Presently, African Americans remain the most disadvantaged group in Indianapolis and, as Blomquist and Parks acknowledged: "In particular, the structure of public finance under Unigov does not reflect significant efforts to use the larger jurisdiction of the city-county government to effect wealth or income redistribution."[32]

The establishment of Unigov has solidified Republican political control over the city-county; Republicans have gained a decided advantage in local elections. Since the establishment of Unigov, Republicans have retained the mayor's office and a majority of the seats on the city council, usually by a substantial margin.[33]

Conclusion

Although each consolidation is unique, a number of generalizations may be made concerning the city-county consolidated governments of the Baton Rouge, Nashville, Jacksonville, and Indianapolis metropolitan areas. First, service problems associated with the increase and spread of population—involving the provision of sewer and water, fire and police protection, and/or primary and secondary public education—served as a catalyst for promoting the concept of and need for city-county consolidation. In this regard, in all four regions, the goal of metropolitan reorganization, which was correctly perceived by its proponents at the outset as a political issue requiring the mobilization of a coalition of support, was primarily led by leadership closely identified with the business community and "good government" groups, such as the League of Women Voters and organizations dedicated to the advancement of effective and efficient local government.

Second, in neither Baton Rouge, Nashville, Jacksonville, nor Indianapolis did a complete consolidation of the city and county governments take place, and in each of these regions a number of suburban local governments retained their independent status and, along with some independent or quasi-independent governmental bodies, continued to provide various services.

Third, each city-county governmental structure has the strong mayor council form of government, which confers on the mayor substantial administrative, budgetary, and personnel powers. This arrangement ensures that the mayor can function as a strong policy leader and preside over and manage an integrated bureaucratic structure. In addition, in terms of governmental structure, it should be noted that each of the city-county consolidated governments utilizes largely district elections for electing members to the council, ensuring that all the significant political interests of the community are represented.

In conclusion, the city-county consolidated governments of the Baton Rouge, Nashville, Jacksonville, and Indianapolis metropolitan areas may be credited with: (1) promoting and ensuring more orderly growth and development of their regions through more effective comprehensive planning, and the adoption of stronger building codes and zoning ordinances; (2) providing more effective and uniform public services throughout the region, especially with regard to mass transportation, sewers, and water; and (3) achieving a substantial amount of economic and job growth by attracting a range of new business enterprises to the region.

CHAPTER FIVE

Metropolitan Government II: The Urban County and Limited Regional Structures

Unlike the Baton Rouge, Nashville, Jacksonville, and Indianapolis areas, where metropolitan governments were brought into being by city-county consolidation, in the Miami area, a metropolitan government was implemented in 1957 by enhancing the fiscal, management, and service capacity of the county. This resulted in a two-tier, or federative, governmental structure for the Miami–Dade County area, which is unique in the United States. Under this federative structure, Metro Dade County, known simply as "Metro," is responsible for the delivery of all services in the unincorporated portions of the county and for services throughout the county that lend themselves to a regional approach, while the county's thirty municipalities (originally twenty-six) carry out services of a local character.

In addition, in 1967 the Minnesota state legislature enacted legislation establishing the Metropolitan Council of Minneapolis–St. Paul, a limited regional structure, which initially enjoyed significant policy review powers, but no direct service responsibilities. Similarly, a limited regional structure, originally labeled the Metropolitan Services District, later renamed Metro, was established in the Portland area by the Oregon state legislature in 1979. It should be stressed that these bodies are not comprehensive metropolitan governments, but regional governmental organizations that possess limited, though important, responsibilities.

This chapter provides an overview of the general and political circumstances accounting for the establishment of Metro Dade County, the Metropolitan Council of Minneapolis–St. Paul, and Metro of the Portland region. In addition, a review of their structures, responsibilities, and funding, and an assessment of their experiences is set forth. Finally, drawing on the material in this chapter and in Chapter 4, this chapter concludes with an overall assessment of the various metropolitan governments and limited regional structures and their contribution to metropolitan governance.

Metro Dade County

Prior to the advent of Metro, the governmental structure of Dade County consisted of an assortment of officials elected under a commission form of government.[1] The voters elected a total of thirty-nine officers, including five commissioners, ten department heads, fourteen judges, five constables, and five justices of the peace. Candidates for these offices

88

generally ran without partisan designation, relying on their personal attributes, political base, and past political experience. As all of this would suggest, there was an absence of an effective countywide agency responsible for long-range planning pertaining to economic development, recreation, welfare, and the physical environment. The lack of adequate planning was further compounded by the widespread perception that local planning boards were ineffective because of inadequate staffs, meager financial support, and the inability of the public to comprehend the planning function. Seeking to correct these deficiencies, the local governments of the area created the Dade County Coordinating Planning Council in 1944. However, this body failed to fully achieve its intended goal and objectives because it was unable to supersede assorted parochial local interests.

Adding to local governmental structural problems prior to the establishment of Metro were the service demands of the rapidly growing suburban population, especially among those residing in the unincorporated areas of the county. Unable to fully meet their service needs, the residents of the unincorporated areas entered into a multiplicity of contracts with local governments for the provision of services, including water, firefighting, and police protection. However, the officials of the municipalities providing these services repeatedly complained that their governments did not receive adequate payment for providing these services.

Notwithstanding the maze of local governments throughout the region, instances of functional service consolidation were achieved in the 1940s. In 1943, a countywide health department was created; this was followed in 1945 by the establishment of the Dade County Port Authority, which assumed the assets and responsibilities of the Greater Port Authority, an agency created several years earlier by the city of Miami. In the same year, a multiple number of local school districts were merged into one county school system, responsible to the County Board of Public Instruction. This body was given the power to levy, with the approval of the electorate, a countywide property tax, not to exceed a rate of ten mills. Most of the citizens of the area favored the merger, with the exception of residents of Miami Beach, where educational standards had long exceeded those in the other parts of the county. In 1949, control over the major public hospital in the region was relinquished by the city of Miami to Dade County, due to financial problems and expanded space needs.

In a more sweeping fashion, a number of determined attempts, all unsuccessful, were made to establish a regional government in the Miami area between 1945 and 1953. In 1945, Miami's mayor set forth a consolidation proposal to merge the governments of all the cities and the county into a single city-county government of Miami. This proposal was defeated in the State Senate. Three years later, in 1948, the electorate of Dade County rejected, by a vote of 23,513 to 27,821, an amendment to the Florida constitution, which would have resulted in the merger of Dade County, the city of Miami, and the four small localities of North Bay Village, Virginia Gardens, West Miami, and Flager City. In 1953, the voters defeated in a referendum by a scant 908 votes a proposal to abolish the city of Miami and transfer its assets, functions, and responsibilities to Dade County.

The small margin by which the latter effort was defeated stimulated the creation by Miami on July 1, 1953 of the Metropolitan Miami Municipal Board (3M Board), charged with exploring the feasibility of governmental reorganization in the region. Miami designated eleven members of this organization, the Dade League of Municipalities selected eight, and the Board of Public Instruction chose one. The 3M Board, as it was popularly labeled, was assisted in its work by the passage of state legislation placing a moratorium on the creation of any new municipalities in Dade County. The 3M Board retained the well-respected Public Administration Service for technical assistance. Upon the completion of its work, the Public Administration Service recommended to the 3M Board the creation of a two-tiered, or federated, form of metropolitan government for the region. Under the proposal, the cities were to be responsible for local functions, with minimum standards established by the county, while a reorganized and fiscally strengthened county government would be responsible for the delivery of regional services, including water, sewer, solid-waste disposal, transportation, traffic, and metropolitan planning. The Public Administration Service recommendations were by and large accepted by the 3M Board, which then proceeded to prepare an amendment to the Florida constitution, providing home rule for Dade County. The state legislature approved the proposed amendment in June 1955 and subsequently created and appointed a Metro charter board. When a number of legal technicalities were raised about this board, it was abolished and replaced by a seventeen-member board appointed by the governor.

The proposed home rule amendment was passed by a two-to-one margin by the Florida electorate on November 6, 1956. The amendment provided the legal basis for the charter board to establish a metropolitan government for the region. The board officially completed its work on April 15, 1957 and released to the public its proposed charter, which was strongly supported by the Dade County Chamber of Commerce, the League of Women Voters, and the *Miami Herald* and the *Miami News* newspapers. Despite some opposition to the charter, principally from the Dade County League of Municipalities, the referendum was passed by the voters on May 21 by a small margin.

Governmental Structure, Service Delivery, and Funding

At the outset, the Board of County Commissioners was designated to serve as the metropolitan policy-making agency. Initially, the board consisted of eleven members, five commissioners elected at-large—each required to be a resident of a different commission district—five commissioners elected by the voters of each district, and one commissioner elected from the city of Miami. Each commissioner served a four-year term. In 1963 the charter was amended, reducing the membership of the board to nine commissioners, with eight elected at-large, subject to the requirement that each commissioner had to reside in a different district. The ninth member, who served as the mayor and chairman of the board, was elected at-large by all the voters of the county. In 1992, the charter was amended to provide for an executive mayor, elected at-large, who may veto the actions of the commissioners and with their approval may hire and dismiss the county manager. In 1993, as a result of a federal court order triggered by African-American and Latino concerns involving their perceived lack of equitable representation, the board was enlarged to thirteen members, each elected from single-member districts. Commissioners and the mayor are elected on a non-partisan basis and serve four-year terms.

The charter designates that the county manager is responsible for managing the county government and implementing the policies of the board. Four departments—finance, personnel, planning, and law—serve under the direct supervision of the manager, and the charter provides that the manager has the discretion to establish additional departments in order to facilitate more efficient administration. The elective status of the assessor, tax collector, surveyor, purchasing agent, and county supervisor was abolished. The charter established a metropolitan court, the judges of which are appointed by the Board of Commissioners to serve six-year terms.

The powers and service responsibilities of the county government may be divided into four broad categories: first, municipal-type services provided throughout the county; second, additional services provided to unincorporated areas; third, county responsibilities related to the establishment of minimum service standards; and, finally, broad elastic powers enjoyed by the county. Direct municipal-type service responsibilities include tax appraisals and collections, law enforcement, election services, some public works, regional parks, recreational and cultural services, civil defense, public health, agricultural services, mass transit, environmental protection, water and sewer, animal services, traffic engineering, solid-waste disposal, libraries, fire and emergency rescue services, development planning and housing, the administration and operation of airports and seaports, and mental health services. In addition to these responsibilities, the county government delivers to the unincorporated areas the following services: garbage and trash collection, zoning enforcement, and neighborhood parks and recreational programs. Funding for these services is provided by revenues raised from real estate and personal property taxes, other assorted local taxes, water and sewer charges, various user fees, and state and federal funds. Metro levies an additional tax on citizens residing in the unincorporated areas for services that it does not provide to city residents.

Further, the county government possesses broad regulatory powers involving the establishment of minimum service standards throughout the county, and powers of an open-ended or elastic nature. The county government may establish service standards for all municipal governmental units; if a local government does not comply with a particular service standard, the county may take over and perform, regulate, or grant a franchise to operate the service. Finally, regarding its elastic powers, the charter authorizes the county government to exercise all powers granted to municipalities, counties, and county officers by state laws and the state constitution, and to adopt ordinances and resolutions that are in the common interest of the people of the county.

In the federative, or two-tier, system of metropolitan governance in Miami–Dade County, the cities have a number of service responsibilities and the guarantee of perpetuity. Services provided by cities include police patrol and some law enforcement; zoning, planning, and enforcement; and neighborhood parks and recreation programs. Four cities provide their own fire protection and nine cities operate their own library systems. Three cities manage their own housing authorities. Importantly, the county government cannot abolish a municipality without the express permission of its voters, nor can it arbitrarily change municipal boundaries. Municipalities retain the right to modify the provisions in their charters, provided that any proposed revision does not conflict with the county charter. Each municipality may exceed county minimum standards for zoning, regulating taxis and rental vehicles, establishing the hours of sale of alcoholic beverages, and for the provision of fire and police protection.

Assessment

At the outset, the Dade County Metro engendered a great deal of political controversy and litigation in the courts, principally concerning issues involving its federal character, and the authority and allocation of services between the county and the cities. In its early years,

Metro Dade adopted a number of countywide regulatory ordinances relating to public works, traffic control, building, and zoning, which drew strong political opposition from many municipal officials, who contended that Metro should be more decidedly involved in the improvement of services in the unincorporated areas. An early suit brought against Metro involved a new countywide traffic code, which transferred jurisdiction over traffic violations from the municipalities to the metropolitan court. In the lawsuit, the municipality of Miami Shores challenged the right of the county government to exercise its power in this policy area. The Circuit Court, in a decision handed down in 1958, dismissed the Miami Shores grievance and stated that the municipalities must enforce the Metro traffic code, which, the Court declared, superseded all municipal traffic ordinances. This decision provided enhanced political legitimacy for Metro Dade and served as a valuable legal precedent.

A broad legal challenge to Metro in 1957 involved adding a local autonomy amendment to its charter. Miami and a number of other municipalities, acting through the Dade League of Municipalities, advanced a proposed amendment to the metropolitan charter stipulating that "neither the political autonomy nor the right of self-government or self-determination of any of the municipalities of Dade shall be infringed upon, disturbed, or interfered with, and that the municipalities shall maintain their continuous right to exercise all powers. . . ."[2] The Dade League of Municipalities and the cities spearheaded a strong campaign seeking to convince the electorate to vote in favor of the amendment. Forces opposing the amendment included the Miami–Dade Chamber of Commerce, the League of Women Voters and a "Vote No" Committee, consisting of a group of prominent citizens. The amendment was overwhelmingly defeated by the electorate in a referendum conducted in September 1958.

In the 1960s and 1970s, several determined attempts were made to amend the charter. In a referendum conducted in 1961, the electorate defeated the so-called McLeod amendment, which constituted a serious organizational threat to Metro, involving thirty-seven changes to its charter.[3] These changes would have done away with the council-manager form of government, and virtually terminated Metro's control over sewerage, water supply, transportation, and central planning services. In the 1970s, the Dade County Metropolitan Study Commission, established by the Board of Commissioners in 1970, offered a series of recommendations to the voters, which would have resulted in the county adopting a strong mayor form of government; establishing an ombudsman to deal with citizen complaints; creating service districts in the unincorporated areas; and creating a Metro zoning review board. However, in a 1972 referendum the electorate turned down these recommendations.

As a result of a rising crime rate, a Citizens Charter Review Committee, composed of economic and political notables, was established in the 1980s and charged with determining how Metro might be better structured to more effectively deal with the problem of crime.[4] The Citizens Charter Review Committee was funded by a number of large corporations, including the Ryder System, Knight-Ridder newspapers, Southern Bell, and Florida Power and Light. Upon the conclusion of its deliberations, the Citizens Charter Review Committee recommended in 1992 that the Metro mayor be elected at-large and that the mayor be invested with increased authority, including the right to veto actions by the Board of Commissioners. This recommendation was supported by a score of prominent citizen activists and approved by the voters in a referendum.

In 1996, a citizen activist movement in Miami, in response to corruption and financial problems associated with the city, began an effort to abolish the city of Miami and merge its functions into Metro. Supporters of the movement argued that the city was too poor and mismanaged to survive on its own, and they argued that if Metro assumed the city services of police protection, firefighting, and garbage collection, local property taxes would be reduced. Some opponents of the proposal suggested that the attempt to abolish the city was a thinly disguised attempt to undermine the political power of Latinos, who had become the dominant element in Miami's politics. In September 1997, the electorate overwhelmingly defeated the proposal in a referendum.[5]

Notwithstanding the political controversy surrounding Metro, soon after its establishment it made significant progress, including the integration and professionalization of the formerly haphazard county administrative organization. Metro implemented modern management practices in the county administration and staffed the departments with well-trained professionals. Metro's first county manager cited a score of improvements made by Metro, including a reduction and coordination of county departments, improved budget practices, and upgraded services involving tax reassessment, water and sewers, mass transit, traffic planning, and law enforcement.[6]

Metro achieved a number of accomplishments in the early 1970s. It established, in 1970, the Citizens' Information Service to receive and respond to citizen concerns. In 1972, Metro ensured the passage of a large general obligation capital bond issue for the implementation of a "Decade of Progress" program, involving capital facilities improvements. That same year, Metro established a countywide water and sewer system, operated by a semi-autonomous board created by the merger of a county agency and the Water Board, the latter established by the state legislature to manage sewer and water services for the city of Miami. Also in 1972, Metro began operating the South Dade Governmental Center, facilitating the delivery of services to citizens in that part of the county; services included public works, pollution control, traffic and transportation, water and sewer, and housing and urban development. In 1974, Metro created the Department of Human Resources, assuming the responsibilities of the former Office of Human Resources.[7]

Throughout the 1970s and 1980s, Metro continued to make progress. First, and most important, toward the end of the 1970s, Metro had defeated its most adamant opponents and had become a broadly accepted governmental structure; there were no longer any serious movements underway to threaten its existence or curtail its powers.[8] Second, reflecting its increasing service role, in the early 1980s Metro emerged as the sole provider of the following services: tax assessment and collection, court services, mass transit, traffic engineering, voter registration and other election services, regulation of water and sewer companies, corrections, and building and traffic codes. In addition, Metro provided most waste disposal, public housing, and community development services. Third, Metro successfully promoted economic development, especially in the unincorporated areas, throughout the 1980s. And, fourth, in the same decade it provided the key leadership for the planning and construction of a rapid rail transit system.

Metro made more progress in the 1990s. First, as a result of the reorganization of the county government, it eliminated twelve departments and reduced the work force by 1,500 positions. Second, Metro achieved greater equity in county property taxes by increasing the tax rate for citizens residing in the unincorporated areas and maintaining the same countywide rate. Third, it strengthened its public safety policies, resulting in an absolute decrease in the crime rate. Fourth, Metro constructed a score of new parks and implemented an enhanced level of park services. Finally, Metro continued to successfully promote the Miami region as an international trade center, serving as a gateway for business in Latin America.

In sum, Metropolitan Dade County has proved to be a successful venture in a federative, or two-tier, structure of metropolitan government. As early as 1972, Melvin B. Mogulof concluded that: "[T]he facts are that Metro Dade County has moved toward areawide influence and achievement in every function that one may consider a proper interest of a metropolitan government."[9] Metro has been particularly successful in promoting a regional perspective on policy issues, modernizing the county government, improving the public infrastructure, providing more uniform services throughout the county, promoting economic growth, and facilitating better land-use planning and development.

Metropolitan Dade County, however, has not escaped serious criticism. Several of these criticisms are basically of an institutional or structural nature. First, although far less acute than during Metro's early years of existence, the federal character of local government in the region continues to provoke suspicion and political conflict between the county and the cities, concerning their authority and service obligations. Mogulof noted in this regard: "[T]he heart of the problem is the failure to reach an accommodation between the county and the cities as to who does what."[10]

The second structural criticism of Metro is that it fails to encompass the entire metropolitan area, which includes not only Dade County, but also the counties of Broward and Monroe. Due to Metro's geographical limitations, some scholars have argued that Metro should not be understood or characterized as a metropolitan government. On this score, Genie Stowers has written: "The region Metro Dade governs is still merely a county, not the full region. Although many consider Metro Dade County a regional government, it is more accurately described as neither a regional government nor as merely a metropolitan county government. Instead, it is a hybrid, perhaps called a 'regional county' government. . . . Its role goes beyond that of a traditional county government and even beyond a metropolitan county government in that it provides the entire county with some services and also supplies metropolitan services often provided by special districts. It is not quite a regional government because its powers stop at its limited borders. It provides some regional services but only within one county; therefore, it is more of a 'regional county' structure."[11]

In addition, Metro Dade County over the years has been criticized for lacking strong, effective, and resourceful political leadership. As long ago as the early 1960s, Edward Sofen, a political scientist who carefully followed and wrote about the metropolitan political experience, noted: "During Metro's approximately five years of existence, it has been plagued by the problem of inadequate leadership."[12] In order to fill this leadership void, Sofen recommended that Dade County be led by a popularly at-large elected mayor.[13] This perspective was eventually favorably acted upon by voters many years later in 1992 when they supported a charter amendment to this effect and directly elected the mayor for the first time in 1996. The popularly elected mayor should be able to provide Metro with the strong political leadership it has long lacked.

Finally, Metro has been taken to task for its somewhat strained relationship with the African-American community. To a degree, the nature of this relationship was due to the lack of African-American representation on the county board until 1992, when the federal court ordered Dade County to abandon at-large elections in favor of district elections, thereby guaranteeing an African-American presence on the county board. In addition, the relationship between Metro and the African-American community has proved troublesome because of the widely held perception among African Americans that Metro does not treat them fairly or provide them with their fair share of services.[14] In her perceptive study of the dynamics of ethnic relationships and rivalries in the area involving Anglos, Latinos (primarily Cubans), and African Americans, Sheila L. Croucher has noted that past outbursts of racial violence were partly due to: "a sense of despair among blacks with regard to their social and economic plight and a complete lack of trust in a political and legal system that was unwilling or unable to curb the persistent injustice."[15]

Twin Cities Metropolitan Council: Minneapolis–St. Paul

Unlike the areas of Baton Rouge, Nashville, Jacksonville, Indianapolis, and Miami, which have comprehensive metropolitan governmental structures, the Twin Cities Metropolitan Council, which encompasses seven counties, was originally established in 1967 by the Minnesota state legislature as a limited regional governmental structure with substantial policy review powers, which, however, depended on other governmental agencies for program implementation.[16] John J. Harrigan, a leading scholar of metropolitan politics and a close observer of the Metropolitan Council, referred to this division of responsibilities as constituting an excellent example of a bifurcated model of metropolitan governance.[17]

Commencing in the late 1950s, the Minneapolis–St. Paul metropolitan area, due to population growth and the flight of a substantial number of citizens to the suburbs, experienced a variety of problems involving sewers, waste disposal, transportation services, and inadequate housing. However, the local governments were unable to effectively confront these problems because (1) many of the problems, such as water pollution, were of a metropolitanwide character, involving the jurisdiction of a multiplicity of local governments; (2) a response to these problems was beyond the fiscal capacity of each local government; and (3) there was a lack of a regional governmental structure with the authority to make policy decisions for the entire metropolitan area.

The establishment of the Metropolitan Council may be attributed to several factors and developments. First, the Minneapolis–St. Paul area, reflecting Minnesota's strong moralistic political culture, has a legacy of civic involvement and good government, ensuring that reforms designed to make local government more efficient have been positively received by the public. Second, the establishment of the Metropolitan Council was preceded by the creation of governmental entities that carried out their functions on a regional basis; therefore, these agencies provided political legitimacy for regionalism. For instance, the Minneapolis–St. Paul Sanitary District was established in 1933 and, a decade later in 1943, the Metropolitan Airports Commission was organized. After repeated lobbying efforts by the League of Minnesota Municipalities, the Metropolitan Planning Commission (MPC) was established in 1957, responsible for producing plans designed to ensure the coordinated physical, social, and economic development of the metropolitan area. The work of the MPC eventually resulted in a "metropolitan guide" for guiding overall metropolitan growth. The Metropolitan Planning Commission possessed only advisory powers and, therefore, largely depended on its power of persuasion to promote cooperation between local governments.

In the early 1960s, several developments stimulated the local political leadership in Minneapolis–St. Paul and members of the state legislature to consider more seriously the need to establish a regional governmental structure for the Twin Cities. First, because of the reapportionment of the state legislature, resulting in greater numerical representation from the Minneapolis–St. Paul area, state legislators became more aware of the various problems of the Twin Cities area and the need to structure a regionwide governmental institution and process that could effectively formulate policies to respond to these problems. Second, a variety of service problems became more serious and complex; this was especially true with regard to the lack of sufficient suburban sewer services. Third, the passage by the federal government of the Demonstration Cities and Metropolitan Development Act in 1966, requiring the establishment of a regional agency in metropolitan areas to review and comment on local applications for federal funds, served as a stimulus to local leaders to devote more attention to metropolitan governmental reorganization. And, finally, the elimination by the state legislature of "home rule" facilitated metropolitan governmental reorganization, since it eliminated the need for popular concurrence on whatever action was taken.

A consensus developed among the political leaders for the establishment of a regional review policy council, as distinct from a comprehensive metropolitan government. Political leadership for promoting the regional council was provided by a coalition of groups. First, the Citizens League, a long-established, nonpartisan, good government organization, composed of prominent business leaders, played a major role in developing throughout the metropolitan area a favorable public opinion toward the concept of governmental regional-ism. Second, the Metropolitan Planning Commission promoted the virtue of metropolitan-wide planning and set forth several specific metropolitan governmental reorganization proposals. In addition, the Citizens League and the Metropolitan Planning Commission were assisted by the League of Minnesota Municipalities, the League of Women Voters, various business groups, and the mass media. By contrast, political opposition to the regional council was fragmentary, involving a scattering of suburban county officials and the suburban press.

Structure, Responsibilities, and Funding

After a debate focusing on whether the members of the governing board should be directly elected by the voters or appointed by the governor, the state legislature enacted and the governor signed a bill in 1967 establishing the Metropolitan Council of the Twin Cities Area. The Metropolitan Council is neither an agency of state government nor an agency of local government, but a unique agency situated between the state and local governments and possessing some of the powers and characteristics of each level of government. In brief, the Metropolitan Council may be viewed as a local regional government because its governing board members are drawn from the area and it is designed to promote areawide interests and services. Further, the Metropolitan Council was granted the power to collect an area *ad valorem* tax to finance its operations. On the other hand, the Metropolitan Council may be considered to some degree a state agency, since the governor appoints (and more recently has gained the power to fire) council members, while the state legislature provides its powers, monitors its finances, and requests periodic reports from the Metropolitan Council. In a pragmatic working sense, upon the establishment of the Metropolitan Council, the Twin Cities metropolitan area embarked upon a three-tier local governmental structure, consisting of the Metropolitan Council, strengthened counties, and cities and towns.

The Metropolitan Council is composed of sixteen (originally fourteen) members, appointed (and, since 1994, subject to firing) by the governor, who serve overlapping six-year terms. Each council member represents a district of the metropolitan area of equal population size. The chairperson, drawn from the metropolitan area, is appointed by and serves at the pleasure of the governor. Legislation introduced into the state legislature providing for the direct election of council members has been repeatedly defeated. In 1994, the state legislature established the position of regional administrator, who is expected to serve as a sort of city manager for metropolitan governance.

Initially, the Metropolitan Council, along with its general metropolitan planning function, was charged with three tasks, including that of reviewing all plans and projects of special districts, independent commissions, boards, and agencies, in order to ascertain their compatibility with regional needs. The Metropolitan Council may indefinitely suspend any project that it finds to be in violation of its metropolitan development guidelines. Second, the Metropolitan Council is charged with reviewing and commenting on long-term municipal comprehensive plans and their relationship to overall metropolitan growth and development. Although the Metropolitan Council cannot exercise veto power over the comprehensive plan of a municipality, if it does determine that a plan is in conflict with the metropolitan public interest, or if a plan draws the objection of another municipality, it may conduct a public hearing, or a series of public hearings, for the purpose of mediating the conflicting concerns. And, third, the Metropolitan Council was given the responsibility of providing an advisory evaluation, in terms of regional criteria, of local governmental applications for federal funding.

The general responsibility of the Metropolitan Council is to conduct regional planning and to encourage local governmental units to adhere to metropolitan development guidelines in their own planning. In line with this, the Metropolitan Council has established a variety of committees including: (1) Human Resources Committee; (2) Physical Development Committee; (3) Personnel and Work Program Committee; and (4) Environmental and Transportation Committee. Assisting the Metropolitan Council are three metropolitan commissions (which are organizationally distinct but subordinate to the Metropolitan Council), composed of eight members selected by the Metropolitan Council and a chairperson appointed by the governor, and six metropolitan advisory boards, consisting of elected officials and private citizens, which provide policy planning assistance.

As part of its general regional planning responsibilities, the Metropolitan Council is charged with conducting studies in the following areas: (1) air pollution; (2) regional parks and open space; (3) water pollution; (4) solid waste disposal; (5) areawide tax disparities; (6) metropolitan tax assessment practices; (7) storm water drainage facilities; (8) consolidation of local governmental services; (9) future public land acquisition; and (10) local governmental organization.

Initially, all policies of the Metropolitan Council were implemented by regional agencies. These agencies, organizationally distinct from the Metropolitan Council but responsible to it, included the Metropolitan Airports Commission, the Metropolitan Transit Commission, the Metropolitan Sewer Board, the Metropolitan Waste Control Commission, the Metropolitan Sports Facility, and the Metropolitan Mosquito Control Districts. The Metropolitan Council appoints the members of these bodies and defines their working relationships, which vary to a considerable degree from one commission to another. However, in 1994 the state legislature abolished the Metropolitan Transit Commission (along with the Regional Transit Board, which the state legislature had established in 1989 to carry out transportation planning) and the Metropolitan Waste Control Commission, and turned their operating functions over to the Metropolitan Council.

The state legislature passed the Fiscal Disparities Act in 1971, providing for the sharing among the localities of the region the taxation benefits of economic growth. This legislation, administered by the Metropolitan Council, designates that 40 percent of the growth of the commercial valuation of each community in the region is placed in a metropolitan fund. The distribution of tax revenues from this fund is allocated in a manner designed to disproportionately benefit the less affluent communities of the metropolitan area.

Assessment

In the first decade of its existence, the Metropolitan Council was credited with an impressive list of achievements, earned substantial political legitimacy, and gained national attention. First, the Metropolitan Council provided regional political leadership and incorporated a regionwide dimension into independent agency operations. This was especially true in regard to policies and services involving sewers, mass transportation, airports, housing, parks, and open space. Second, it facilitated state and local intergovernmental dialogue and cooperation on a wide range of policy issues. Third, the Metropolitan Council, making use of its regional review powers, achieved substantial savings in the public sector by curtailing various proposed construction projects, including a second international airport and a rapid transit system. Fourth, it developed a Development Framework Plan, creating a Metropolitan Urban Services Area designed to curb suburban sprawl. Fifth, the Metropolitan Council formulated and successfully ensured passage by the state legislature of the innovative Fiscal Disparities Act. And, finally, the Metropolitan Council garnered wide public praise by serving as a valuable forum for the discussion of areawide issues and by promoting a regional response to these challenges. As Harrigan noted: "In sum, by the tenth anniversary of the Metropolitan Council in 1977, the bifurcated governance model had gained considerable legitimacy, had evolved an innovative governing structure that fit the desires of regional elites, and had scored an impressive array of accomplishments in carrying out its mission."[18]

However, in the 1980s and 1990s the Metropolitan Council encountered difficult times and lost a substantial amount of its earlier stature and political support, for a variety of reasons. First, the Metropolitan Council was severely criticized in the 1980s for not making more extensive use of its policy-review powers to formulate major land-use decisions involving the construction of a domed stadium, race track, world trade center, velodrome, large shopping mall (the largest in the nation), basketball arena, and numerous industrial parks and festival marketplaces. In addition, in the 1980s and 1990s, the Metropolitan Council was taken to task for extending the line of the Metropolitan Services Area (MSA) and for not aggressively seeking and gaining a higher political profile among the general public. And, as Harrigan underscored, for an assortment of reasons, political support for the Metropolitan Council diminished in the state legislature, the business community, and in the Democratic and Republican political parties. Adding to its difficulties, the Metropolitan Council has not been able to acquire a position of metropolitan leadership in recent years.[19] Indeed, by 1991 the fortunes and the political legitimacy of the Metropolitan Council had plummeted so severely that, according to one well-placed observer, it was in danger of being abolished by the state legislature.[20]

However, in 1994 the state legislature somewhat reversed itself by enacting legislation providing a stronger role for the Metropolitan Council, especially in terms of service delivery. This legislation abolished a number of agencies and made the Metropolitan Council responsible for the planning, administration, and provision of mass transit and waste-water services. In addition, the legislature created the position of regional administrator for the Metropolitan Council and the governor was given the authority to dismiss as well as appoint members of the Metropolitan Council.[21] However, notwithstanding some strong political appeals, the legislature refused to pass legislation providing for the direct election of the members of the Metropolitan Council.[22] By failing to take this action, Harrigan noted: "[T]he 1994 legislature increased the dependence of Council members on the governor. This means that the Council's ability to address the growing central city/suburban disparities will depend primarily on the goodwill of the governor. If the governor favors taking the political risks to address those issues and is willing to back up the Council's efforts along those lines, then it is conceivable that considerable progress could be made. . . . In the long run, however, tying the Council so closely to the governor makes action on metropolitan issues dependent on the whim of the governor, who has little to gain politically from involving himself or herself in the divisive issues of regional disparities and growth control."[23]

Portland, Oregon: Metro

In the 1950s, the Portland, Oregon metropolitan area witnessed, in response to various service needs, a proliferation of single-purpose special districts, adding to its maze of local governments.[24] Responding to this development, the League of Women Voters in the late 1950s conducted a study of local governmental structure and service delivery and released a report, titled *A Tale of Three Counties*, underscoring the need for more accountable and efficient local government in the region. Partly in response to this report, the state legislature established in 1961 the Portland Metropolitan Study Commission (PMSC), composed of elected officials, business leaders, and citizen activists. The responsibility of the commission was to review local governmental structure and service delivery and to set forth appropriate recommendations.

A number of other important regional developments took place in the area during the decade from 1960 to 1970. First, a council of governments was established in 1966—called the Columbia Region Association of Governments (CRAG)—given the mandate of promoting local intergovernmental cooperation and conducting long-range planning. However, CRAG was viewed as a somewhat ineffective organization, primarily because of its voluntary membership character and substantial reliance on federal funding. However, these deficiencies were partially overcome by state legislation in 1973 mandating local governmental membership in CRAG and local dues to be paid on a per capita basis. Second, a United Sewerage Agency was created in 1970, which assumed the service responsibilities of twenty-three independent sewer districts, largely serving the western suburbs of Portland. And, third, due to a financial crisis in a suburban county, Portland, along with a neighboring smaller city, annexed a large amount of unincorporated territory and entered into a variety of intergovernmental contracts, providing urban-type services for citizens residing in the remaining unincorporated areas.

The Portland Metropolitan Study Commission existed from 1963 to 1971. In 1969, the commission recommended the establishment of the Metropolitan Service District (MSD), with an appointed board of ten members. According to its recommendation, the MSD was to assume the responsibility for areawide planning, sewerage treatment, solid-waste disposal, and drainage and flood control. In addition, the commission recommended that, in the future, the MSD should assume responsibility for criminal justice, open-space preservation, parks, water supply, library services, and the administration and operation of sports facilities. Further, the commission advocated the establishment of a regional transportation authority, Tri-Met, for the operation of mass transportation services. After some debate, the state legislature adopted the recommendations and in May 1970 the electorate approved the establishment of the MSD and Tri-Met. In 1976, the MSD took over operational responsibility for the area zoo, which had been formerly managed by the city of Portland.

A grant from the National Academy of Public Administration, along with leadership and financial support from the business community, provided the impetus for the creation in 1975 of a second local governmental study commission, charged with ascertaining the best way to manage regional problems without undermining the role of local governments. This commission, labeled the Tri-County Local Government Commission, was composed of sixty-five members, drawn from the public and private sectors. The commission proposed to the state legislature a plan for a two-tier governmental structure in the Portland region. The state legislature modified and passed the proposal, with the stipulation that the new governmental structure would be confined to the urban and urbanizing portions of the metropolitan area. In May 1978, the electorate approved the proposal passed by the state legislature, resulting in a newly structured Metropolitan Service District, which assumed the responsibilities of the Columbia Region Association of Governments. The Metropolitan Services District commenced operations on January 1, 1979. In 1992, the electorate approved a home rule charter for the Metropolitan Service District and the name of the organization was changed to simply "Metro."

Structure, Responsibilities, and Revenues

Metro, which encompasses twenty-four cities and three counties, is the only regional body in the United States that has a governing body directly elected by the voters. The Metro Council consists of seven members, elected on a nonpartisan district basis, each for a four-year term. The council is responsible for policy formulation and the preparation of the budget. An executive officer, elected on a nonpartisan, at-large basis for a four-year term, is responsible for overall management. Metro officeholders may seek indefinite terms of office. Metro derives its revenues from a variety of sources, including solid-waste tipping fees, zoo admission fees, a regional property tax dedicated to the operation of the zoo, retiring revenue bonds utilized to finance the construction of a convention center, and a transient occupancy tax imposed to support the operations of the convention center. Subject to the approval of the electorate, Metro may be authorized to realize revenues from an income and/or sales tax.

Metro is responsible for coordinating growth management, land use, and transportation planning. In addition, it provides regional solid-waste disposal services, manages the regional zoo, and operates a regional tourism development program. Further, Metro has been authorized to assume the direct management and operation of mass transportation services, an option that it has not yet exercised.

Assessment

Metro has effectively promoted the concept of regionalism, provided regional political leadership, and made the interrelated issues of growth and development a central part of the political agenda. On this point, Alan Ehrenhalt has written: "Over 20 years, the existence of an independent regional government, gradually taking on new powers and electing its leadership, has changed the underlying psychology of the area's civic life. Growth and development issues have a visibility in Portland that they simply don't have in other parts of the country. . . . Portland's jurisdictions conceive of themselves as a combined entity, a problem-solving unit, in a way that they were unable to do so two decades ago, and communities elsewhere still are unable to do."[25]

Secondly, Metro has limited suburban sprawl by establishing a metropolitan urban growth boundary (UGB) in 1979, which was approved by the Oregon Land Conservation and Development Commission, a state agency. The establishment of the UGB has drawn national attention and has facilitated the implementation of the tenets of the "New Urbanism" development philosophy, emphasizing mixed-use development, transit-oriented design, neotraditional planning, and efficient resource development. The development effect of the implementation of these principles has been more intensive land use and development within the boundary—Portland and the inner suburbs—and the limitation of suburban sprawl beyond the boundary.[26]

And thirdly, Metro has served as an effective policy "umbrella," coordinating local and regional interests in the policy process. It has played a key role in allocating fair-share housing units throughout the region, distributing transportation funds, planning a light rail transit system, promoting the issuance of bonds to acquire farmland outside the UGB (therefore ensuring the farming use of these lands in the future), and selecting a convention center site. In sum, by functioning as a regional policy umbrella, Metro has played a major role in protecting and enhancing the high living standards of the region.[27]

Presently, Metro is under considerable pressure, due to escalating real estate and housing costs in Portland, to expand the UGB. Ehrenhalt has noted: "Homebuilders and allied growth advocates argue that the rigid boundary has forced up real estate prices and made the construction of affordable new housing virtually impossible. . . . Arrayed against them are environmentalists, downtown Portland interests and most of the region's local officials, who argue that an expanded UGB will magnify the suburban sprawl that planning has so far limited, and impose infrastructure costs that the suburban governments cannot afford."[28]

Conclusion

Our review of the metropolitan governments of Baton Rouge, Miami, Nashville, Jacksonville, and Indianapolis, and the limited regional governmental structures of Minneapolis–St. Paul and Portland underscores the uniqueness of these institutions and the fact that metropolitan governmental reorganization in the United States has followed no set formula (see Table 5.1). Further, each of these governmental organizations was established because of a particular set of circumstances and a coalition of local and state political forces. Although peculiar to their regions, they share the characteristic of being evolutionary in character; as these institutions have developed over time and gained a greater degree of political legitimacy, they have acquired larger political, policy, and service roles in their respective metropolises.

The establishment of metropolitan governments in Baton Rouge, Miami, Nashville, Jacksonville, and Indianapolis, and the limited regional structures of Minneapolis–St. Paul

Table 5.1
METROPOLITAN GOVERNMENTS AND LIMITED
REGIONAL STRUCTURES: SUMMARY DATA

Metropolitan Area	Date of Establishment	Type of Regional Structure	Voter Approval Required	Governing Structure	Functional Responsibility
Baton Rouge	1949	City-county consolidation	Yes	Mayor; 12 council members; chief administrative officer	Multifunctional
Indianapolis	1970	City-county consolidation	No	Mayor; 29 council members	Multifunctional
Jacksonville	1968	City-county consolidation	Yes	Mayor; 19 council members	Multifunctional
Miami	1957	Two-tier urban county	Yes	Mayor; 13 council members; county mamager	Multifunctional
Minneapolis–St. Paul	1967	Regional council	No	Chairperson; 16 council members (all appointed by governor); regional administrator	Policy review; limited functions
Nashville	1962	City-county consolidation	Yes	Mayor; 40 council members	Multifunctional
Portland	1979	Multi-service district	Yes	Executive officer; 7 council members	Policy review; limited functions

and Portland was due to a variety of factors and a coalition of political forces. First, in each region the migration of a large number of people to suburbia aggravated existing service problems, particularly with regard to system-maintenance services, such as sewers and water. Citizen demands for these services were inadequately met and the establishment of special districts to meet these demands simply resulted in further governmental fragmentation. Second, the quest for metropolitan government, particularly in Jacksonville and to a somewhat lesser degree in Nashville, was stimulated by the widely held popular perception that the government of the former city was incompetent and corrupt and was incapable of providing a reasonable level of services. Third, in all seven regions, business leaders, assisted by various "good government" groups, metro-inclined scholars and public administrators, and elements of the mass media served as vigorous advocates of metropolitan reform. And, fourth, sympathetic state legislators played a decisive role in establishing these metropolitan institutions.

It should be stressed that these metropolitan structures did not come into being without precipitating a substantial amount of political conflict. This underscores the fact that the quest for metropolitan governmental reform involves a good deal of political struggle over the locus of political power and policy making. Groups and individuals in Baton Rouge, Miami, Nashville, Jacksonville, Indianapolis, Minneapolis–St. Paul, and Portland, therefore, who perceived metropolitan reform as a threat to their political power and economic well-being resisted metropolitan governmental reform. For example, politicians in Jacksonville associated with old-style machine politics perceived metropolitan reform as undermining their political position, while many Democrats in Indianapolis viewed metropolitan reform simply as a way for Republicans to solidify their local political power.

Due to the lack of comparative studies, it remains somewhat problematic to set forth definitive general statements concerning the experience of the metropolitan governments of Baton Rouge, Miami, Nashville, Jacksonville, and Indianapolis, and the limited regional governmental structures of Minneapolis–St. Paul and Portland. However, on the basis of the tangential evidence presented in this chapter, it may be concluded that these regions are better off because regional institutions were established. The various metropolitan governments have realized a number of accomplishments, including, first, promoting a sense of regional identity and introducing a regional factor into the local policy process. Second, by serving as a critical component of a "growth machine," they have been successful in promoting economic development and attracting large companies to their region, resulting in substantial private investment and additional jobs. Third, the metropolitan governments have implemented a substantial degree of governmental modernization, administrative centralization, and functional integration, resulting in service efficiencies and savings in governmental operations. Fourth, they have provided more uniform and better quality system-maintenance services throughout their regions and promoted more orderly regional development and growth. And, finally, these metropolitan governments may be credited with being innovative in their operations. For instance, Indianapolis has been in the forefront in incorporating the concepts of competition and privatization into the delivery of public services; Jacksonville has developed structures to facilitate citizen participation in government; and all five metropolitan governments have made novel use of taxing and service districts.

On the other hand, the metropolitan governments of Baton Rouge, Miami, Nashville, Jacksonville, and Indianapolis may be criticized on several grounds. First, the metropolitan governments of Baton Rouge, Nashville, Jacksonville, and Indianapolis, brought about by city-county consolidation, are somewhat structurally wanting, since these mergers involved only partial consolidation, allowing for the continuing existence of a variety of local governmental units. Second, in all five regions—although less acute in the instance of Jacksonville—the metropolitan government over time has increasingly failed to encompass the entire socioeconomic metropolitan region. Third, although metropolitan government advocates have promoted metro as a way of enhancing local governmental efficiency, in all five regions the expenses of government and the taxes paid by citizens over the years have increased. Regarding this matter, Melvin B. Mogulof, in his assessment of the metropolitan governmental experience twenty-five years ago, wrote: "Reorganizations are sold as efficiency devices. But once in operation, a prime purpose is to raise the level of community services, not lower them. . . . In short, metropolitan government expenses have risen."[29] And, finally, and perhaps most critically, these metropolitan governments should not be considered as panaceas for the problems of the former core cities, since they have not served to redistribute wealth and have been only marginally successful, at best, in responding to the economic and social problems of the disadvantaged. Mogulof's observations on this matter, penned a quarter of a century ago, still remain true: "There appears to be inconsistent evidence of interest in or a capacity to redistribute locally raised revenues to serve the poorest and neediest citizens. On the contrary, such redistribution as does occur among constituent jurisdictions often works to the disadvantage of the central cities where the poorest citizens are most highly concentrated. . . . The regressive nature of certain user charges and property taxes likewise suggests that the burden of supporting metro governments falls heaviest on those least able to pay. This is not to say that metros are worse than other local governments, but neither do they appear to be much better in these respects."[30] Perhaps our expectation that metropolitan governments should serve as redistributive mechanisms is unwarranted since, as Paul Peterson reminded us two decades ago, local governments are primarily involved in the implementation of allocative policies.[31] And, further, as Edward C. Banfield and Morton Grodzins advanced in 1958, we need to remember to distinguish between (1) the problems that exist in metropolitan areas, and (2) problems that exist by virtue of the inadequacies of the governmental structure in metropolitan areas.[32]

In a far less sweeping and institutional sense, the experience of the limited regional structures of the Metropolitan Council of Minneapolis–St. Paul and Metro of Portland, Oregon has paralleled that of the metropolitan governments. Although the Twin Cities Metropolitan Council has been severely criticized over the past decade for not making greater use of its extensive policy-review powers concerning several controversial land-use decisions, the Metropolitan Council and Metro have been credited for promoting regional leadership, developing a sense of regional community, stimulating horizontal and vertical intergovernmental relations, containing urban sprawl, and ensuring the more orderly growth and development of their regions.

CHAPTER SIX

Public Choice: An Alternative Perspective

As underscored in Chapter 2, the reform perspective concerning governmental structure in metropolitan areas early on gained the allegiance of practically all scholars of urban affairs and held a virtual intellectual monopoly well into the 1960s. However, in the early 1960s scholars identified with the political economy approach began to develop a forceful intellectual defense of the fragmented character of government in the metropolis. Vincent Ostrom, Charles M. Tiebout, and Robert Warren, in their seminal contribution "The Organization of Government in Metropolitan Areas: A Theoretical Inquiry," published in the *American Political Science Review* in 1961, drew on concepts associated with democratic administration and political economy to sharply criticize the consolidationist argument and defend the plurality of governments or the polycentric character of government in the metropolis. According to Ostrom, Tiebout, and Warren, fragmented governmental structure allows and stimulates competition between local governments functioning as service providers and the ability of citizens, by "voting with their feet," as they phrased it, to choose for their place of residence that community which best meets their private and public needs.[1] This well-crafted intellectual attack began the undermining of the intellectual hegemony of the reform perspective.

This chapter sets forth the origins, development, and contributions of the public choice argument toward our understanding of metropolitan governance. At the outset, attention is given to the writings of James Madison, Alexander Hamilton, and Alexis de Tocqueville in framing the general principles of democratic administration and the political economy school of politics. This discussion is followed by a review of the specific theoretical and empirical contributions of political economy scholars to the public choice argument. The chapter concludes with a summary and an evaluation of the contribution of public choice scholars to our understanding of metropolitan governance.

The Broad Philosophical Basis of the Public Choice Perspective

In a broad philosophical sense, the public choice argument is based on the principles of self-government and democratic administration, and the economic approach to the study of politics. The principles of self-government and democratic administration are found in the writings of Alexander Hamilton, James Madison, and Alexis de Tocqueville. Ostrom, in his important work *The Intellectual Crisis in American Public Administration*, has nicely summarized the principles of self-government and democratic administration as set forth by Hamilton and Madison in *The Federalist Papers*.[2] These principles include: the origin of government and the right to change it are derived from the people; the right of the people to change their government requires a constitutional process involving an extraordinary majority; the constitutional conditions of government are binding on governmental authorities; governmental authorities enjoy limited powers; each unit of government has a defined constituency with governmental authorities directly or indirectly chosen by the constituents; collective decision making in a governmental unit is divided among diverse offices, with all important decisions considered by the members of a common council, elected by their constituents; in larger units of government, authority is allocated to diverse structures, which are each subject to a veto, thereby requiring that collective action be authorized by a concurrent majority; the legal and political competence of each unit of government is limited in relation to other governments, and individuals are citizens of several governments; and, finally, conflicts among governments concerning their jurisdiction, constitutional exercise of authority, and the provision of public services are subject to a judicial remedy.

As Ostrom pointed out, principles of self-government and democratic administration underscore that each individual may participate in the conduct of public affairs and have a voice in constitutional decision making, electing public officials, and holding officials accountable for their interests when making major decisions. Further, as he noted, individuals have the right to make demands on public officials through administrative, legislative, judicial, political, and constitutional structures. In addition, important decisions are reserved for consideration and resolution by the members of the community and their elected representatives. The power of command is restricted by the scrutiny of officials in decision structures within each unit of government, by the allocation of authority among different units of government, and by the presumption that the exercise of all governmental authority is limited by conditions set forth in constitutional law. Ostrom noted that the principles of self-government and democratic administration advocated by Hamilton and Madison provide for a system of administration that is part of a complex structure of decision making.[3]

Augmenting the writings of Hamilton and Madison in framing the broad principles of self-government and democratic administration are the contributions of de Tocqueville, as set forth in his classic work *Democracy in America*, also nicely summarized by Ostrom. De Tocqueville observed that the American tradition of self-government was first realized in townships and was subsequently reflected in the governmental structure of the states and the national government. He characterized the political and administrative affairs of each state as being centered in three governmental arenas of action: the township, the county, and the state. De Tocqueville noted that the township, the county, and the state are governed on the principle that individuals are the best judges of their own private interests, and that no society has the right to limit individual preferences unless such preferences represent a threat to the common good or unless the public interest commands the assistance of the individual. He underscored that public administration is confined to those instances where centralization and hierarchy can be best held to a minimum. Instead of a single hierarchy of public administrators, de Tocqueville advocated that executive power should be dispersed and given to numerous officials and that the populace should participate in the making of their laws through their selection of legislators. Political responsibility, he concluded, is secured to a greater degree by the principles of election than by accountability to central authority through a hierarchy of control; and popular political control should pervade both the government and its administration. The essence of American democracy, noted de Tocqueville, is that of a system of democratic administration organized and bound by the principles of voluntary association and self-government.[4]

In addition to the principles of self-government and democratic administration, the economic approach to the study of politics, also labeled the political economy approach, has played a significant role in framing the public choice perspective. Three major political economy studies were published in the 1950s: Robert Dahl and Charles E. Lindblom, *Politics, Economics, and Welfare*;[5] William J. Baumol, *Welfare Economics and the Theory of the State*;[6] and Anthony Downs, *An Economic Theory of Democracy*.[7] Findings advanced in these works were augmented in the 1960s by political economy scholars studying a wide range of nonmarket phenomena. Representative studies include: James M. Buchanan and Gordon Tullock, *The Calculus of Consent*;[8] Mancur Olson, *The Logic of Collective Action*;[9] Gordon Tullock, *The Politics of Bureaucracy*;[10] William H. Ricker, *The Theory of Political Coalitions*;[11] Charles E. Lindblom, *The Intelligence of Democracy*;[12] and R. L. Curry and L. L. Wade, *A Theory of Political Exchange: Economic Reasoning in Political Analysis*.[13]

Although political economy studies have investigated a wide range of subjects, each was predicated on a number of basic assumptions about the importance and character of human behavior. These assumptions include: first, individual behavior should constitute the basic unit of analysis; second, individuals are primarily motivated by rationality and self-interest; third, individuals adopt maximizing strategies to realize their private and public goals; and, finally, the level of information that an individual has pertaining to a decision varies considerably from complete certainty to uncertainty. These assumptions undergird the public choice argument concerning metropolitan governance.

Metropolitan Government and Governance: The Public Choice Perspective

General principles inherent in self-government, democratic administration, and the political economy approach to the study of politics provide the basic framework for the public choice argument. In a more specific sense, however, a number of early scholars, building on this broad intellectual framework, made important theoretical and empirical contributions to the development of this perspective. Among these contributions, Charles M. Tiebout's paper "A Pure Theory of Local Expenditures,"[14] published in 1956, is regarded as a landmark work.

Tiebout began by stressing that the pattern of local public expenditures better reflects the public policy preferences of the population than its federal counterpart. This is true, he argued, simply because the local political leadership has a base self-interest in maintaining the optimal, or most advantageous, size of the community and therefore ensuring that "each locality has a revenue and expenditure pattern that reflects the desires of its residents."[15]

Tiebout succinctly advanced his argument as follows:

> The consumer-voter may be viewed as picking that community which best satisfies his preference pattern for public goods. This is a major difference between the central and local provision of public goods. At the central level the preferences of the consumer-voter are given, and the government tries to adjust to the pattern of these preferences, whereas at the local level various governments have their revenue and expenditure patterns more or less set. Given these revenue and expenditure patterns, the consumer-voter moves to that

community whose local government best satisfies his set of preferences. The greater the number of communities and the greater the variance among them, the closer the consumer will come to fully realizing his preference position.[16]

Although Tiebout never specifically utilized the terminology, his argument was soon characterized by scholars as that of citizen-consumers "voting with their feet" regarding their choice of residence. It should be acknowledged that Tiebout regarded his model as one of a purely theoretical nature and recognized that: "Consumer-voters do not have perfect knowledge and set preferences, nor are they perfectly mobile."[17]

Importantly, Tiebout's contribution, implicitly defending the polycentric character of government in the metropolis, constituted a rebuke to the reform argument which called for the consolidation of local governments. On this score, he commented in regard to the usual failure of metropolitan governmental proposals: "The general disdain with which proposals to integrate municipalities are met seems to reflect, in part, the fear that local revenue-expenditure patterns will be lost as communities are merged into a metropolitan area."[18]

However, although the thrust of Tiebout's argument defends the usual fragmented nature of metropolitan governmental structure, he acknowledged that either positive or negative economic effects on a community could stimulate a limited amount of political integration: "In cases in which the external economies and diseconomies are of sufficient importance, some form of integration may be indicated."[19] Specifically, Tiebout used as an example the function of law enforcement: "Not all aspects of law enforcement are adequately handled at the local level. The function of the sheriff, state police, and the FBI—as contrasted with the local police—may be cited as resulting from a need for integration."[20]

In 1961, Ostrom, Tiebout, and Warren contributed their seminal paper "The Organization of Government in Metropolitan Areas: A Theoretical Inquiry" to the metropolitan governance debate.[21] They initiated their discussion by sallying forth with a biting critique of the reform argument:

> This view assumes that the multiplicity of political units in a metropolitan area is essentially a pathological phenomenon. The diagnosis asserts that there are 'too many governments' and not enough government. The symptoms are described as 'duplication of functions' and 'overlapping jurisdictions.' Autonomous units of government, acting in their own behalf, are considered incapable of resolving the diverse problems of the wider metropolitan community. . . . The political topography of the metropolis is called a 'crazy quilt pattern' and its organization is said to be 'organized chaos.' The prescription is reorganization into larger units—to provide 'a general metropolitan framework' for gathering up the various functions of governments.[22]

In sharp contrast to the reform argument, Ostrom, Tiebout, and Warren defended the polycentric character of government in the metropolis, suggesting that the interaction among governments is far less chaotic than is usually portrayed, constituting a system: "To the extent that they (governments) take each other into account in competitive relationships, enter into various contractual and cooperative undertakings or have course to central mechanisms to resolve conflicts, the various political jurisdictions in a metropolitan area may function in a coherent manner with consistent and predictable patterns of interacting behavior. To the extent that this is so, they may be said to function as a 'system.' "[23] Ostrom, Tiebout, and Warren, continuing their argument, asserted that the primary responsibility of government is to provide its citizenry with public goods and services, defined as "the maintenance of preferred states of community affairs."[24] They further emphasized that the *production* of goods and services needs to be analytically distinguished from their *provision* to the citizenry. A local government, rather than directly producing a particular service, may deliver a service to its citizens by contracting with another government or a private vendor. In addition, the appropriate geographical scale, or scope, of a governmental unit should be determined by the criteria of control, efficiency, political representation, and local self-determination. Bearing these criteria in mind, Ostrom, Tiebout, and Warren argued that different scales of governmental organization are required to provide different public services. They further advanced: "Contrary to the frequent assertion about the lack of a 'metropolitan framework' for dealing with metropolitan problems, most metropolitan areas have a very rich and intricate 'framework' for negotiating, adjudicating, and deciding questions that affect their diverse public interest."[25]

The contribution of Ostrom, Tiebout, and Warren called into question many of the basic tenets of the reform perspective, most importantly the assertion that the fragmented nature of government in the metropolis constituted a dysfunctional condition and that public services could be more effectively and efficiently provided by a single, areawide government. In a very real sense, Ostrom, Tiebout, and Warren cast considerable doubt on the reform argument, provoking a wider scholarly debate about metropolitan governance.

In 1964, Werner Z. Hirsch published a paper titled "Local Versus Areawide Urban Government Services," providing further support for Ostrom, Tiebout, and Warren's argument that the appropriate geographical scale of governmental organization for the delivery of services varies for each service.[26] According to Hirsch, factors relating to economics (scale economy), politics (people government), and administration (multifunctional jurisdictions sufficient in scope to resolve conflicting interests) should be taken into consideration when determining governmental service responsibilities. He noted: "Certain programs are carried out more efficiently on a larger scale than on a smaller scale. In a few instances the opposite can be true, while in others scale of operation is unimportant."[27] Elaborating on the factor of political considerations, Hirsch advanced: "Proximity of people to government can help in the prevention and exposure of graft; it can promote new avenues of operation, improved management practices, greater efficiency and better services. It can ensure that change is evolutionary rather than revolutionary."[28] He concluded: "In short, an effective citizen-consumer feedback into the government sector can produce better services for the same amount of expenditures than could be obtained in its absence."[29]

Although Hirsch concurred that the use of multifunctional jurisdictions was somewhat in conflict with the principles of scale economy and political proximity, he recommended the establishment of these bodies for some types of service delivery and conjectured: "The most we can hope to do is to assign to a given government unit a number of services with similar scale economy and political proximity characteristics."[30]

In addition to economic, political, and administrative concerns, Hirsch argued that welfare considerations involving spatial benefit (and cost) spillovers and income redistribution should be taken into account in the assignment of service responsibilities. Concerning the former, Hirsch advanced: "Government services differ as to their spatial cost and benefit spillovers. If any portion of the costs or benefits resulting from services provided in one urban government jurisdiction is ultimately realized by residents of another, we speak of spatial cost or benefit spillover."[31] He noted: "The flow can move in both directions—into the jurisdiction and out of it. In the first case we have spillins and in the second, spillouts.

If major spillins and spillouts occur and are not offset by one another, welfare inequities and malallocation of resources can result."[32] Hirsch suggested in regard to mitigating the effects of spillovers: "Our strategy . . . will be to identify those services for which major benefit spillovers can be expected, as well as identify their geographical dimensions, and suggest that fiscal arrangements be made which are consistent with equity and efficiency objectives."[33] Regarding his parallel concern for income redistribution, he noted that "all urban government services which do not play an important income redistribution role are to be largely financed according to the benefit taxation principle."[34]

Hirsch, applying the above economic, political, administrative, and welfare criteria, concluded that local governments could best provide the following services: education, libraries, public housing, public welfare, fire and police protection, refuse collection, parks and recreation, urban renewal, and street maintenance. By contrast, he suggested that an areawide unit of government would more effectively provide air pollution control, sewage disposal, transportation, power, public health, water, planning, and hospital services. He further stressed that although income redistribution considerations mandated that education, welfare, public housing, and public health services should be provided by local government, these services should be significantly financially underwritten by the federal government and to a lesser extent by state governments.

In conclusion, Hirsch provided further support to Ostrom, Tiebout, and Warren's argument that the delivery of community services should be entrusted to a variety of governments, differing in geographical and organizational scale, and his contribution served to further undermine the reform perspective that the provision of services should be the sole responsibility of a single metropolitan government. Reflecting this sentiment, Hirsch concluded: "Our present system (of government) is not as illogical and irresponsive to need as is so often claimed."[35]

Following Hirsch's work, public choice scholars made further theoretical contributions to their argument. Robert Warren, in 1964, elaborating on the municipal services market model of metropolitan organization, stressed that municipal buyers, that is, local governments, "can be looked upon as sets of consumers, collectively organized and represented by a city council and professional staff."[36] He noted that his model was "constructed to explore the theoretical consequences of competitive behavior and decentralization under stipulated conditions."[37] Warren wrote of his model: "The market model assumes that a metropolitan area is composed of diverse communities of interests which are territorially distinct from one another which have different preferences for goods and services in the public sector. It is further presumed that consumers of public goods will seek the most favorable net payoff of benefits in relation to costs in attempting to satisfy their preferences."[38] Elaborating, he wrote: "A consumer may be an individual, an organized group of individuals who are residents of the jurisdiction producing the services (such as a neighborhood improvement club), or may be a public agency utilizing an external producer."[39]

Warren noted the various alternatives that citizens residing outside or within a municipality may consider for obtaining services: "The possible options for residents outside the boundaries of a municipality can be annexation, incorporation as a city, or continued unincorporated status. In the latter case, various combinations of municipal services may be obtained from the county government and special districts."[40] Warren wrote in regard to citizens residing in municipalities: "Organization as a municipality does not end the range of choices of a community. Control over the provision of services does not require that they be produced by the same jurisdiction. Thus a small municipality can realize economies of scale by separating production from control over the provision of services and utilizing external producers."[41] He added: "This can be achieved by such arrangements as contracting with a large unit for public health or law enforcement, by voluntary membership in a special fire, library, or sewerage-disposal district, or purchases from private firms. Under such arrangements, the community has the right to negotiate the service levels provided to its residents and, in all cases, has the right to withdraw and utilize other options."[42]

Warren noted: "[B]argaining and accommodation among units pursuing their own interests will result in a sorting out and allocation of services between regional and local production. These adjustments will reflect a balancing of economic and social criteria."[43] And he added: "While territorial boundaries will differ in the adjustments which are made to obtain various services, it can be predicted that regional or sub-regional systems for the production of such services as public health, sewerage disposal, water supply, library services, transportation, law enforcement, and specialized public works functions will be developed through contracts, special districts, or joint management arrangements."[44]

Warren defended the fragmented nature of government in the metropolis by maintaining that it places each group of consumers in a position where they are receiving public goods and services that fit their individual preferences, and where the production of services is allocated rationally between regional and local levels. In a direct attack on the reform position he noted: "[T]he viability of decentralized governmental systems has been greatly underestimated, and . . . expectations concerning the benefits of integrated government exceed what can be predicted on the basis of existing evidence."[45] Warren added: "The prediction that governmental fractionalization will lead to breakdown and failure in the public sector has stood long enough to cast doubt on its validity."[46]

Warren strongly asserted that the municipal market model for the delivery of services is not at variance with, or unmindful of, the need to resolve regional issues: "Just as the presence of numerous jurisdictions in an area does not mean that production inefficiencies necessarily exist, neither does the absence of a centralized decision-making mechanism mean that regional issues cannot be resolved. Evidence indicates that decisions are made, agreements reached, and disputes settled in a variety of ways."[47] Specifically, these ways include: "Bargaining, informal understandings, formal intergovernmental agreements, and the creation of new agencies with a region, usually with local support, are all possible methods of acting upon issues which extend beyond the scope of individual jurisdictions. Furthermore, local entities are not sovereign, but are subordinate to general political systems at the state and national levels and to the judiciary."[48]

Following Warren's elaboration of the municipal market service model, Vincent Ostrom and Elinor Ostrom published several papers, which, while not singularly concerned with metropolitan governance, implicitly contributed to the theoretical advancement of the public choice argument. In their work "A Behavioral Approach to the Study of Intergovernmental Relations," published in *The Annals of the American Academy of Political and Social Science* in 1965, they argued: "The study of the systemic character of intergovernmental relations requires that we begin to search for the nature of the order which exists in the complex of relationships among governmental units and abandon the assumption that all of these relationships are unique or random."[49] In a strong backhanded slap at the metropolitan reform argument, Ostrom and Ostrom asserted: "[A] scholar undertaking such a search assumes the obligation to understand the patterns of behavior in systems composed of many governmental units before predicting their imminent failure and recommending the creation of alternative structures."[50] And, further: "The concept of the single self-sufficient public firm producing all of the public goods and services for its resident population is no longer a tenable concept for understanding the structure and conduct of the public service economy."[51] In their paper "Public Choice: A Different Approach to the Study of Public Administration," published six years later in the *Public Administration Review*, Ostrom and Ostrom reiterated many of the arguments found in their preceding paper and concluded: "Most political economists in the public choice tradition would anticipate that no single form of organization is good for all social circumstances."[52]

Robert L. Bish and Robert Warren in "Scale and Monopoly Problems in Urban Government Services" elaborated on Warren's municipal market service model, contending that because large city governments enjoy a monopoly position over public services and are guided by professional values, they lack a measure of responsiveness to the diverse service preferences of individuals.[53] Bish and Warren emphasized that: "Individual choices differ for public goods and services as well as for private. Some consumers want more freeways; others want a rapid transit system instead. Some prefer local parks; others, larger private back yards."[54] Bish and Warren took to task the seeming inability of large cities to adequately respond to the service needs of all individuals, especially the disadvantaged, resulting in the demand for the decentralization of city services and the establishment of neighborhood governments. Implicitly attacking the reform argument, they wryly advanced: "If existing big cities are perceived by many residents as exhibiting monopolistic behavior, these citizens will find it difficult to see how an even larger governmental unit will improve their position."[55]

Bish and Warren argued that civic reformers, administrators, and social scientists advocating metropolitan consolidation have failed to adequately take into account the problems associated with regional governmental service monopolies and have neglected to consider institutional alternatives, such as contracting between governments, the establishment of special districts, and the use of private vendors, which often achieve the benefits associated with large-scale organizations, without creating monopolistic structures. They argued that the most effective urban governmental structure would facilitate the following: (1) providing an effective mechanism for soliciting citizen service preferences; (2) inducing producers, both public and private, to adequately respond to these preferences; and (3) ensuring that services are provided at the least cost.[56] Bearing these goals in mind, and stressing the utility of separating demand-articulating units from producing units, Bish and Warren stated: "The conclusion must be reached that the production of public goods and services will be most efficiently undertaken by varying units with boundaries appropriate to the particular good being produced. Similarly demand is most efficiently articulated by a variety of sizes of political units, again depending on the nature of the good or service."[57] And they added: "Thus, a rather complexly organized public economy may be more efficient for meeting citizens' demands in metropolitan areas than would the simple, single-unit structures usually recommended by political reformers."[58] In a final swipe at the reform argument, Bish and Warren concluded: "Proposals that would have the effect of expanding bureaucracies which are unresponsive and inefficient within large cities to a regional scale without introducing constraints upon monopolistic behavior is a strange solution to urban problems."[59]

In 1973, Vincent Ostrom made a major contribution to the public choice argument. In his work *The Intellectual Crisis in Public Administration*, Ostrom provided at the outset an overview of the reform perspective, followed by a severe attack on a prominent publication of this persuasion: "[T]he CED [Committee for Economic Development] report completely discounts *any* costs associated with institutional weaknesses and institutional failure in large-scale public bureaucracies. No recognition is given to the substantial literature in organization theory on the problem of goal displacement and bureaucratic dysfunctions. The concept of bureaucracy as an ideal-type solution pervades the CED analysis."[60]

Elaborating, Ostrom argued:

Citizens in a democratic society will run a very substantial risk if they are asked to stake their future upon ideal-type formulations. Anyone offering perpetual-motion machines for sale would be exposed to a potential charge of fraud. Perhaps it is a reflection upon the contemporary state of political science that a distinguished group of political scientists can recommend that eighty percent of the units of local government should be eliminated without making any efforts to assess the opportunity costs inherent in such a solution. Sixty thousand units of local government represent a major investment in decision-making facilities among the American people. Their elimination would be destructive of the basic infrastructure of American democratic administration.[61]

Ostrom noted that Americans, by eliminating a good share of the infrastructure of democratic administration, could expect "increased measures of corruption associated with bureaucratic free enterprise."[62] By contrast, he defended the polycentric metropolis, with its array of local governments, as enhancing economies of scale in the delivery of services: "Optimal size will vary with the boundary conditions of *different* fields of effects inherent in the provision of *different* public goods and services. Under these conditions, optimality can be attained only by reference to multiple agencies and overlapping jurisdictions."[63] Finally, Ostrom argued that the polycentric metropolis provides local governments a variety of alternatives for providing services, including the use of contracts, and that competition between governments functioning as service providers promotes effectiveness, efficiency, and citizen responsiveness.

Bish provided a comprehensive discussion of the public choice argument in his work *The Political Economy of Metropolitan Areas*, published in 1971.[64] At the outset, he set forth a public economy paradigm (model) for understanding the public economy of metropolitan areas and proceeded to identify and discuss the structures and coordinating mechanisms found in the public sector. This is followed by material contrasting the public economy of the relatively unified governmental structure of Miami–Dade County with Los Angeles County's polycentric governmental structure. Bish then directed his attention to the provision of education, air pollution, and income redistribution services in the two metropolitan areas. He concluded that the public economy paradigm provides a far more adequate and useful framework for understanding the realities of informal and formal governmental structure, and the functioning of local governments. Bish, on a number of grounds, characterized the reform model as far too simplistic, misleading, and inaccurate.[65]

In the early 1970s, Elinor Ostrom and her co-investigators at Indiana University, as a result of their studies of law enforcement in two metropolitan areas (Indianapolis, Indiana, and Grand Rapids, Michigan), provided a measure of empirical evidence in support of the public choice argument. In a general sense, they found, through the employment of various statistical measures and analysis and survey research, that the per capita cost of police services in large core cities was significantly greater than in suburban communities, and that citizens residing in smaller suburban jurisdictions rated the quality of their law enforcement services higher than their core city counterparts. In sum, they argued: "The major conclusion which can be derived from the analysis presented above is that proposals for the elimination of suburban police departments by consolidation are *not* based on firm empirical evidence."[66]

In 1973, Robert Bish and Vincent Ostrom presented a succinct overview of the public choice argument in their work *Understanding Urban Government: Metropolitan Reform Reconsidered.*[67] Reiterating many of the well-honed public choice arguments, they asserted that individuals are primarily motivated by rationality and self-interest, but hold various combinations of preferences. Some of the goods and services that individuals seek are best provided under private market arrangements, while others must be provided by the public sector. The willingness of an individual to pay the cost of a private good substantiates a preference. In the public sector, in contrast, the preference of an individual for a public good is made evident through voting, lobbying, and other mechanisms of opinion. Bish and Ostrom underscored: "Citizen demands can be more precisely indicated in smaller units rather than larger political units, and in political units undertaking fewer rather than more numerous public functions."[68] However, they acknowledged that since citizens are not able to articulate a preference to a single small unit for each public service, "the optimal situation is more likely to be one in which each of several units performs multiple services."[69]

Regarding the supply side of government, Bish and Ostrom perceived government as a natural monopoly, with little incentive to operate efficiently, to innovate, to reduce costs, or to be responsive to consumer demands. Nevertheless, they argue that the adverse effects of a public monopoly can be minimized by the institution of competition between local governments: "If ample fragmentation of authority and overlapping jurisdictions exist sufficient competition may be engendered to stimulate a more responsive and efficient economy in metropolitan areas."[70] This competition may be stimulated through electoral contests and by citizens "voting with their feet," that is, moving to a governmental jurisdiction that has the set of services and taxes they find most attractive. Service competition may be further enhanced by the utilization of private and public producers or vendors.

Advancing a well-developed theme, Bish and Ostrom argued that both small and large governmental units are needed for the delivery of services:

> Different public goods and services are most efficiently provided under different organizational arrangements. Services which involve proportionately large expenditures for physical facilities may be provided most efficiently by large organizations. Economies in such services can often by realized by serving large populations and large areas. Other services, such as education and police, are best provided in person-to-person situations. These services are both more difficult to manage and highly sensitive to individual preferences and localized conditions. Diseconomies are likely to accrue when these services are organized on a large scale.[71]

Bish and Ostrom concluded: "A governmental system of multiple, overlapping jurisdictions can take advantage of diverse economies of scale for different public services. A public economy composed of multiple jurisdictions is likely to be more efficient and responsive than a public economy organized as a single area-wide monopoly."[72]

With the publication of *Understanding Urban Government: Metropolitan Reform Reconsidered*, the public choice argument emerged as a well-developed, serious competitor to the reform perspective. By this time, public choice advocates had succeeded in framing a broadly respected alternative position to the reform argument. There no longer prevailed among scholars of urban affairs a consensus that all local governments should be consolidated into a single metropolitanwide structure.

Following the publication of *Understanding Urban Government*, scholars further developed and refined the public choice perspective. In 1977, Elinor Ostrom and Vincent Ostrom integrated with greater force into the argument the concept of the coproduction of services, and argued that coproduction is best facilitated by the polycentric metropolis, with its abundance of local governments and numerous arenas for citizen participation. They define the coproduction of public services as involving those instances in which citizen-consumers assist in some fashion in the production of the services they receive. Hence, coproduction involves a mixing of the productive efforts of regular (public or private) and consumer producers.[73]

Elaborating on the definition advanced by Elinor Ostrom and Vincent Ostrom, Gordon P. Whitaker cited three examples of coproduction: (1) citizens requesting assistance from government; (2) citizens providing assistance to government; and (3) citizens and governmental representatives negotiating through a mutual adjustment process and subsequently agreeing to a public policy decision. An example of the first occurs when citizens request an increase in the frequency of police patrols in their neighborhood; the second type is realized when citizens alert their fire department of potential fire hazards in their neighborhood; and the third type takes place when citizens and public officials agree, after an extended period of negotiations, to a local zoning change. Whitaker noted that services particularly susceptible to coproduction include: (1) public safety and security; (2) elementary, secondary, and higher education; (3) fire protection; (4) recreation; and (5) solid-waste collection and disposal. He reminds us that the coproduction of services is especially useful in those instances which involve the goal of modifying the behavior of the citizens being served.[74] In this regard, Gina Davis and Elinor Ostrom found that students who function as significant coproducers of their education generally achieve higher levels of success.[75]

Elinor Ostrom and Vincent Ostrom stress that one benefit of coproduction is that it serves to modify the service decisions of professionals, resulting in more relevant services and a higher level of services. As they explain: "When professional personnel presume to know what is good for people rather than providing people with opportunities to express their own preferences, we should not be surprised to find that increasing professionalization of public services is accompanied by a serious erosion in the quality of these services."[76] Elinor Ostrom and Vincent Ostrom further noted: "High expenditures for public services supplied exclusively by highly trained cadres of professional personnel may be a factor contributing to a service paradox. The better the services are, as defined by professional criteria, the less satisfied citizens are with those services. An efficient public service delivery system will depend upon incentives to assist citizens in functioning as essential coproducers."[77]

A major liability of metropolitan government, according to Elinor Ostrom and Vincent Ostrom, is that since it functions as a monopoly service provider—albeit dominated by professional values—citizens are deprived of a range of alternative service provision choices, hampering their involvement in the production of services. In contrast, in the polycentric metropolis, served by a variety of public service industries, citizens are provided with a multiplicity of service provision alternatives, facilitating their involvement in the production of services.

In addition to tempering professional values, public choice advocates have advanced a number of other benefits resulting from coproduction. According to Stephen L. Percy, these benefits include: (1) a higher level of services; (2) lower costs for current services; (3) the enhanced responsiveness of service agencies to citizen preferences and needs; (4) increased citizen cognizance of service production technology and constraints; and (5) increased citizen participation in the other areas of local government.[78]

In the 1980s, public choice scholars made additional theoretical contributions to their argument, especially with regard to the legal and political relationship between the state and local governments. The most insightful of these contributions are set forth in a paper written by Ronald J. Oakerson and Roger B. Parks and published in the *American Review of Public Administration*.[79] At the outset of their paper, Oakerson and Parks argue that although states provide the legal framework and political process for the establishment of local governments, states do not create these entities. They advanced: "Local citizens create and sustain—which is to say, govern—local governments through processes of constitutional choice, a role that extends well beyond electing local officials."[80]

According to Oakerson and Parks, two levels of constitutional choice are found in a local government constitution: an *enabling* level, provided by the state, which sets forth a set of rules that local citizens may utilize to create and modify local governments; and a *chartering* level that determines the specific character of a local government as citizens act to bring it into existence in accordance with enabling rules.

Enabling rules consist of four types: (1) rules of association, pertaining to a process such as municipal incorporation, which enable citizens to create a general-purpose or single-purpose government, vested with certain powers; (2) boundary adjustment rules, which enable local citizens and officials to change the boundaries of an existing unit; (3) fiscal rules, which determine the revenue-raising authority of a local unit; and (4) interjurisdictional rules, which enable a local unit to enter into relationships with other governments and with private firms. As Oakerson and Parks observed, the enabling rule-making capabilities of state legislatures involving these matters allow them to structure a form of areawide governance in metropolitan areas. They noted: "Attention can be given to metropolitan-wide concerns in a way that does not entail a bias toward any particular local government unit but is, nevertheless, a form of 'local' governance. A metropolitan-wide unit of decision making, because it operates at a constitutional level, can be operative in a multijurisdictional setting without displacing local provision units."[81]

Rules of association pertaining to the chartering level of local constitutional choice involve: (1) classificatory decision rules, which allow for the creation of different types of governmental units, such as municipalities, school districts, and special districts, for different objectives; (2) constitutive decision rules, which permit citizens to establish a new government; and (3) reconstitutive decision rules, which modify the charter of an association, or allow disassociation. Closely related to these rules of association are rules pertaining to boundary adjustment, especially boundary extension, and a permissive set of interjurisdictional rules facilitating joint action among units of government and with the private sector.

According to Oakerson and Parks, the nature of governance in metropolitan areas may be best understood in terms of citizens making use of enabling and associational rules, resulting in complex "local public economies,"[82] consisting of a variety of governments dependent on one another in the provision of local public goods and services. Simply stated, a local public economy is an array of provision and production units linked by a variety of interorganizational arrangements, comprising a system of governance. Therefore, as Oakerson and Parks noted: "[R]egional or metropolitan government does not depend upon the establishment of a single regional government that has provision and production responsibilities."[83]

The Public Choice Argument: Summary and Evaluation

In direct contrast to the reform perspective, public choice scholars—adhering to the principles of self-government and democratic administration, and the political economy approach to the study of politics—defend the polycentric character of government in the metropolis, represented by the multiplicity of local governmental units. Their defense is predicated on the following arguments: (1) a variety of local governments is more responsive to diverse citizen service needs and preferences than a single metropolitan government; (2) citizens, acting on a rational and self-interested basis, are able, by "voting with their feet," to reside in a community that best meets their service and tax preferences; (3) services may be delivered by a variety of governments and private vendors in terms of geographical size, thereby realizing the benefits of more efficient, effective, and responsive services and economies of scale; (4) the multiple number of governments and private vendors providing services diminishes the problems associated with monopoly providers, facilitates competition in terms of service delivery, and underscores the role of governments as both service producers and providers; (5) multiple governments provide more opportunities for citizens to become involved in government and to assist in the coproduction of public services; and (6) the frequency and regular interactions between governments constitute a system of metropolitan governance that can successfully respond to metropolitanwide service and policy challenges.

Public choice scholars have played a major role in structuring the current debate on metropolitan governance; indeed, the most recent publications of the U.S. Advisory Commission on Intergovernmental Relations (ACIR), including *The Organization of Local Public Economies*,[84] *Metropolitan Organization: The St. Louis Case*,[85] and *Metropolitan Organization: The Allegheny County Case*,[86] strongly reflect the tenets of the public choice argument. This recent stance of the ACIR is in direct contrast to its general defense of the reform position which it advanced for a quarter of a century between 1960 and 1985.

Scholars aligned with the public choice argument have advanced a number of important insights contributing to our better understanding of metropolitan governance. First, by providing us with a comprehensive portrait of metropolitan government and politics, taking into account both public and private, and formal and informal aspects, public choice advocates have wisely directed our attention away from an excessive preoccupation with formal structure and toward a focus on individual needs and preferences. This is a truly welcome development, given the past penchant of scholars of urban affairs to believe that by simply re-engineering the governmental structure of metropolitan areas along the lines of consolidation, socio-economic problems would be substantially alleviated.

Second, public choice scholars have seriously eroded the legitimacy of totally consolidated metropolitan government, casting asunder an alternative that has enjoyed very little real political viability. Currently, few scholars of urban affairs defend the notion of a single consolidated government for a metropolitan area, endorsing instead some sort of federative, or two-tier, governmental structure. Even the prestigious Committee for

Economic Development, which initially recommended massive governmental consolidation in metropolitan areas in its report *Modernizing Local Government*,[87] issued in 1966, retreated from this position four years later when it released the publication *Reshaping Government in Metropolitan Areas*,[88] recommending a federative metropolitan governmental structure. In a parallel way, Victor Jones, a long-time distinguished scholar of the government and politics of metropolitan areas, in "From Metropolitan Government to Metropolitan Governance" beseeched his audience to forgive him for his past sins for supporting metropolitan governmental consolidation and urged greater acknowledgment of the virtues of the polycentric metropolis.[89]

Third, in sharp contrast to the reform advocates, public choice scholars have widened the debate on metropolitan governance by stressing the positive features and consequences flowing from the polycentric character of government in the metropolis. As they underscore, the decentralized governmental structure, with its variety of general-purpose and limited-function governments, allows citizens to better realize their particular public and private needs. In addition, the multiplicity of local governments offers a vast number of opportunities and political arenas for citizens to assist in the production of services and to practice their democratic citizenship. And, finally, the polycentric political metropolis provides the best guarantee for limiting the rise and effects of governmental monopolies, which tend to be marked by inefficiency, ineffectiveness, and a lack of responsiveness to citizens' concerns and demands.

Fourth, advocates of public choice have correctly noted that the maximization of economies of scale in terms of service delivery requires governmental units of varying geographical size for the provision of various services. Evidence clearly indicates that a single, consolidated government cannot realize economies of scale with regard to all services. Studies have substantiated that capital-intensive services, such as water, sewage disposal, and mass transportation, must be provided on a regionwide basis to realize economies of scale, whereas the delivery of public education and other services involving a good deal of human interaction are most effectively delivered on a local or perhaps even on a neighborhood basis.

Fifth, public choice scholars, as a result of their work analytically separating out the production function of government from its provision function, have played a major role in providing us with a more sophisticated understanding of the functional operation and service-rendering role of government. As a result of this analytical divide, they entertain a far greater appreciation than their reform counterparts of the utility and resourcefulness of incremental change in the metropolis, implemented by oral agreements, intergovernmental contracts, regional councils, special districts and authorities, the transfer of functions from one governmental unit to another, and the use of private vendors. As public choice scholars have correctly pointed out, the massive use of incremental change by local governments has put in place a system of metropolitan governance that discredits the longstanding belief that only political chaos prevails in the metropolis.

Finally, public choice scholars certainly are on the mark in reminding us that widespread political alienation prevails among a good segment of the urban citizenry and that, perhaps, the most pressing need in the metropolis is not the establishment of a regional government but, rather, the institution of neighborhood governments, as recommended by Milton Kotler in his work *Neighborhood Government: The Local Foundations of Political Life*[90] and Alan A. Altshuler in his volume *Community Control: The Black Demand for Participation in Large American Cities*,[91] each published more than three decades ago. According to this line of reasoning, the establishment of neighborhood governments, especially in the less affluent sectors of the metropolis, would serve to facilitate the ability of the citizens to articulate their particularistic policy preferences and have an impact on the policy-making process, resulting in more effective and relevant public policy and services.

The public choice argument, notwithstanding the major role it has played in contributing to our better comprehension of the government and politics of the metropolis, may be criticized on a number of grounds. First, public choice scholars place far too much emphasis on the belief that citizens, in terms of their general political behavior, their quest to maximize public and private goods, and their choice of residence, are largely guided by the virtues of rationality and self-interest. As Michael Keating has advanced: "The status of the premise that humans are rational individual utility maximizers is not always clear. If it is intended as a descriptive statement about human motivation, then it is demonstrably false."[92] And, further: "The notion of interest, too, is a difficult one. Individuals' perception of their self-interest in a particular matter is governed in many ways by the structure in which they find themselves."[93] Certainly, it is not unreasonable to state that factors other than rationality and self-interest—factors more emotive and pedestrian—come into play when citizens make political, policy, and residential choices.

Another criticism that may be leveled against the public choice argument is that it fails to adequately provide for a mechanism whereby citizens may discretely communicate their public policy preferences to elected officials. Given the variety of combinations and intensity levels of personal policy preferences held by individuals in a community, the voting mechanism does not adequately meet this need. In this regard, Mark Sproule-Jones and Kenneth D. Hart wrote: "The critical problem in both the practical provision of public goods and services, and also in the public choice literature, is to devise a valid and reliable signalling mechanism of individual preferences comparable to the way the monetary system operates in the perfectly competitive private market place. The most popular candidate to date is a voting mechanism. But votes, as a 'political currency,' is subject to many flaws. . . . It does not, for example, precisely register the strength of preferences that a citizen-consumer may have over a whole range of public goods and services provided by any one political institution."[94] Perhaps, to overcome the deficiencies of the voting mechanism, public choice scholars should incorporate into their argument the utility of annual public opinion surveys in order to determine more precisely individual policy preferences.

Third, perhaps no other phrase in the public choice literature has been more repeatedly cited by scholars of metropolitan politics than "voting with your feet," emphasizing that citizens choose their place of residence on the basis of seeking to maximize their policy preferences. Yet, in choosing their place of residence, citizens are constrained, to a greater or lesser degree, by monetary, place of occupation, and other considerations. Keating, elaborating on this point, noted: "Unfortunately to make the model work, Tiebout had to make some simplifying assumptions. He had to assume that mobility was costless and, to cope with the objection that people's choice of residential location is based on work rather than the pattern of local government services, he assumed that all citizens lived on dividends."[95]

Fourth, a common criticism advanced by scholars against the public choice argument is that it does not consider the need for redistributive politics in the metropolis, whereby the more affluent sectors of the metropolitan area provide a financial subsidy to fund services for citizens dwelling in disadvantaged areas. This criticism is not entirely meritorious since, as Keating has noted: "A serious objection sometimes raised against public choice approaches is that they do not allow for redistributive politics. It is not true that public choice theorists all deny the need for or possibility of redistribution."[96] The flaw in the argument of the public choice advocates is not their failure to consider the need for redistributive politics, but their dependence upon the belief that this need can be adequately met with intergovernmental revenues from the state and federal governments. Especially given the general decline in federal funding for urban areas and the growing political supremacy of suburbs in state legislatures, we have little real assurance that these levels of government will meet this redistributive need.

Fifth, although public choice scholars have made more repeated and serious attempts than their reform counterparts to measure the efficiency and effectiveness of services, public choice literature remains insufficient in terms of empirical evidence. This deficiency is partly due to the difficulties of measuring service performance. Keating noted: "Measuring the public choice school's claims to allocation and service efficiency has proved as difficult as measuring those of the consolidationist school. The evidence for the effect of local spending and taxation on economic growth is patchy and inconsistent."[97]

Sixth, the public choice argument may be challenged for being excessively parochial, in both a territorial and a functional sense. In its defense of the polycentric metropolis, it strongly underscores the utility of local governments as maximizers of individual needs and preferences, and downplays the alternative of responding to policy issues on a regional basis. This political emphasis bestowed upon local governments, in contrast to regional ones, makes for parochial political leadership. Keating has written: "The problem with local government fragmentation may not be that it produces a poor 'quality' of leadership as the consolidationists argued in the past, but that it produces a parochial leadership and defines the policy agenda in narrow terms."[98]

Moreover, the public choice argument may be challenged as being parochial in a functional sense. It tends to portray services in a discrete or single sense, each delivered by a public or private agency, rather than as a collection or package of coherent services provided by local governments. The public choice approach perhaps places an excessive amount of faith in the ability of local government bureaucrats, functioning as service coordinators and guided by their own internalized professional values, to obtain from the public and private markets and deliver to citizens a wide range of compatible and appropriate services.

In addition, although public choice scholars may be applauded for suggesting that citizens should practice coproduction and become more involved in assisting in the production of services they utilize, this involvement, somewhat ironically, may well result in greater service inequalities in the metropolis. This is simply because empirical studies have demonstrated that advantaged citizens are much more apt to practice coproduction than their disadvantaged counterparts. Cognizant of this problem, Percy has noted that: "[C]oproduction may have some negative influence on service equity if no compensating strategy is adopted by local government."[99]

A final and more serious criticism of the public choice argument is that in its defense of the polycentric metropolis—with its numerous local governments, its analytical distinction between the production and provision functions of local governments, and its promotion of incremental mechanisms, such as intergovernmental contracts and special districts, and the use of private vendors for service delivery—the public choice alternative results in a bewildering maze of service arrangements incomprehensible to the average voter. This condition serves to undermine accountability to the citizens and local democracy.

Notwithstanding the above criticisms, public choice scholars have immeasurably contributed to our understanding of the government and politics of the metropolis, by centering our attention on the concept of *metropolitan governance*, and its inclusive richness of public and private relationships, rather than formal governmental structure. Much more than structure, it is the quality and relevance of metropolitan governance—and the inclusiveness of that governance—that will determine the future of our metropolitan areas.

CHAPTER SEVEN

Incremental Change and the Metropolis

The one constant in the American federal system is change: change in the roles played by the federal, state, and local governments; shifts in public policy; alterations in intergovernmental relations; change in the power and influence of citizens and groups; and variation in obligations relative to the benefits and liabilities of the system.

In a 1987 article, David B. Walker lists the reasons metropolitan areas need some measure of integration and the seventeen approaches that have evolved to partially integrate the services of the nation's urban regions.

> Snow White nearly lost her heart. But she overcame the hostility of her stepmother and was kept alive in the forest by a family of dwarfs. Metro America is Snow White. Migration to suburban areas nearly took the heart out of her. Federal hostility toward taking a role in metro governance has driven metro America into a temporary disappearance from public view. The good news is she is being kept alive by 17 distinct types of interlocal approaches, on a spectrum from intergovernmental cooperation to full regional governance.[1]

Walker listed several reasons metropolitan areas need some level of integration, particularly with respect to system-maintaining services. With updating and adaptation, these include: (1) more metropolitan areas, up from 174 in 1957 to 315 by 1992, an increase of 83 percent; (2) an increase of 111 percent in the number of residents, from 56 percent of the population to 80 percent over the last four decades; (3) growth has not meant consolidation in most cases but, rather, continuing fragmentation of local government, with the number of local units in metropolitan areas more than doubling since 1957; (4) increasing diversity in population, territory, the mix of private economic functions and public services, the position of the central city versus the suburban and fringe areas, and increased jurisdictional complexity; (5) reduced federal aid to local governments since the 1970s without a corresponding reduction in federal mandates; and (6) more recently, reduced state aid for non-educational services.

The list of seventeen approaches to regional problems is arranged from the easiest to the most difficult (see Table 7.1). Most metropolitan areas utilize three or more of these approaches to help solve interlocal and areawide service problems. Most are discussed in this and previous chapters. These approaches range from informal interlocal cooperation to the three-tier approach used in Portland, Oregon, and the Minneapolis–St. Paul MSA. These partial "successes" have not reduced jurisdictional fragmentation, but are neverthe-less helpful. Walker notes that these actions reflect "an ad hoc, generally issue-by-issue, incremental pattern of evolution. . . . [M]ost of the major reorganizations were triggered, in part at least, by a visible crisis of some sort."[2]

Table 7.1
REGIONAL APPROACHES TO SERVICE DELIVERY[1]

Easiest

1. *Informal Cooperation.* Involves collaborative and reciprocal actions between two or more local jurisdictions, but usually does not require fiscal action. Probably the most common regional approach.

2. *Interlocal Service Contracts.* Voluntary formal agreements between two or more local governments. Used more by local governments in metropolitan areas than other areas.

3. *Joint Powers Agreements.* Agreements between two or more local governments to provide for the joint planning, financing, and delivery of a service to the residents of the jurisdictions involved. All states authorize such agreements.

4. *Extraterritorial Powers.* Thirty-five states permit some cities to exercise regulatory authority to a distance beyond their respective boundary. It does not apply to incorporated areas beyond their boundary.

5. *Regional Councils/Councils of Governments (COGs).* These are the approximately 530 voluntary councils of elected officials drawn from the local governments in metropolitan areas or, in some cases, for more rural areas. Their creation was stimulated by federal requirements for grants, most of which have now been cut back or eliminated.

6. *Federally Encouraged Single-purpose Regional Bodies.* Though quite a large number of these entities were created in the late 1970s and early 1980s by some twenty federal aid programs (1,400–1,700), only a limited number remain because of budget cuts, notably related to economic development, Appalachia, aging, job training, and transportation.

7. *State Planning and Development Districts (SPDDs).* Established in the late 1960s and early 1970s by states to bring order to the proliferation of federal special-purpose regional programs. There are approximately forty-three SPDD systems. Practically all SPDDs conform to the confederate style of COGs. Many COGs have been folded into the SPDD systems. They perform mostly a clearinghouse function. Only five SPDD systems have respectable funding.

8. *Contracting (Private).* Contracting with the private sector for service delivery is quite common. Most states authorize local government contracting with private service providers.

Middling

9. *Local Special Districts.* In 1992 the Census listed 29,036 single-purpose special districts, two-thirds with boundaries that are not coterminous with other local jurisdictions. These entities are discussed elsewhere in this chapter.

10. *Transfer of Functions.* This is the permanent transfer of a specific function to another local unit or the state. It is more common in metropolitan areas. In some cases voter approval is mandated. It became more common in the 1980s.

11. *Annexation.* This was the most common method of aligning regional needs in the nineteenth century and is still used today, but most involve only a few square miles. It is used most extensively for city expansion in Texas, where unilateral annexation is allowed, but most states require voter approval in the area to be annexed, which limits its usefulness. Annexation in Virginia is a judicial decision.

12. *Regional Special Districts and Authorities.* These are often areawide or nearly areawide units providing a single service. They often provide sewer or water service, though other common services are mass transit, hospitals, and airports.

13. *Metropolitan Multipurpose Districts.* Most commonly, these units provide sewer and water services, though about one-third are involved in other combinations of services.

14. *The Reformed Urban County.* About three-fourths of counties located in metropolitan areas have modernized their administrative structure and many provide supplementary urban-type services to their unincorporated ares. Some provide selected urban-type services countywide. Even though twenty-nine states have authorized home-rule charters, only about eighty such entities exist.

Hardest

15. *The Consolidated City-County.*[2] The major city and the county government consolidate and the reorganized unit serves as both a county and a municipal government. Small suburban municipalities, special districts, and school districts are often left out of the consolidated government. Though there were a half-dozen city-county consolidations in the nineteenth century, starting in 1804, most by state legislative fiat, since 1947, starting with Baton Rouge, there have been about twenty such creations.

16. *Two-tier Restructuring.* This is the federative approach, where areawide functions are separated from more local interests. The prime examples include the Miami, FL–Dade County reorganization of the 1940s and the municipality of Metropolitan Toronto in the 1950s.

17. *Three-tier Reforms.* There are only two three-tier examples involving local governments, a metropolitan council with some authority and the state government—Minneapolis–St. Paul area with its Metropolitan Council and the Portland, OR Metropolitan Service District. Both of these arrangements are discussed in Chapter 5.

[1]This is an adaptation of the listing by David B. Walker in "Snow White and the 17 Dwarfs: From Metro Cooperation to Governance," *National Civic Review*, vol. 76, no. 1 (January–February 1987): pp. 14–28.
[2]The forty "independent cities" in Virginia are really city-counties. Though they are not labeled as city-counties, counties in both Virginia and Maryland provide 90 percent or more of all local services.

The Changed Role of States vis-à-vis Local Government

At the turn of the twentieth century, states were our least active level of government, but between 1927 and 1942 they more than doubled their level of activity vis-à-vis local government. State governments responded earlier and more effectively to the problems caused by the Great Depression than the federal government, as measured by Stephens's index of state centralization and a comparable index of federal activity vis-à-vis state and local governments.[3] The state/local division of responsibility leveled off between 1942 and 1952, then states gradually increased their activity until 1987, when another period of stability or even slight decline in the state position vis-à-vis local government occurred. It is open to conjecture what will happen over the next decade as a consequence of increasing federal abdication of responsibility for domestic public services as the result of efforts to balance the budget and cut taxes at the same time. In all probability, some states will accept more responsibility while others will devolve these problems to their political subdivisions (see Figure 7.1).

Since the 1950s, state governments have gone through something of a metamorphosis. These changes were stimulated by three key factors: (1) the states becoming much more important as service-providing entities; (2) federal court rulings of the 1960s that referred to the principle "one-man, one-vote," which reduced the representation of central cities in state legislatures while increasing that of suburban areas; and (3) federal requirements

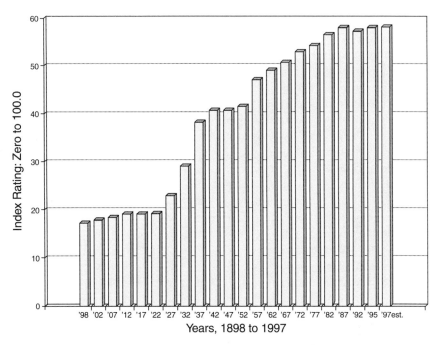

Figure 7.1. State Centralization for the Average State, 1898–1997. This graph uses Stephens's index of state centralization, which measures services delivered, financial responsibility for public services, and personnel adjusted for state and local differences in labor inputs versus inputs of cash and capital. Local services tend to be about twice as labor intensive as those of state governments.

for the administration of federal grant funds. In any case, over the last forty or fifty years, nearly all states have updated and broadened their revenue systems, adopted the principle of one-man, one-vote in their systems of legislative representation, and reorganized their administrative structures, their court systems, and their legislative procedures. States are no longer the backwater of American politics.

Using an entirely different approach from that of Stephens's typology (Figure 7.1), Stephen S. Jenks and Deil S. Wright document the increased administrative activities of states by counting the number of states with administrative agencies concerned with different functions from the 1950s through the 1980s. They list the functions that are the focus of administrative agencies in at least thirty-eight states. By the end of the 1980s, the number of functions had nearly doubled, from fifty-one by the end of the 1950s to one-hundred by 1989. In the early 1990s, up to 1992, at least twenty-five states, but less than thirty-eight, had added an additional eight activities. As the authors point out:

> . . . [S]tate government has experienced considerable growth in new functions and activities over the past three decades. Further, this growth has encompassed a broad range of policy areas some of which include responsibilities that many people thought more likely to be limited to national (e.g., international trade) or local (e.g., mass transit) jurisdictions.[4]

After listing these changes, it should be pointed out that states are giving less attention to the problems of central cities because of demographic changes over the last three or four decades. With representation primarily based on population, the influence of suburban representatives in state legislatures has increased substantially over this period. In the 1960s U.S. population was evenly divided among core cities, suburban and fringe areas, and non-metropolitan areas. By the late 1990s, half the population resided in the suburban/fringe area portion of our metropolitan regions, with less than one-third in central cities (see Figure 7.2). With states applying the "one-man, one-vote" principle in redistricting their legislatures, suburban/fringe and rural/small town areas are overrepresented in state legislatures, as well as in the U.S. Senate, given the state-by-state distribution of residents. As noted earlier, only two states have a majority of residents living in central cities and in only another two are central-city residents even a plurality, yet three-tenths of the population still resides in core cities. Suburban/fringe areas are dominant in twenty-eight states, rural/small town areas in eighteen states. Suburban and rural areas have much more influence in state legislatures. By 1997, half the population resided in suburban/fringe areas, with 20 percent living in rural/small town portions of the nation. This is another reason metropolitan restructuring is more difficult than might otherwise be the case, because state legislatures are usually required to pass enabling legislation.

For small states like Connecticut and Rhode Island, where over 90 percent of the population resides in metropolitan areas, the state government itself may serve in lieu of metropolitan government. This could also be the case for Hawaii, with 83 percent of the state population resident in Honolulu, or even for Delaware, with 66 percent of the population

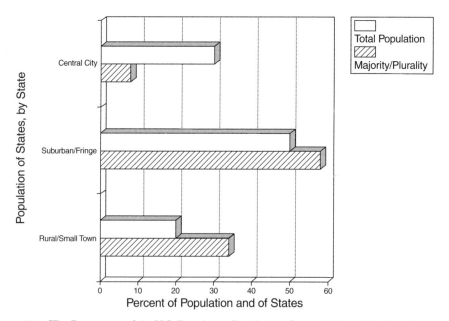

Figure 7.2. The Percentage of the U.S. Population Residing in Central Cities, Suburban/Fringe Areas and Nonmetropolitan Areas and Percentage of the Fifty States Where Each of These Sectors is Dominant, 1997. Central cities have a majority or a plurality of the resident population in only 8 percent (4) of the states with 30 percent of the U.S. population; 56 percent (28) of the states have suburban/fringe areas comparable majorities or pluralities and 50 percent of the population; while 36 percent (18) of the states have majorities or pluralities for nonmetropolitan areas, with only 20 percent of the residents.

residing in the Wilmington metropolitan area. For small states, metropolitan governments might constitute an unnecessary layer between local government and the state, except where there are substate regional needs for a particular service.

An article published in *Connecticut Government* in 1970 noted:

Connecticut provides a good case study of where the state government has taken more responsibility in the provision of services which in other places are considered local functions. After World War I, the state gradually assumed the functions previously performed by county governments and in 1960 counties were abolished.[5] State government in Connecticut is the primary provider of such services as public welfare, health and hospitals, correctional institutions, major airports, water transport facilities, water pollution control, and natural resources. It does more than many other states in such fields as highways, urban renewal, planning, education, and even police protection. Further it spends a larger portion for such broad categories as financial administration, general control, and interest on bonded debt. . . .

Connecticut is a prime example of a state that is building a statewide administrative structure for the handling of problems that many have classed as urban. In 1967, the Department of Community Affairs was established, but unlike so many states that have gone this route, Connecticut funded the agency so it could make a concerted attack on the problems facing local government. . . .

Connecticut is evolving in the direction of a *de facto* metropolitan government. It is a small urban state and it is quite logical for the state itself to act in this capacity.[6]

Moreover, small states tend to be more centralized and to have simpler systems of local government with fewer overlapping local jurisdictions and fewer local governments per unit of population. Ten of the twelve most centralized states, with index ratings ranging from 63.7 to 83.1 in 1995, had a 1995 population ranging from 585,000 to 1.8 million (Hawaii, 83.1; Delaware, 71.1; Rhode Island, 68.0; Vermont, 67.8; West Virginia, 66.6; Maine, 65.3; Montana, 64.9; North dakota, 64.8; and New Mexico, 63.7). The other two states of the twelve most centralized, Arkansas, 65.3, and Connecticut, 63.8, are also much below average in terms of population, with 2.5 million and 3.3 million residents respectively (see Table 7.2).[7].

Neither the national government nor the states are organized for collective action concerning the problems of governing metropolitan areas. Like the national government, all states have a "presidential" arrangement utilizing a separation-of-powers system with a rather clearcut division between the legislative, executive, and judicial branches. To further complicate this situation, all states except Nebraska have bicameral legislatures. Each of these sectors is elected or selected by different constituencies or methods of appointment. For some important issues, voter approval is required. These divisions frustrate state responsibility for the manner in which we govern ourselves locally and in metropolitan areas. This is one reason states have seldom taken major initiatives to solve the problem of governing metropolitan areas. Moreover, the establishment of effective metropolitan government could rival the authority of state government in some instances. As a result, most state action in terms of solving local and metropolitan problems tends to be the lowest common denominator—the minimum necessary to alleviate some of the worst aspects of a particular situation.

Canadian provinces, with the powers of government effectively unified in the legislature under a parliamentary system, have been far more effective in solving the governmental

Table 7.2

COMPOSITE RANKING OF THE 50 STATES IN TERMS OF
STATE CENTRALIZATION, 1957 AND 1995[1]

Category and Number of States, 1957/1995	States	
	1957, Index Rating	1995, Index Rating
Centralized (4/17)	HI 71.6, DE 66.1, NM 60.8, WV 60.4	HI 83.1, DE 71.1, RI 69.3, AK 68.0, VT 67.8, WV 66.6, ME 65.3, AR 65.3, MT 64.9, ND 64.8, CT 63.8, NM 63.7, MA 62.4, PA 62.4, WA 62.2, KY 62.1, LA 60.4.
State Services (5/14)	AK 59.9, LA 58.2, NC 57.7, AR 57.1, OK 55.0	SC 59.9, MD 58.7, NH 58.4, OK 58.3, UT 58.1, ID 57.7, SD 57.5, OR 57.4, AL 56.7, MI 56.2, OH 56.1, MS 55.9, NJ 55.8, VA 55.4.
Balanced (20/18)	CT 54.4, KY 54.1, ME 53.6, SC 53.1, VT 52.4, MT 51.6, OR 51.5, AL 51.3, MS 51.3, RI 51.3, NH 51.2, NV 51.0, VA 50.9, ND 50.0, WA 49.2, SD 49.1, UT 49.1, ID 48.8, WY 47.0, AZ 45.4	WY 54.6, IA 53.6, TN 53.6, NC 53.4, IL 53.1, MO 53.0, KS 52.9, WI 52.9, IN 52.8, TX 51.8, GA 51.2, MN 50.9, NE 50.2, NY 50.0, NV 49.7, AZ 49.3, FL 47.8, CO 47.1.
Local Services (8/1)	PA 44.9, MO 44.8, GA 44.1, FL 42.5, MI 41.7, TN 41.5, MD 40.6, KS 40.3	CA 44.4.
Decentralized (13/0)	IA 39.8, IN 38.9, MA 38.6, TX 38.0, CO 37.6, OH 37.1, MN 34.1, IL 33.4, NE 33.4, CA 32.4, WI 31.6, NJ 29.9, NY 28.9	
Average State	47.1	58.0

[1]Alaska and Hawaii are included in the 1957 data even though they had not quite achieved statehood at that time.

problems of their metropolitan areas. In the 1930s, Ontario ordered the consolidation of Windsor and its suburbs because of severe financial problems. This decision was upheld when appealed all the way to the Privy Council in England in 1938. In 1952, the Ontario Municipal Board (OMB) ordered the creation of a metropolitan government for the Toronto area, as a result of the breakdown in essential public services, and the parliament subsequently passed legislation implementing this decision. The OMB is a regulatory agency with powers over local government. Since that time, government in the Toronto area has been further integrated. Additional metropolitan entities have been created by other provinces since the 1950s. Originally the OMB was the Ontario Railroad Commission, but when the national government took over the regulation of railroads, it assumed the regulation of local governments in terms of planning and finances. No U.S. state has created a state agency with authority comparable to the OMB, though there have been one or two attempts to do so.

"Toy Governments"

Nearly 35 percent of all local governments in the United States operate without paid personnel. In other words, their paid part-time employees add up to zero. A total of 29,522 such entities are listed by the 1992 *Census of Governments*.[8] Only 3 of the 3,043 county governments operate without paid personnel, but 3,737—or over 19 percent of the 19,279 municipalities—can be so classified:

Governmental Units	Units with Zero FTE Personnel	Percentage of Units with Zero FTE
Counties	3	0.1%
Municipalities	3,737	19.4%
Towns & Townships	7,678	46.1%
New England, Middle Atlantic	320	7.7%
Midwestern Townships	7,358	59.8%
School Districts	317	2.2%
Special Districts	17,787	56.4%
Total	29,522	34.8%

The school districts listed are called non-operating school districts; they provide this service by contracting with adjacent districts or school systems. An unknown number of these municipalities operate by contracting for all the services they provide; some exist only on paper and provide no services, though they may exist primarily to prevent annexation to adjacent cities and suburban municipalities. The situation for townships is discussed below. While over 56 percent of special districts operated with zero FTE employees in 1992, this is a decline from an estimated 84 percent over the previous three decades. One reason so many special districts operate without personnel is that these districts are often used primarily as a funding mechanism for infrastructure improvements. They are also used to add to the taxing ability and bond-issuing capacity of general-purpose local governments—municipalities, counties, and, in some cases, towns and townships. The number of special districts could be greatly reduced if states could find a way to fund local facilities for prescribed areas without creating separate local governments for this purpose.

Special District Governments

As noted earlier, ours is a system of add-on, ad hoc local government, and nothing reflects that situation better than special district governments. The number of special districts increased from 8,299 in 1942 to 31,555 by 1992, with 1992 revenues and expenditures ranging from a few hundred dollars each for cemetery districts in Kansas to over $2 billion for the Port Authority of New York and New Jersey, which provides major transportation systems and economic development for the New York–New Jersey portions of the New York metropolitan region. By 1997 an additional 3,128 districts were created, which is the largest five-year increase since the period of 1957 to 1962. The number of districts ranges from fourteen in Alaska and fifteen in Hawaii to 3,012 in California and 3,068 in Illinois. Slightly more than 92 percent perform but a single function. These districts are used for almost every conceivable function of local government, but their use and the functions performed vary widely from one state to the next. Their adaptability results from the fact that they are normally created to fill specific needs of local areas and to fill in service gaps left by state and other local governments. In creating enabling legislation, states normally allow territorial flexibility. In other words, they can be very small or very large, depending on the need for a specific service or combination of services.[9]

While most of the functions performed by special districts are in the public interest, they are sometimes employed for what some would call dubious purposes. In Connecticut, beachfront property owners have used this device to prevent public access to "their beaches." In Kansas, special-assessment districts are at times used by developers to make adjacent property owners share in the cost of new streets needed for the developer's project. This is possible in Kansas because the vote for approving this levy is based on the area covered by each piece of property within the district. In one case involving subdivisions in Leawood, the vote was 185 against, 3 for—the 3 won because they owned 51 percent of the land area involved.

Special districts are often used simply as a funding mechanism for needed facilities. This is emphasized by the fact that 56 percent of special districts have no employees at all—a higher percentage than any other type of local government except Midwestern-type (weak) townships. It appears, however, that these districts are being increasingly used for the purpose of providing specific services, because in 1962 an estimated 84 percent functioned with zero FTE employees. If absolute change is defined by an index that measures the size of the bureaucracy in terms of FTE employees per 10,000 residents, revenue as a percent of gross domestic product (GDP), and direct expenditures as a percent of GDP, special districts increased their relative role 183 percent between 1957 and 1992. Over this same period, county governments rose 99 percent, school districts 60 percent, townships 31 percent, and municipalities 21 percent. The average for all local governments was 60 percent, states increased 109 percent, while the role of the federal government declined 1 percent.

As measured by per capita revenues, per capita direct expenditures, and FTE employees per unit of population, converted to an index where the average state receives a rating of 100.0, 1992 special-district activity ranged from a low 0.03 in Hawaii, with its sixteen soil and water conservation districts, to 455.3 in Nebraska, where a considerable portion of the state's electric power is delivered by special districts. The District of Columbia's Metropolitan Area Transit Authority gives that nonstate entity a rating of 643.8 on this scale (see Table 7.3). While there is a significant association between the number of districts in a state and district activity, the number is more closely related to the population of the state and the population of metropolitan areas, core cities, and suburban areas.[10]

Partly as a result of the increase in the number of metropolitan areas (MAs), the number of special districts located in MAs increased from 3,180 in 1957 to 13,614 by 1992, up 328

Table 7.3

NUMBER OF SPECIAL DISTRICTS AND THE SPECIAL DISTRICT ACTIVITY INDEX, 1992[1]

Activity: Above Average to Hyperactive		(Number)[2]	Activity: More and Less Average		(Number)	Activity: Below Average to Insignificant		(Number)
DC	643.8	(1)	MA	122.1	(396)	VA	69.9	(129)
			NC	111.9	(321)	OH	67.7	(513)
NE	455.3	(1,047)	ID	105.2	(728)	IN	65.7	(939)
WA	373.5	(1,157)	MO	104.8	(1,386)	NY	57.6	(980)
GA	329.8	(421)				MD	56.2	(223)
			Average			CT	56.1	(368)
UT	214.3	(329)	State	100.0	[631]	ND	54.8	(722)
CA	209.6	(2,797)				TN	52.5	(477)
AL	203.4	(487)	SC	94.9	(291)			
IL	192.6	(2,920)	KS	79.7	(1,482)	KY	48.4	(590)
			NV	79.7	(156)	MT	40.1	(556)
WY	178.8	(373)	NJ	78.6	(374)	RI	38.0	(83)
OR	168.0	(835)	ME	76.6	(199)	WV	34.4	(350)
CO	162.9	(1,272)				DE	33.9	(196)
AZ	162.4	(261)				WI	32.5	(377)
						SD	27.6	(262)
PA	149.0	(2,006)				MI	26.9	(277)
MN	139.7	(377)						
TX	137.7	(2,266)				AK	24.7	(14)
FL	133.5	(462)				VT	23.1	(104)
						MS	22.0	(320)
						AR	21.1	(561)
						OK	21.1	(524)
						LA	18.3	(30)
						NH	17.8	(116)
						NM	17.8	(116)
						IA	7.5	(388)
						HI	0.03	(16)

[1]This activity index is the average for three subindices that measure different variables for special district governments: (1) full-time equivalent employees (FTE) per 10,000 residents, (2) per capita own source revenue, and (3) per capita direct expenditures for each state compared to the national average (excluding the District of Columbia). Because it is impossible to obtain population data for districts, and would not be meaningful for this purpose if they were available, state population is substituted. Washington, DC is not included in the calculation for the state average, but the same data are used to indicate the role of special districts for this nonstate entity.
[2]The simple linear correlation coefficient (r) for district activity and the number of districts is +.42; the rank-order correlation coefficient (p) is +.52.
Sources: U.S. Bureau of the Census, 1995 *Statistical Abstract of the United States*; 1992 *Public Employment*, GE/92-1; and 1992 *Government Finances*, GF/92-5 (Washington, DC: Government Printing Office).

percent, while those outside MAs rose 60 percent; with the total increasing 119 percent. The increase per MA was 119 percent. Over the same time span, those increasing the most rapidly involved system-maintaining or system-augmenting services like sanitary and storm sewers, water supply and distribution, solid waste, airports, and gas and electric utilities. Multifunction districts rose at a faster pace than single-function districts. Seven out of ten of the 2,519 multifunction districts provide sewer and water services. Only highway districts declined in number over this thirty-five-year period (see Table 7.4).

Table 7.4
CHANGE IN NUMBER OF SPECIAL DISTRICTS, 1957 TO 1992

	Number of Districts		Percentage Change
	1957	1992	
U.S. Total	14,405	31,555	+119.1%
Inside metropolitan areas	3,180	13,614	+328.1%
Outside metropolitan areas	11,225	17,941	+59.8%
Increase per metropolitan area	18.3	51.4	+181.1%
Single-function districts	13,723	29,036	+111.6%
Multiple-function districts	682	2,519	+269.4%
Change in Number by Function[1]			
Airport	29	435	+1,400.0%
Sewer and water	144	1,344	+833.3%
Solid waste	43	395	+818.6%
Gas & electric utility	97	461	+375.3%
Water supply	787	3,302	+319.6%
Sewerage	451	1,710	+279.2%
Parks and recreation	316	1,156	+265.8%
Housing, community development	969	3,470	+258.1%
Library	322	1,043	+223.9%
Health	223	584	+161.9%
Transit, water transportation	105	235	+123.8%
Hospitals	345	737	+113.6%
Fire protection	2,624	5,260	+100.5%
Cemeteries	1,107	1,628	+47.1%
Natural resources	5,543	6,228	+12.4%
Highways	782	636	-18.7%

[1] *Census of Governments* classification is not entirely comparable for 1957 and 1992.
Sources: 1957 *Census of Governments*, "Government in the United States," vol. 1, no. 1; 1992 *Census of Governments*, "Government Organization," vol. 1, no. 1 (Washington, DC: Government Printing Office, 1957 and 1994).

For 1992, the Census separated out 1,800 large special districts for more detailed consideration.[11] Large districts are those that had revenues or expenditures of $5 million or more or outstanding debt of $20 million for FY 1992. Large districts tend to be located in metropolitan areas. Moreover, there is a close association between the number of large special districts per million population and the district activity index for the forty-seven states with large districts.[12] This would seem to indicate that the special district device is particularly applicable for the alleviation of service deficits in metropolitan areas.

For 1992, three factors explain nearly all—96 percent—of the state-by-state variation in the use of special districts, using the special district activity index (based on per capita own source revenue, per capita direct expenditures, and FTE personnel per unit of population). Districts are more active in states that are less centralized and in states where county governments are less active. In addition, they are more active in states with more complex state systems of local government (ranked on a scale from the simplest to the most complex in terms of overlapping and discrete local jurisdictions, excluding special districts from this scale).[13]

Clearly, special districts help solve local service deficiencies, but they also further complicate the structural problems of metropolitan areas. They fail the test of democratic norms and public accountability. Very few citizens are aware of the functional importance of special districts or even realize they exist. Of the 157,543 members of district governing boards in 1992, only 52 percent are elected to that position, while 48 percent are appointed, most by other local officials, with a few appointed by the governor of the state. Some are appointed by a rather circuitous process. Decidedly few citizens are aware of and participate in the governance and politics of special districts. Nancy Burns reported that, following their establishment, special districts usually have a minuscule number of voters participating in their elections, with involvement of 2 to 5 percent of the electorate considered a high turnout.[14] Several years ago a friend of one of the authors decided, after three terms, not to run for re-election to the Vandalia, Ohio Board of Public Utilities. He was re-elected anyway because three people wrote in his name.

The Changing Role of County Government

Though the origin of county government can be traced back a thousand years to the English shire, the settlers of North America adapted the county to the geographic and economic circumstances they found in the New World. Even in England at that time, counties served as agents of the Crown and as the providers of some minimal local services.[15] In this country they developed as both agents of the colony—later agents of the state—and local service providers. Counties are area-type units that range in size from 26 to 159,000 square miles, but average somewhere between 400 and 600 square miles. Most of the largest counties are in western states. The number of counties in each state averages 64, but ranges from 3 in Delaware to 254 in Texas. They range from less than 200 residents to 9.1 million in Los Angeles.

As pointed out above, in absolute terms counties doubled their level of activity in terms of own source revenue, direct expenditures, and personnel between 1957 and 1992. As units that generally serve a larger geographic area, counties are usually in a position to provide services to a larger jurisdiction than the majority of central cities and almost all suburban municipalities, in spite of the fact that counties were not originally created to provide ordinary urban-type services. In many parts of the country, county governments began as agents of the state, providing courts, recording deeds, assessing property and collecting property taxes for the state—and often for other local governments—electing a sheriff, and providing a jail. Over the years most counties located in metropolitan areas have adapted their governmental structures to accommodate the provision of urban services to outlying unincorporated areas or, in some instances, to provide countywide services. For a number of more urban counties, this process started after World War I. This is particularly true for counties located in states where annexation of territory by central cities became more difficult after states abandoned special legislation and as voters in the areas to be annexed had to approve absorption into the core city or where the central city was surrounded by incorporated suburban municipalities. As urban areas expand in terms of geographic extent and population, counties are often left to provide services to increasingly populous unincorporated areas.

The most common type of county governing body is a three- to five-member elected county commission, though in some states the governing body is called a board of supervisors. The board of supervisors system is used primarily in Michigan, New Jersey, New York, Virginia, and Wisconsin and can have as many as forty-seven members. At the other extreme is Georgia where fourteen counties have but a single elected member of the governing body.[16] In most counties the governing body often serves in both legislative and executive capacities.

The level of county government activity varies significantly from one state to the next. Activity is measured by the average per capita own source revenue, per capita direct expenditures, and FTE personnel per unit of population, converted to an index where the national average is 100.0. Counties do not exist as civil governments in Connecticut and Rhode Island. Connecticut counties were abolished in 1960 and the state took over the largely judicial services formerly performed by county governments.[17] Counties in Rhode Island were never more than judicial districts. County activity ranges from a rating of 1.6 in Vermont to 359.4 in Maryland, with New Jersey counties at the national average (see Table 7.5).[18] Counties in Maryland, Virginia, Hawaii, Alaska, North Carolina, Tennessee, and Nevada are more like municipal corporations than the more traditional county units in other states.

Excluding insignificant special districts, counties and the city-county of Honolulu-Oahu are the only units of local government in Hawaii. Counties and city-counties in Maryland and Virginia (called "independent cities" in Virginia) constitute over 90 percent of local government activity. Baltimore is the only city-county in Maryland, but Virginia has forty "independent cities." In Alaska, counties (called boroughs) and city-counties (Anchorage, Juneau, and Sitka) constitute 72 percent of all local government activity based on this measure. Counties in New England have always been rather minor entities compared to counties in other states and compared to towns in New England. Municipalities in New England are really only towns that choose to call themselves cities, as both are incorporated places.

Again, particularly in urban areas outside of New England, county governments have increasingly adapted their organizational structures to accommodate increased levels of activity and to increase administrative responsibility. Historically, in most states, county governments have been a collection of separately elected officials and judges who just happen to occupy the same courthouse. In many states these elected officials include the three-member county commission (sometimes called a county court, as well as thirty-two other names), the county clerk, sheriff, prosecuting attorney, minor court judges (in states where judges are elected), recorder of deeds, assessor, tax collector, court administrator, etc. Even in more rural counties in states where counties have significantly above average levels of activity, they have been adapting their organizational structure. For example, ninety-four of the ninety-five non–city-county counties in Virginia now employ a professional administrator.[19]

In metropolitan counties, structural change is more evident. The three counties with nearly three-fourths of the population of the Kansas City, MO-KS metropolitan area

Table 7.5
INDEX OF COUNTY ACTIVITY BY STATE, 1991[1]

County Government Activity Compared to the National Average, in Each State's System of Local Government											
Hyperactive 150 plus		**Above Average 120–150**		**Average 80–120**		**Below Average 50–80**		**Low 25–50**		**Negligible Less than 25**	
MD	359.4[2]	MS	133.0	CA	112.9	AR	79.0	MO	49.8	ME	16.4
VA	349.0[2]	WY	129.0	LA	111.9	WV	78.2	NH	32.3	MA	10.9
HI	331.6[2]	FL	123.7	MT	111.2	ND	75.1			VT	1.6
AK	298.4[2]			SC	110.8	NM	74.5			CT	0.0[3]
NC	279.3			WI	100.7	DE	72.7			RI	0.0[3]
TN	226.4[2]			NJ	100.0	MI	69.1				
NV	178.6			ID	99.4	NY	68.4				
				GA	95.1	CO	67.2				
				MN	93.4	TX	64.0				
				OH	92.8	OR	63.9				
				IN	88.3	SD	60.9				
				KS	85.4	OK	60.5				
				IA	84.1	WA	57.6				
				KY	83.0	UT	56.3				
				AZ	81.7	NE	53.4				
						AL	52.0				
						PA	50.7				
						IL	50.3				
(7)		(3)		(15)		(18)		(2)		(5)	

U.S. Totals	100.0
Average State	102.5
Median State	80.4

[1]Based on three subindices where the national average equals 100.0: (1) county per capita own source revenues as a percentage of total local revenue to show relative fiscal independence; (2) county per capita direct expenditures as a percentage of total local expenditures as an indication of services delivered; and (3) county full-time equivalent (FTE) personnel per unit of population to indicate the degree to which counties actually deliver the services they pay for.

[2]City-counties in these states are more like other county governments than other municipalities in terms of the criteria listed in Footnote 1. Thus, they are so classified. Ordinary counties in these states exhibit much above average levels of activity and are more like municipal corporations than traditional county governments in other states.

[3]Counties do not exist as civil governments in Connecticut and Rhode Island.

have adapted to increased urbanization. The Kansas City, Kansas–Wyandotte County consolidation was covered earlier. Johnson County, Kansas has a five-member county commission with an appointed professional administrator. In the early 1970s, Jackson County, Missouri adopted a county charter with an elected executive and a fifteen-member legislature (later reduced by discontinuing the four at-large positions) that eliminated all other elected positions except those of prosecuting attorney and judges.[20]

In 1949, St. Louis County, outside the city-county of St. Louis, adopted a charter that created an elected executive and a seven-member county council. Over the years, St. Louis county has eliminated most other elected officials. It now provides some services on a countywide basis, some services primarily to unincorporated areas, and still other services to county municipalities on a contractual basis. Across the nation, counties have been adapting to urbanization since at least the 1950s, with the appointment of county administrators in states like Ohio and county managers in California as well as many other states.

For example, in addition to the normal county functions, Milwaukee County started assuming areawide services with the consolidation of parks and recreation services and welfare in the 1930s. In the 1940s the county took over pollution control, airports, and expressways. In 1960 the county went through a structural reorganization that eliminated a number of separately elected officials, created an elected county executive, and consolidated the administrative organization by placing urban and areawide services under the elected executive. The legislative body was elected on the basis of state representative districts. The Milwaukee County area also exhibited another kind of adaptation with the creation of a city-suburban sewerage authority in the 1920s. This city facility provides services to suburban areas with suburban representation on the governing body and revenue collection authority over the areas served.[21]

Twenty-seven states allow the adoption of county charters, usually called county home-rule charters, while seven of these states also provide optional forms of county government. Another dozen states allow optional forms of county government. Only about 119 counties have adopted home-rule charters, most in urban areas, though over 1,300 are eligible to do so. Many more have adopted optional forms of county government. In some of the remaining states, those that still allow special legislation, change for individual county governments can be achieved by act of the state legislature.[22] Nearly 800 counties have what might be labeled the "commissioner-administrator" form of county government, with a council-manager, chief administrative officer, or county administrative assistant adaptations. At least another 385 counties now have a council-elected executive system, often with an elected executive having veto power over council decisions, which can only be overridden by an extraordinary majority vote. The latter adaptation is comparable to a strong mayor-council system in municipalities.[23]

Municipalities, Towns, and Townships

Using the Census classification of local governments, municipalities increased their absolute role by 21 percent since 1957, but relative to other local governments they declined by 25 percent. This relative decline is largely due to the difficulty and/or inability of large cities to annex territory because they are ringed by suburban municipalities or because annexation procedures have become more difficult over time. As with other types of local governments, the levels of municipal activity are highly disparate from one state to the next and often from one municipality to the next.

Virtually all townships in New England, New Jersey, and Pennsylvania are municipal corporations and hence are classified as such in Table 7.6, making this presentation different from the usual Census typology. City-counties in Alaska, Hawaii, Maryland, Tennessee, and Virginia are more like other county governments in those states and are classified as counties rather than municipalities, even though hyperactive county governments can be considered corporate entities.

The Census classification of local governments is confusing for at least fourteen states. This is partly due to the fact that states often use the same terminology for different types

Table 7.6
INDEX OF MUNICIPAL ACTIVITY BY STATE, 1991[1]

				Relative Role of Municipal Corporations in Each State's System of Local Government							
Hyperactive 150 plus		**Above Average 120–150**		**Average 80–120**		**Below Average 50–80**		**Low 25–50**		**Negligible Less than 25**	
CT	265.4[2]	NH	135.0[2]	OK	117.5	IA	79.9	VA	35.0[3]	MD	18.5[3]
RI	255.7[2]	TN	121.0[3]	NM	116.7	OH	79.3			HI	0.0[3]
MA	253.9[2]			AL	108.7	MI	78.6				
ME	240.0[2]			CO	102.9	PA	76.3[2]				
NY	201.9			AK	94.8[3]	FL	75.5				
				MO	94.5	IN	75.5				
				VT	93.5[2]	WI	75.5				
				MN	90.6	MS	71.1				
				TX	90.4	NC	71.0				
				LA	90.3	DE	70.5				
				IL	89.7	ND	69.8				
				KS	88.0	WA	69.8				
				KY	88.0	WV	68.7				
				SD	87.1	NE	65.5				
				AZ	84.7	OR	64.3				
				CA	83.8	UT	62.5				
				AR	83.6	ID	61.3				
				NJ	83.6[2]	MT	59.0				
						WY	58.4				
						GA	57.0				
						NV	55.0				
						SC	51.1				
(5)		(2)		(18)		(22)		(1)		(2)	

U.S. Totals		100.0
Average State		94.2
Median State		81.8

[1]Based on three subindices where U.S. totals equal 100.0: (1) municipal own source revenues as a percentage of total local own source revenue to show relative fiscal independence; (2) municipal direct expenditures as a percentage of total local direct expenditures as an indication of services delivered and/or paid for out of total revenues; and (3) municipal full-time equivalent (FTE) personnel per unit of population to indicate the degree to which municipalities actually deliver the services they pay for.
[2]All or virtually all townships in these states are classed as municipalities because they are municipal corporations.
[3]City-counties in these states are classed as counties because they are more like other county governments than other municipalities. Hyperactive county governments are really municipal corporations, but are not normally classified as such.

of local government and different terminology for the same type of local unit. It is also compounded by the fact that local units, particularly counties, have evolved over time. While reclassifying data for these fourteen states does not make a lot of difference in national totals, the changes for the fourteen states as well as those for individual states are considerable. Table 7.7 illustrates the changes brought about by reclassifying hyperactive county governments in five states and townships in eight states as municipal corporations and school districts in southern New England as dependent entities. Since the time of this research, county governments in New York have all been given municipal corporate status, thus there are fifteen states where the census classification is from moderately to seriously in error concerning the roles played by different types of local government.

Townships exist in only twenty states. In these states they represent one-third of all local governments, with a population that rivals that of municipalities. In addition, they constitute one-fourth of local governments in the metropolitan areas of these states. In 1982, they exhibited a range of activity from 11 to 961, where the twenty-state average was 100 using an index that measured, state by state, per capita own source revenue, FTE personnel, and services delivered. Personnel appeared to be the critical variable, as FTE personnel per township for 1992 almost achieved unity with the 1982 index (with a simple correlation of +.99, see Table 7.8). In 1992, the average number of FTE personnel per township varied from 0.1 in North Dakota to 352.1 in Connecticut. The most inactive townships are on a line running from Minnesota through the Dakotas, Nebraska, and Kansas to Missouri.

Townships are most active in southern New England and weakest in the Midwest. For these states, there is a high negative association between the level of township activity and that for county government; as township activity increases, that for county governments declines. As mentioned earlier, virtually all townships are municipal corporations in New England, New Jersey, and Pennsylvania. Ninety-six percent of the 7,678 townships with zero FTE personnel are located in the Midwest. Some townships in Minnesota, Michigan, and New York also have municipal authority comparable to villages or small cities.[24] The number of weak Midwestern-type townships is gradually declining as their territory is annexed by cities and suburban municipalities or as they incorporate as villages or small cities.

Public Education

Expenditures for public education are exceeded only by spending for defense and social security, and are by far the largest expenditure item for state and local governments. Education represents only 3 percent of federal outlays; for states, 30 percent; and for local governments, 36 percent. Because education is labor-intensive, it accounts for 44 percent of all government employees in the United States, nearly all at the state and local levels of government. Public education accounts for 37 percent of state FTE employees and 55 percent for local governments. Of the 65 million students enrolled in the nation's schools from kindergarten through college in 1995, 86.5 percent were in public institutions; for K–12 it was nearly nine out of ten. Moreover, 85 percent of those enrolled in public institutions reside in the nation's metropolitan areas. Almost four out of five college students attend public institutions; at the same time private colleges and universities and their students receive significant amounts of money for research and student aid from federal and state governments.[25]

Table 7.7

SUMMARY OF CHANGES IN PERCEPTION OF LOCAL ROLES BROUGHT ABOUT
BY RECLASSIFYING CENSUS DATA FOR FOURTEEN STATES, 1991[1]

I. Census Classification:

Activity as a Percent of Total Local

State	Counties	Municipalities	Towns and Townships	School Districts	Special Districts
CT	—	41.1%	52.4%	2.0%	4.5%
MA	2.8%	42.3	40.8	4.9	9.2
RI	—	54.1	39.8	2.1	4.0
ME	3.6	28.6	32.8	28.3	6.7
NH	8.2	27.8	20.0	42.5	1.5
VT	0.3	15.0	16.5	65.7	2.5
NJ	22.2%	19.8%	10.7%	40.7%	6.6%
NY	14.3	57.4	4.6	20.9	2.8
PA	13.3	20.8	5.4	47.9	12.6
MD	74.2%	21.0%	—	—	4.8%
VA	53.4	41.0	—	—	5.6
NC	67.1	23.2	—	—	9.7
AK	34.4%	64.2%	—	—	1.4%
HI	40.1	59.9	—	—	*

II. Reclassifying Census Data:

State	Counties	Municipal Corporations	Weak Townships	Independent School Districts	Special Districts
CT	—	95.5%	—	—	4.5%
MA	2.8%	87.9	—	—	9.2
RI	—	96.0	—	—	4.0
ME	3.6	61.4	—	28.3%	6.7
NH	8.2	47.7	—	42.5	1.5
VT	0.3	31.5	—	65.7	2.5
NJ	22.2%	30.5%	—	40.7%	6.6%
NY	14.3	62.0	—	20.9	2.8
PA	13.3	26.2	—	47.9	12.6
MD	—	95.2%	—	—	4.8%
VA	—	91.8	—	—	8.2
NC	—	90.3	—	—	9.7
AK	—	98.6%	—	—	1.4%
HI	—	100.0	—	—	*

[1]These data are the average of the average percent distributions for own source revenues, direct expenditures, and FTE personnel.

*An asterisk is an item too small to be shown in these terms.

Source: G. Ross Stephens, *State Systems of Local Government and the Census Typology*, research report to the Research Board of the University of Missouri System, June 18, 1995.

Table 7.8

TOWN AND TOWNSHIP PERSONNEL, 1992, AND TOWNSHIP ACTIVITY INDEX, 1982[1]

	Number of Townships, 1992		1992		1982 Township Activity Index	Number of Townships 1997 (Preliminary)
State	with Zero FTE Personnel	Total Number of Townships	Average FTE per Township[2]	Percent of Townships with Zero FTE		
CT	0	149	352.1	0.0%	960.6	149
RI	0	31	333.7	0.0%	892.3	31
MA	1	312	242.2	0.3%	806.7	307
NJ	3	247	121.9	1.2%	337.0	243
NY	11	929	37.7	1.2%	137.7	929
ME	93	468	26.0	19.9%	176.3	467
NH	19	221	22.1	8.6%	147.5	221
PA	178	1,548	10.4	11.5%	70.5	1,546
VT	15	237	9.5	6.3%	94.6	237
MI	291	1,242	7.1	23.4%	57.4	1,242
OH	205	1,314	5.6	15.6%	27.6	1,310
IL	350	1,433	3.6	24.4%	12.1	1,433
WI	306	1,266	2.2	24.2%	44.6	1,266
IN	760	1,008	1.9	75.4%	11.2	1,008
MO	208	324	0.6	64.2%	14.4	324
SD	928	969	0.6	95.8%	23.9	956
KS	1,086	1,353	0.3	80.3%	18.6	1,370
MN	1,532	1,803	0.3	85.0%	26.2	1,794
NE	367	452	0.2	81.2%	15.9	455
ND	1,325	1,350	0.1	98.2%	20.0	1,341
Twenty-state average	384	833	16.0	46.1%	100.0	831
Number of townships		16,656			16,734	16,629

[1]The data shown for 1982 are taken from an article by G. Ross Stephens, "The Least Glorious, Most Local, Most Trivial, Homely, Provincial, and Most Ignored Form of Local Government," *Urban Affairs Quarterly* 24, no. 4 (June 1989): 501–12; from the U.S. Bureau of the Census, 1992 *Census of Governments*, vol. 3, no. 2, Table 19 (Washington, DC: Government Printing Office, 1994); and from a preliminary count of special districts by the Governments Division of the Census Bureau, May, 1998.

[2]The correlation between average 1992 FTE per township and the 1982 township activity index is r = +.992. The 1982 activity index is based on FTE per 10,000 population, per capita own source revenue, number and importance of services delivered, and legal status, with the twenty-state average pegged at 100.0.

In 1992, there were 15,834 public school systems in the United States; 14,422 were run by separate school district governments, and 1,412 were dependent school systems, operated by state (28) and local (1,384) governments, according to the 1992 *Census of Governments*. County governments operated 581 school systems; municipalities, 225; and 578 were run by town (township) governments—575 in Connecticut, Maine, Massachusetts, and Rhode Island. In addition, there were 757 special district governments, most located in Indiana,

Pennsylvania, and Texas, that financed school building construction. Nearly 6,000 or forty-two percent of all school districts were located in metropolitan areas, as were 778, or 55 percent, of all dependent school systems. The 1997 Census lists 13,726 independent school districts.

The number of school districts declined from over 128,000 in 1932, to 108,000 in 1942, to a little over 50,000 in 1957. Since then the number decreased to 13,726 as a result of state government policies promoting school district consolidation, mostly during the three decades between 1942 and 1972. Unfortunately, all of this restructuring brought about relatively little equalization of local financial resources between districts, because rich districts usually consolidated with rich districts, middle-class districts consolidated with middle-class districts, while poor districts were either left out of the process or consolidated with other poor districts. There has been some equalization of resources through state aid, but there are still wide discrepancies among school systems in terms of their ability to fund public education. One reason for this is that more school districts are located in suburban areas, where half the population resides, and they tend to have both more resources and more political clout in state legislatures than central-city districts.

All or almost all public education is provided by separate local school district governments in thirty-seven states. For these states, school districts are the most important unit of local government in terms of expenditures and employment, but not necessarily relative to own source revenue. For five states (Alaska, Maryland, North Carolina, Tennessee, and Virginia) and the District of Columbia, public education is provided by counties and/or municipalities; in southern New England by municipalities and town (township) governments;[26] while in Hawaii education is a state function. In New Hampshire and New Jersey, about four-fifths of public education expenditures come from school districts, the rest from dependent school systems. For Maine and New York, the division is about 50/50 between districts and dependent systems. Nationally, public education is heavily subsidized by state governments, less so by the federal government. Only a little more than one-fourth of the cost of public education is paid for by local governments and school districts, yet education constitutes over 36 percent of all direct expenditure by local governments.

In 1994, average per pupil expenditure for K–12 education was $5,363, with a range from a low of $3,328 in Utah to a high of $8,902 in New Jersey. In other words, for every $100 spent by the average state, New Jersey spent $162 and Utah $62. On the other hand, Utah ranks seventh among the states in expenditures per $1,000 of personal income. Among the states, general revenue per pupil available to pay for public education ranges from less than $4,000 to nearly $10,000. Unfortunately, within many states the differences among individual school systems are even greater. Because education is labor-intensive, half of public education expenditures are for salaries and wages and another 10 percent for employee benefits (see Table 7.9).

A Dynamic Model of the "City"

The roles played by different types of local governments vary greatly from state to state and from one metropolitan area to the next. There is no standard pattern. Local government in the United States is continually improvised. Further, the one constant in the American system is change—change in the environment in which local governments operate as well as

Table 7.9
INDEX OF SCHOOL DISTRICT ACTIVITY BY STATE, 1991[1]

	**Relative Role of School Districts in Each State's System of Local Government**												

Relative Role of School Districts in Each State's System of Local Government

Hyperactive 150 plus		Above Average 120–150		Average 80–120		Below Average 50–80		Low 25–50		Negligible Less than 25	
VT	197.0	IA	146.1	AZ	118.1	NY	70.0			TN	1.5
WY	165.4	KS	144.3	KY	117.8	NC	70.0			AK	0.0
MT	162.9	AR	144.1	NM	117.4					CT	0.0[2]
OR	160.9	TX	143.7	MN	116.1					HI	0.0[3]
PA	160.9	ID	140.4	GA	114.7					MD	0.0
SD	160.3	OH	137.6	LA	114.6					MA	0.0[2]
MI	159.4	IL	137.3	UT	112.6					DC	0.0
WV	154.9	SC	135.1	FL	110.3					RI	0.0[2]
WI	152.5	MO	134.6	AL	101.0					VA	0.0
ND	152.1	IN	134.5	NV	95.4						
		NH	134.2	WA	90.5						
		NJ	132.8	CA	88.0						
		MS	131.7	ME	85.8						
		OK	129.0								
		NE	124.5								
		CO	124.3								
		DE	120.5								
(10)		(17)		(13)		(2)				(9)	

U.S. Totals	100.0
Average State	108.9
Median State	124.4

[1]Based on three subindices where U.S. totals equal 100.0: (1) district own source revenues as a percentage of total local own source revenues to show relative fiscal independence; (2) direct expenditures as a percentage of total local direct expenditures as an indication of services delivered and/or paid for out of total revenues; and (3) full-time equivalent (FTE) personnel per unit of population to indicate the degree to which the districts actually deliver the services they pay for.

[2]Regional school districts are not independent, as they must depend on the individual member towns to raise and appropriate money for their needs.

[3]State operated school system.

Note: Though five states (Arizona, California, Mississippi, Tennessee, and Wisconsin) have a few dependent school systems, from 95.2 percent to 99.6 percent of education expenditures are by independent school districts. For other states: New Hampshire and New Jersey, four-fifths of spending is by independent school districts; while there is roughly a 50/50 division in Maine and New York.

changes in terms of the structure and numbers of local governments. This is particularly true for governments located in the nation's metropolitan areas. In addition, there is constant change in intergovernmental relations, as federal and state policies are altered, both vertically (on the state and national governments levels) and horizontally (in local units), including state-to-state relations. The United States has the world's most dynamic and most complex federal system as well as the one with the most state and local governments per unit of population.

Many factors affect individual units of local government. Each must be cognizant of changes, not only in their respective local situations and the myriad of factors that influence their own situations (dependent variables), but also those of adjacent and overlying local political entities (endogenous variables), and those of larger governments and other social, economic, and political institutions (exogenous variables). Individual local governments are affected by the character of local politics and public policy, their own tax and revenue structures, the types of services performed, legal and/or constitutional arrangements, economic activity and patterns of ownership of wealth, quasi-governmental institutions, systems of transportation, social institutions, social and demographic characteristics, and success or failure in the establishment of public policy as well as geography, topography, geology, and climate. Most of these factors also influence other local governments in the area, the state, and the nation.

Moreover, all these factors and actors are constantly changing, some gradually, others at a more rapid pace. If we think of the individual unit as a city, then, as shown in Table 7.10, the local political environment of a metropolitan area becomes exceptionally complex, with interaction between the city and other local areas as well as with larger governments in terms of demands, resources, and restrictions. In addition, the city is also affected by the bypassing interaction between the local environment, other local units, and the state and national governments, not to mention the world at large, multinational corporations, and other institutions.

With over 87,000 local governments, 50 states and several statelike entities, the federal government, and half a million elected officials, the United States is replete with organizations called "public interest groups" (often referred to by their acronym as PIGs) that try to influence public policy. PIGs are organizations of both elected and appointed officials, civil servants, and state and local governments, such as the Council of State Governments, the National Association of Counties, the International City Managers Association, the National League of Cities, the National Association of Towns and Townships, organizations of state or local judges, labor unions whose members work for government, the National Governors Association, state and county sheriffs associations, the National Conference of State Legislatures, the National League of Cities, and so on.

These entities influence public policy not only at their own level or unit of government, but also at other levels of government. They are often quite influential politically, particularly given the relatively weak political party structure at all levels of government in the United States. Additionally, there are a significant number of professional associations for occupations associated with government. In one sense, these interest groups are a kind of "shadow government." Many specialized or technical policy decisions are made by what some refer to as "functional triads" or "iron triangles" at all levels of government. These are: (1) the specialized government agencies, (2) comparably specialized legislative committees or subcommittees; and (3) associated public and private interest groups. Functional triads are active at all levels of government and many operate at multiple levels of government. Though they did not call them that, Wallace S. Sayre and Herbert Kaufman documented their activities in a 1960 study of New York City.[27]

Table 7.10
A DYNAMIC MODEL OF THE CITY

[Exogenous Variables] The State and Nation	[Dependent Variables] The City, the Local Public Sector	[Endogenous Variables] The Local Environment
1. *Federal and state political characteristics* political parties, factions, interest groups, PIGs[1], the electorate 2. *Federal and state legal environment* 3. *Services, programs, and taxes* 4. *Intergovernmental relations* interlevel political activity, grants, shared taxes, mandates, accountability, coordination 5. *National and state economic activity and structure* 6. *Quasi-governmental activity* government corporations, special authorities, government contractors 7. *National and state transportation systems* highways, air, water 8. *Social institutions,* including all organized interest groups particularly those associated with major corporations and large religous entities 9. *The world beyond and multi-national corporations*	1. *Local politics and public policy* 2. *Taxes and other revenue sources* including intergovernmental receipts and payments 3. *Services and regulatory activity* 4. *Legal jurisdiction and legal environment* 5. *Failure to establish public policy* 6. *Economic structure and activity* types of activity and land-use, commercial-industrial-residential development, public employment 7. *Quasi-governmental activity* publicly owned utilities and enterprises, government contracts 8. *Systems of transportation* streets, highways, airports, water transportation and terminals 9. *Geography, topography, geology, and climate* 10. *Social institutions,* particularly organized interests or corporations with economic or political clout within the city 11. *Social and demographic characteristics* including service populations	1. *Other local governments* 2. *Political characteristics and activity* political parties, factions, interest groups, PIGs, the electorate 3. *Social and demographic characteristics* service populations, inmigration, outmigration, social rank 4. *Economic structure and activity* types of activity and land-use, commercial-industrial-residential development, public employment 5. *Quasi-governmental activity* publicly owned utilities and enterprises, government contracts 6. *Systems of transportation* 7. *Geography, topography, geology, and climate* 8. *Social institutions,* especially those concentrated within the individual units of government 9. *Residential community associations,* also known as homeowners and condominium associations

DIRECT INTERACTION
Demands
Resources
Restrictions

DIRECT INTERACTION
Demands
Resources
Restrictions

BYPASSING INTERACTION
Demands
Resources
Restrictions

DYNAMICS OF CHANGE
Growth, stability and decine; separately
and in combination; alteration of the mix

[1]PIGs stands for "public interest groups," i.e., organizations of governments, government employees, or public officials that are organized to influence the public policies of their own or other governments in the complex of federal, state, and local governments that exist in the United States.

Contracting and Other Methods for Providing Services

Textbooks on American government tend to emphasize the services provided directly by all levels of government, but particularly those delivered directly by local governments using their own facilities and personnel. As Robert Stein pointed out, local governments use a variety of techniques to ensure that residents receive a larger package of public services.[28] Traditional delivery arrangements include direct delivery by the local government, contracting with private firms or other local governments for the delivery of services, and cooperating with other local units in developing joint contracts with private firms or other public agencies for services. Direct delivery by a local unit usually applies to what Stein calls "collective goods," such as public safety and pollution control, where everyone benefits, but there is really no way to put a price on a unit of service. Even so, some municipalities do contract for collective goods using cost of inputs as the basis for the contract.

Some services to urban residents are provided by private and semiprivate entities. Electricity, gas, and sometimes water services are provided by private business. In addition, local agencies often contract for services such as road construction and maintenance and garbage collection. Contracting out by local governments is increasingly common as private business does not need to provide various benefits and pension plans for their employees, which sometimes makes it cheaper to farm out some public services. Construction of all types is usually done by private contractors. Some municipalities, townships, and special districts contract out for all the services they provide. Over 13 percent of local direct expenditures are for capital outlay, most in the nation's metropolitan areas. This compares to 10 percent for states and 7 percent for the federal government. Local capital outlays amounted to between $84 billion and $87 billion in the period from FY 1992 to FY 1994. The cost of contracting for public services by all three levels of government amounts to well over $200 billion annually. Whole industries rely on government for sustenance.

Other, less direct, methods of providing or making services available to residents Stein calls "regulatory." These include the use of vouchers for housing, providing franchises, and the use of volunteer help. Large municipalities, those with populations of 250,000 or more, are increasingly using subsidies and tax incentives such as tax increment financing (TIF) to attract economic development. For these larger municipalities—mostly central cities— the use of subsidies and TIFs increased 7.7 times between 1982 and 1988, from 1.48 percent to 11.43 percent. The International City Managers Association (ICMA) survey of 604 cities for these years reveals that direct service delivery for large cities declined from 56 percent to 46 percent while contracting remained the same, at about 36 percent. The largest cities in this survey are increasingly using nontraditional methods of service delivery—the use of volunteers increased 6.3 times over this short period, from 0.87 percent to 5.51 percent. Cities under 250,000 increased direct service delivery, while contracting declined slightly from 30 percent to 28 percent. The latter group tends to include more expanding suburban municipalities.[29] Not mentioned above is the fact that homeowners in many areas contract with private firms for the delivery of some services without the intervention of local government or RCAs. This is quite common for services such as utilities and garbage and refuse collection.

As we pointed out in Chapter 1, the development of an estimated 180,000 residential community associations (RCAs), often known as "homeowners" or "condominium" associations, allows for the provision of services traditionally associated with local governments. These entities contract with private service providers or local governments for the services they render their members. RCAs are usually created by developers for the purpose of maintaining property values as well as providing a limited number of services. RCAs often maintain a number of rather specific controls over the use of property within their jurisdictions. On occasion, another objective of the RCA is to prevent annexation by adjacent municipalities, where residents might be subject to higher property taxes. Whatever the reason, these semiprivate entities greatly complicate local intergovernmental and public/private relationships as well as patterns of service provision.

All of this—the state and local governments in all their diversity, the private and semiprivate service providers, the RCAs, the differences in need for public services, the myriad of public and private interest groups—along with the material outlined earlier, makes the pattern of service delivery exceedingly complex for metropolitan areas, with each metropolitan area exhibiting somewhat unique characteristics. As a result, unless state governments take a more proactive role, no one solution to the problems of metropolitan governance and reform is likely to work for more than a few metropolitan areas—perhaps only for a few county areas nationally where there is some commonality within a single state/local system. Nevertheless, most residents of metropolitan areas receive a basic complement of services through a mixture of public, semipublic, and private arrangements.

As if to document this, the "Compendium of Government Finances" of the 1992 *Census of Governments* lists the finances of twenty-seven city-county governments that range in size from 96,000 to 7.3 million inhabitants. Except for the ten "independent cities" located in Virginia, there is no commonality in terms of total and per capita revenue by source, total and per capita expenditure by function, or even in terms of the number and types of services delivered. The seventeen large city-counties outside of Virginia, with the exception of two in Louisiana and the District of Columbia, are all located in different states.[30]

Federal Initiatives, Urban Planning, and Councils of Governments

The United States evolved from a rural society to an urban nation, with the majority of the population residing in metropolitan areas, without any kind of centralized controls over urban development. As a result of the multiplicity of jurisdictions at the local level, coordination of development is still highly decentralized and fragmented, even though there have been attempts on the part of the federal government—and, more recently, state governments—to coordinate and occasionally restrict development in metropolitan areas. Throughout most of American history, most land-use decisions were made by private business people—land developers, realtors, and bankers. There were a few exceptions such as William Penn's 1682 layout for the city of Philadelphia and Pierre L'Enfant's radial plan for Washington, D.C. Hartford, Connecticut created the first municipal planning agency in 1907, and the first national conference on city planning was held in Washington, D.C. in 1909. By 1960, 90 percent of the cities with a population of more than 10,000 had a planning commission or planning agency.

The federal government became more directly involved in local government with slum clearance and housing with the passage of the Housing Act of 1937. With passage of the Housing Acts of 1949, 1954, and 1959, the latter providing money for municipal planning, the federal government became concerned over the lack of areawide planning in urban and metropolitan areas. Virtually all urban planning before 1959 was done by individual municipal and town governments and a few urban counties. Federal efforts to encourage metropolitan and regional planning became more focused after the consolidation of federal programs affecting local governments under the Department of Housing and Urban Development (HUD) in 1965 and the Department of Transportation (DOT) in 1966. Increasing federal grants and the integration of federal agencies related to the activities of local and state governments led to a stimulus for the creation of "regional" planning agencies in some metropolitan areas and the creation of counterpart agencies at the state level.

In 1960, there were only a half dozen voluntary regional councils of elected officials, usually called Councils of Goverments (COGs), that tried to coordinate development in our metropolitan areas, though urban renewal and other federal grants had stimulated the development of regional planning commissions in many metropolitan areas, usually with citizens as members. COGs are *voluntary* associations of elected officials usually representing county and municipal governments of a metropolitan area or other designated region. They are voluntary because local units cannot be forced to join and can resign at any time. COGs were created to develop consensus regarding metropolitan or regional needs and action to be taken in solving area problems.[31] The number of COGs soared to over 660 by 1980, as a result of federal requirements and massive increases in federal aid to state and local governments between 1957 and 1977. Most regional planning commissions were converted to COGs during this period. Model Cities and other legislation required regional review and comment in all metropolitan areas for some types of local grant applications. The Intergovernmental Cooperation Act (1968) built on Model Cities legislation to require a "clearinghouse" system for rural as well as urban areas.

Federal legislation also stimulated the creation of state planning and development districts (SPDDs) in most states. SPDDs were created by state legislation and executive order to bring some order to the proliferation of federal regional programs. About half of the SPDDs were given the right to review and comment on state and locally funded projects. Many COGs either became SPDDs or were folded into SPDDs. Both COGs and SPDDs have a confederate style of operation. Some were denounced as "marching and chowder societies" for the purpose of dividing up federal largesse. This criticism may be too severe, as COGs appear to have stimulated considerable interlocal contact and more cooperation than existed previously.

Since the 1950s, states have become more involved in planning and the control of landuse. This has been a piece by piece, back-door approach, as problems arose relative to local control of development. Increasingly, states are reviewing local plans, but more importantly, they have become involved in coastal-zone, flood-plain, and wetlands management; the location of power plants; problems of the environment; the regulation of surface mining; water resources; and economic development.[32]

With the advent of the Reagan administration, and, over time, the severe reduction in federal aid to local governments, the number of COGs decreased to approximately 530. Federal aid was reduced and much of what remained was redirected to state government for state use or for state distribution to local government. President Reagan, by Executive Order 12372, gave the principal responsibility for the clearinghouse function to state governments if they accepted it, and forty-eight states did. According to David Walker, thirty-nine federal programs had a regional component in 1980. Over the next few years, twelve were scrapped, eleven were cut severely, nine lost their regional orientation, six were revised, and only one was left intact.[33] In order to survive, regional councils had to adapt, and most did so. Some obtained local contributions and became a source of technical services—even, in a few cases, direct services—to local units, though some federal money still exists.

Summary

Walker's seventeen "dwarfs" point up the variety of techniques that are used to solve or at least mitigate some of the service deficiencies in the nation's metropolitan areas, particularly interlocal agreements and contracts, the expanded role of county governments with their assumption of supplementary and/or countywide services, and the use of single- and multipurpose special district governments. The greatly expanded role played by state governments in the United States is another method of alleviating some of the service problems of our urban regions as well as areas where the population is more rural. Small urban states can, and in some cases do, act in lieu of a metropolitan government; in other instances, they financially subsidize local services. Though far from perfect, these devices— plus federal and state aid, and increased state-level activity—have managed to patch together to provide system-maintaining services at some marginally adequate level.

In discussing the so-called "metropolitan problem," as Edward Banfield and Morton Grodzins explained in 1958, we must distinguish between the problems inherent in metropolitan areas and the problems associated with the fragmented pattern of local government. The latter can sometimes be solved by creating a metropolitan government, but the former cannot. Even in cases where metropolitan governments have been established, problems remain. These are often associated with the social, demographic, and economic characteristics of the metropolitan area, and these attributes often vary widely among the 300-plus metropolitan areas.

Problems that have not been solved by the creation of metropolitan governments include those associated with the regressive revenue structure of most state/local systems. Ethnic minorities and the poor are concentrated in core cities, older suburbs, and rural areas. The heavy reliance of states on sales taxes and service charges, and the reliance of local governments on property and sales taxes and service charges, means the burden of state and local taxes falls more heavily on these disadvantaged groups. Very few states make any real attempt to give greater financial support to poorer local governments. Few states make much of an attempt to provide adequate tax relief for the poor, though seven states have a rebate system for sales taxes and most provide some tax relief for the elderly poor through the use of "circuit breakers" that reduce their property taxes. Over the past four decades, state and local tax structures have become more regressive as new sales taxes and service charges have been levied.

CHAPTER EIGHT

Local Government in an Intergovernmental Context

The proper placement of decision making, revenue collection, and service delivery authority between federal, state, and local levels of government is a difficult question even without the contemporary situation where urban regions have evolved with relatively little alteration of the exceptionally complex pre-existing federal system. In the United States, the congruence between resources, taxes, services, and political responsibility is complicated by 300-plus metropolitan regions (MSAs) layered onto one of the world's most complex systems, with over 87,500 federal, state, and local governments.

In order for a complex federal system to function at some acceptable level of effectiveness, if not efficiency, it is necessary for there to be rather extensive interaction between governments and levels of government. There is extensive political, collaborative, confrontational, regulatory, financial, and even, on occasion, social interaction among governments, levels of government, and the private sector in the United States. Given the structure of the federal system, it is indeed a rare situation when either social or economic efficiency is achieved.

In one sense, the federal system is set up *not* to work, given the separation of powers between branches of government, bicameral legislatures at the state and federal levels, semi-autonomous government agencies, and multifarious local units. With more than 300 metropolitan areas, it is more difficult to achieve policy goals considering the political-demographic divisions between core cities, suburban and fringe areas, small towns, and more rural parts of the nation. Add on a political-legal system that has institutionalized limited authority on the part of elected representatives and referenda at state and local levels for both minor and major policy changes, and you have a prescription for inaction on many of the major issues and problems faced by local government.

State and Local Tax Capacity

According to a 1993 report by the U.S. Advisory Commission on Intergovernmental Relations (ACIR), depending on the measure utilized, thirty-one to thirty-two of the fifty states have below average combined state and local tax and revenue capacity, using the commission's representative tax system tax capacity index (RTS) and its representative revenue system revenue capacity index (RRS) for states, including local sources. The U.S. Treasury Department's measure of state/local tax capacity, total taxable resources (TTR), lists thirty-five states with below average state/local revenue capability. Some thirty-two

149

states have below average per capita personal income (PCI). After World War II, the differences among the fifty states in terms of tax and revenue capability declined through the mid- to late 1970s, then started to increase, with more states falling below the national average. No one knows how many local governments have below average ability to raise revenue and thereby have difficulty or are unable to provide public services at some basic level. Listing the national average tax capacity as 100, the range in state/local tax capacity is as follows:[1]

| Measure | 1991 Range in Tax Capacity | | District of Columbia |
	Low State	High State	
PCI (Census)	70 (MS)	136 (CT)	131
TTR (Treasury)	71 (MS)	139 (AK)	224
RTS (ACIR)	68 (MS)	178 (AK)	123
RRS (ACIR)	69 (MS)	240 (AK)	124

The range of differences among the states is probably significantly higher than these data indicate, due to the ability of some states and a significant number of local governments to export taxes to residents or consumers in or from other states. On the flip side, a number of states are saddled with a liability in terms of paying the taxes that are exported to them. The high ratings for the District need some explanation. High levels of personal income are generated in the District, but nonresidents employed in the District are not liable for the District tax on personal income; Congressmen and others who live and work in the District are not liable for the tax if, when counting days, they are not in the District more than seven months a year. Most people who work in the District do not live there. These measures of tax and revenue capacity do not take either of these politically imposed situations into consideration.

Even with federal grants-in-aid to state and local governments in excess of $250 billion for FY 1997, there was little or no attempt at equalization of taxable resources among the fifty states. In the 1980s, where the federal government spent its money for defense and grants explained 80 percent to 86 percent of the differences among state/local systems in their per capita ability to raise revenue. Rather than equalizing taxable resources, federal spending patterns exacerbated these inequalities. There is no reason to believe this situation has changed in the 1990s.[2] Unlike federal systems in Australia, Canada, and Germany, the United States does not have a grant structure that places a floor under the taxable resources of poorer constituent governments.

Ideally, public services should be provided by the level of government most capable of providing a particular service in terms of need, resources, and administration. All of this is complicated by the measures taken by several states, and undetermined numbers of local governments, to export tax burdens to residents of other states by taxing revenue sources that apply primarily to tourists, travelers, and/or goods that are exported to other states. At least eleven states are able to export significant portions of their taxes to tourists or travelers and residents, consumers, corporations, or governments located in other states.[3]

It is harder to avoid or evade state taxes than those of local government and even more difficult to avoid or evade those of the national government. Service delivery for particular services, on the other hand, may be more appropriate to local, state, or regional areas. Given this lack of congruence, as well as a rather extreme level of political fragmentation, relatively few services are delivered on the basis of urban regions, even though urban regions may need a fairly common package of urban-type services delivered on an areawide basis. The need for specific services varies from locality to locality. Further, only the national government can effectively establish policies relating to the overall economy in terms of the allocation of resources and the distribution of income as well as those relating to international economic competition and multinational corporations. In order to understand the problems experienced by many metropolitan areas, it is first necessary to comprehend the fiscal/service structure of the U.S. federal system.

Taxes and Other Revenue

In 1957, each of the three levels of government relied to a considerable degree on different revenues as their primary source of income, but by the mid-1990s the major revenue sources of all three levels had become more diversified, particularly state and local revenue structures. The federal government received 65 percent of its own source revenue in 1957 from taxes on individual and corporate income. Today that proportion has dropped to 49 percent, with nearly another one-third from flat-rate payroll taxes for Social Security, Medicare, and railroad retirement. In fact, federal retirement programs for Social Security and railroad retirement are highly solvent compared to federal civilian and military retirement programs, which are largely unfunded (Congressional and civil service retirement) or almost entirely unfunded (military retirement). States in 1957 received over half (51 percent) their tax revenue from sales taxes and, even with major increases in tax rates, this source brings in only 28 percent today. State income taxes increased from 15.5 percent in 1957 to 22 percent by 1995. Since 1957, state insurance trust revenue, financed by flat-rate payroll taxes, increased from 15.5 percent to over 25 percent; charges for services rose from 5.8 percent to 10 percent. Local governments relied heavily on the property tax, which constituted 58 percent of own source revenue in 1957, but has since declined to a little over 40 percent. Local units now receive one-third of their own source revenue from charges for public utilities and other services.[4] With the exception of income and property taxes, the federal government has increasingly taxed the tax sources of state and local governments by disallowing the deduction of all types of state and local sales taxes. (See Table 8.1.)

One way to measure the progressivity/regressivity of government revenue structures is a simplified regression line index that measures the slope of the regression line between categories of income. A flat-rate structure that taxes all income groups at the same percentage of income paid in taxes and other revenues is given an index rating of 100, with a figure between 90 and 110 considered flat-rate or proportional; anything below 90 is regressive; anything above 110 is considered progressive. A regressive tax or revenue system takes a larger percentage of personal income from lower-income taxpayers, less from higher-income taxpayers. A progressive tax or revenue system takes a higher percentage of personal income from those with higher levels of income. A rating of 200 means the top category, on average, pays twice the percentage of that paid by the bottom group, indicating a progressive tax or

Table 8.1

OWN SOURCE REVENUE OF FEDERAL, STATE, AND LOCAL GOVERNMENTS, FY1995

	Percent of Total[1]			
	Federal	**State**	**Local**	**Total (All Levels)**
Income taxes	49.3%	22.0%	3.0%	33.7%
Individual	39.2	18.1	2.5	27.5
Corporate	10.1	3.9	0.5	6.2
Sales and gross receipts	5.4	28.0	7.7	11.7
Property taxes	—	1.3	40.6	7.8
Current charges	6.9	9.4	20.9	10.1
Publicly owned utilities	0.4	0.6	12.5	2.7
Insurance trusts	32.2	25.2	4.3	25.3
Other	5.8	13.5	11.0	8.7
Total	100.0%	100.0%	100.0%	100.0%
Percent distribution of own source revenue	54.0%	26.5%	19.5%	100.0%

[1]Based on U.S. Bureau of the Census data from the Internet (www.census.gov/govs/estimate/95stlus.txt) and the 1995 *Government Finances*, GF/95-5 (Washington, DC: Government Printing Office, 1996).

revenue system; a rating of 50 indicates that the bottom group pays twice the percentage of the top category for that particular tax or revenue structure indicating regressivity.[5]

As shown in Figure 8.1, state and local tax structures are regressive in their impact on taxpayers across income groups, with an regression line index rating of 43. In other words, individual taxpayers in the lower-income categories pay a much higher percentage of their income in taxes than those with higher levels of personal income—2.3 times the percentage of the top group. This is due to the heavy reliance of state governments on flat-rate sales and payroll taxes, and local reliance on property taxes, service charges, and utility revenues. These measures analyze taxes and other revenues that impact personal income and do not measure corporate income and other business taxes.

Federal taxes are more progressive because of the federal individual income tax, with a rating of 647. While this rating appears sharply progressive, tax payments of 4 percent to 28 percent of adjusted gross income (AGI) are much lower than those of the period during and after World War II. Other federal taxes and revenues are not progressive. The federal income tax is substantially offset by regressive Social Security and Medicare taxes, with a regression line index rating of 31. Stated differently, a person with an adjusted gross income of $9,000 pays 3.2 times the percentage of a person with an AGI of $458,000. The Social Security tax drops to zero above an income in the form of wages and salaries of $65,400 (1997), while the Medicare tax applies across the entire spectrum of wage and salary income. Individuals with incomes so low that they pay no federal income tax must still pay Social Security and Medicare taxes on their wage and salary income. Other forms of income, such

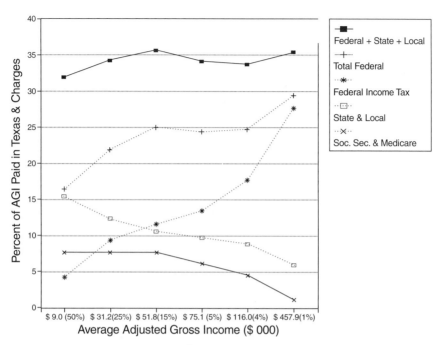

Figure 8.1. Government Revenue as a Percentage of Adjusted gross Income (AGI), 1993. These are average AGI categories for the bottom 50 percent of tax returns, the next 25 percent, the next 15 percent, the next 5 percent; the next 4 percent, and the top 1 percent. These data apply only to personal income. The pattern for 1995 is almost exactly the same except that the regression line index declines from 109 to 105. With recent cuts in the federal capital gains tax and increases in state and local sales taxes there will be further declines in the regression line index for 1997 and later years. *Source:* U.S. Bureau of the Census at www.census.gov/govs/estimate/95stlus.txt and the National Tax Association, *Tax Features* 39, no. 8 (October 1995).

as interest, dividends, and capital gains, are exempt. These payroll taxes bring in nearly one-third of federal revenues, compared to 39 percent for the individual income tax. Overall, the federal revenue structure receives a mildly progressive index rating of 156. The federal individual income tax is the only tax that still keeps the federal-state-local revenue system from being regressive.

The federal tax structure is much less progressive today than in 1950, when the rate paid by the top 1 percent of tax returns averaged 59 percent of AGI and the bottom 50 percent averaged 4 percent of AGI. The top 1 percent of taxpayers have benefited from a drop from 59 percent to less than 28 percent of AGI for the federal individual income tax, while the bottom 50 percent of taxpayers are paying exactly the same rate as in 1957. In 1950, the regressive Social Security/railroad retirement taxes brought in less than 6 percent of federal revenue, compared to 32 percent in the mid-1990s. Federal taxes for very high income taxpayers have declined significantly over the last half-century while low and middle-income groups have experienced an increase in the proportion of taxes on personal income paid to the federal government. In 1950, the Social Security tax represented only 1.5 percent of the first $3,000 of wage and salary income for the employee. In constant dollars, adjusted by the Consumer Price Index (CPI), the Social Security tax has increased fifteenfold between 1950 and 1995. If the Medicare tax is included, the increase is 18.5 times the earlier figure. Using different years, Kevin Phillips notes that the median family's effective federal tax rate (Social Security and the individual income tax) in 1948 was 5.3 percent and by 1989 this had increased to 24.6 percent, whereas over the same period the top 1 percent of taxpayers experienced a decline from 76.9 percent to 26.7 percent.[6] This in itself indicates a nearly proportional tax structure for 1989.

Using Figure 8.1 and the regression line index described above (where a rating from 90 to 110 is a flat-rate revenue structure; above these figures, progressive; below, regressive), it is interesting to compare the federal tax structure with that for state and local governments:

	Regression Line Index
Federal individual income tax, 1950	1,119
Federal individual income tax, 1993	647
Social Security/Medicare/railroad retirement, 1993	31
Total federal taxes and charges, 1993	156
State and local taxes and charges, 1993 (national average)	43
Total federal, state, and local taxes and charges, 1950	209
Total federal, state, and local taxes and charges, 1993	109

These calculations are based on data shown in graphic form in Figure 8.1 and comparable data for 1950. The combined federal, state, and local revenue structure receives a regression line index rating of 109, indicating an overall flat-rate tax structure for all governments, as taxes affect personal income.[7] There has been a significant decline in the progressivity of government revenues since the 1950s. The spate of proposals in the 104th and 105th Congresses and during the 1996 election cycle for a flat-rate federal individual income tax would make the federal-state-local revenue structure regressive, with low- and middle income groups paying significantly higher taxes than the top 5 percent of taxpayers in the United States. This nation already has a flat-rate revenue structure, whereby income groups across the range of adjusted gross income pay basically the same percentage in total taxes and other revenue for the support of government.

Recently released preliminary data for 1995 tax collection as a percent of AGI indicate the same overall pattern of government taxes and revenues that apply to personal income as a percentage of adjusted gross income for federal as well as for state and local governments.[8] Federal, state, and local revenues from personal income were slightly less progressive (or more regressive) in 1995 due to changes in the mix and more reliance on payroll taxes (for Social Security, Medicare, and other retirement systems), all types of sales taxes, and service charges. Between calendar years 1993 and 1995, total adjusted gross income reported by the IRS increased 12.4 percent, but AGI for the average tax return rose only 9.0 percent, indicating an upward redistribution of income.

The overall rating for federal taxes dropped from 156 to 132 on the regression line index, even though the taxes on the top 1 percent of tax returns increased slightly, up 0.85 percent, and the Medicare tax was made applicable across the range of wage and salary income between 1993 and 1995. Most very high income taxpayers receive much of their income in forms other than wages and salaries, which is the tax base for Social Security and Medicare. The overall system—federal, state, and local—is relying more on all types of sales taxes and service charges. The rating for state and local taxes and revenues declined from 43 to 42. For all three levels of government, the regression line index declined from 109 to 105. Given the recent decrease in the capital gains tax, the rating for 1997 and 1998 will probably drop to 100 or less for the tax structure of the American federal system, as it affects personal income. A flat-rate federal income tax or a federal general sales tax, as proposed by some of the Republican leaders in Congress, would make the overall structure of taxes in the United States quite regressive.[9] To paraphrase H. L. Mencken: For every major problem there is a solution that is simple, timely, and . . . wrong.

Service Delivery

Though there is still some separation of services between levels of government, over the course of the twentieth century, federal, state, and local governments have become increasingly involved in the delivery and/or financing of many of the same domestic public services. The federal government is responsible for national functions like defense, international relations, the postal service, air traffic control, as well as space research and technology and grants-in-aid to state governments. Nevertheless, states and even some local governments are increasingly inserting themselves into economic activities that may be considered a part of international relations. Nearly 90 percent of all federal grants go initially to states, though some of this money is passed through to local units. The federal government is the principal player in terms of natural resources. In addition, the federal level provides Social Security, Medicare, and railroad and military retirement.

State governments are the primary providers of higher education and a miscellany of minor educational services, corrections, mental hospitals, unemployment and worker's compensation, and liquor stores, where these are publicly owned. States provide 91 percent of direct grants-in-aid received by local governments. Local governments are the dominant deliverer of K–12 public education, police and fire protection, sewerage and other sanitation services, parks and recreation, libraries, and publicly owned utilities. This allocation of services is based on national data totals, and it should be noted that there is considerable variation among the fifty state/local systems in terms of the division of services between state and local governments.

All three levels share in the delivery of health services, environmental protection, and financial and judicial administration. Roads, streets, and highways are a shared state-local activity. The federal and state levels provide their own employee retirement programs; at the same time most states provide teacher retirement and, in some cases, retirement programs for other local employees. Federal and local governments share the provision of housing and community development, airports, and other transportation services (see Table 8.2).

Intergovernmental Transfers

Most of the intergovernmental political and regulatory activity focuses upon finances and the transfer of funds among governments, both vertically and horizontally, but particularly in relation to grants-in-aid from federal to state and from state to local. These

Table 8.2

DOMINANT SERVICE PROVIDER BY LEVEL OF GOVERNMENT, 1995

Federal	State	Local
Defense and veterans	Higher education	K–12 education
International relations	Miscellaneous education	Utilities
Space research and technology	services and regulation	Police protection
Postal service	Public welfare[1]	Fire protection
Natural resources	Corrections	Sewerage
Social Security	Liquor stores	Other sanitation
Medicare	Protective inspection and	Parks and recreation
Railroad retirement	regulation	Libraries
Aid to state governments	Unemployment compensation	
Regulation of air traffic	Worker's compensation	
	Mental hospitals	
	Aid to local governments	

Shared Services
Health (F/S/L)
General hospitals (F/L)
Highways (S/L)
Airports (F/L)
Other transportation (F/L)
Housing and community development (F/L)
Employee retirement (F/S)[2]
Environmental protection (F/S/L)
Financial administration (F/S/L)
Judicial administration (F/S/L)

[1]The average state is more active in the delivery of public services than national data totals indicate because small states tend to be more centralized and large states less so. National aggregate data indicate that states deliver 62 percent of public welfare services; local government 14 percent. But for the average state the percentage is 78 percent state, 8 percent local.

[2]Nearly all federal military personnel retirement is unfunded, as is most of that for federal civilian personnel and Congress (FY 1995). Most states handle employee retirement for school district personnel, and often pensions for other local government employees.

intergovernmental transfers, often referred to as *grants* or *grants-in-aid*, are handled using a variety of mechanisms and often by a combination of procedures. There are three basic types of intergovernmental transfers, plus at least one other way which resources and/or services are provided:

1. *Grants-in-aid.* These can be (a) *general-purpose grants*, sometimes referred to as "revenue sharing" (a misnomer as they are often appropriated funds), which allow the recipient government to spend the money as it sees fit as long as it is for a public purpose; (b) *functional-purpose grants*, usually called "block grants," which allow fairly wide discretion on the part of the recipient unit to spend the money in the functional area designated; and (c) *specific-purpose grants*, often referred to as "categoricals," which are usually for a narrowly defined purpose or project. Usually these are funds given from the federal government to state or local governments, or state aid given to its political subdivisions. General-purpose grants are usually unconditional or largely so. Categorical grants usually are conditional, in

that they have requirements or mandates that must be met by the recipient government. Block grants also have conditions, though there is usually more freedom of action on the part of the recipient government than with categoricals. These grants may require matching funds from the receiving government, set in dollars, percentages, or a share of the cost. In the case of federal grants, the match can vary from 10 percent to 90 percent. The allocation of money can be by project, by program, or by formula—or by formula and then by project or program. Most grants are for a set amount of money, though a few are open ended.

2. *Shared taxes.* These can also be for general purposes, functional purposes, or highly specific purposes. The federal government has no shared taxes per se, but some state governments do share the revenue from some tax sources with their local governments. This has been fairly common with gasoline and sales taxes; on occasion, a few states share the revenue from state income taxes. Though not technically a shared tax, Maryland allows counties to levy an income tax as a percentage of the state income tax; Iowa has a similar arrangement for school districts. It is more common for states to allow local governments to levy a sales tax, which is then collected along with the the state sales tax.

3. *Contracts*—an increasing element in intergovernmental transfers. As mentioned earlier, local governments often contract with other local governments for the delivery of selected public services, but there is no official data on the extent of this type of local financial interaction.

4. *Services-in-aid.* Sometimes part of state activities, these provide assistance to local governments, particularly in the form of aid for planning activities for smaller local governments, but there is no tabulation of this type of assistance. Occasionally, a larger government will provide commodities or products to its political subdivisions.[10]

The federal government is also heavily involved in loan, credit, and insurance programs. Though not grants, these are another aspect of federal financial activity. In 1996 the federal government operated loan, credit, and insurance programs that amounted to $550 billion in terms of coverage, not in terms of cost. Much of this activity primarily benefits individuals and businesses for things like commodity supports, housing, flood and crop insurance, and small business loans. Occasionally, local governments are the beneficiaries of these programs.

For FY 1997, federal grants to states were $228 billion, while state grants to their local units approached $260 billion, some of which was federal money passed through to local governments. The federal government also gave $25 billion directly to local government. Local governments transferred about $13 billion to their respective state governments, largely unspent money from state grants and/or local collection of state revenue.

There were about 600 different federal grant programs, providing an average of $950 per capita with $855 to state governments and $95 to local units for FY 1997. It should be pointed out that state and local units receive widely varying amounts of per capita federal aid—in FY 1992 the state-local average was $739, with a range from $462 in Virginia to $1,444 in Alaska. Virginia, on the other hand, ranks first among the fifty states in per capita direct federal expenditure. The federal government has only two or three very small general-purpose grants though, in the 1970s, the General Revenue Sharing grant passed out significant amounts of general-purpose money, with one-third going to the states and two-thirds allocated to local governments. General-purpose grants comprise less than 1 percent of federal aid, block or broader-based grants cover about 11 percent, and categoricals constitute the remaining 88 percent.

State aid to local governments averaged $975 per capita for FY 1997, but it is also highly variable. Though detailed information is not yet available for FY 1997, in FY 1992 state aid averaged $776 per person, with a range from $118 in Hawaii, our most centralized state, to $1,358 in Alaska, the state with the highest per capita financial resources. The average state has approximately fifty grant programs, but the range is from about a dozen in Hawaii to nearly one hundred in California. States with more structurally complex and decentralized state/local systems tend to have more numerous grant programs. Federal and state grant programs have very different functional priorities.

In the mid-1990s, the federal government funded 17 percent of general government services delivered by state and local governments, while states financed one-third of those delivered by local governments. Figure 8.2 illustrates the flow of intergovernmental payments between levels of government for FY 1995. At the same time, there are major differences between federal and state grants in terms of priority (see Table 8.3). Nearly 53 percent of federal aid is earmarked for welfare, with a little over 12 percent for education. Less than 10 percent is for housing and community development and less than 9 percent goes for highways. The remaining 16 percent is for a variety of activities. States, on the other hand, give nearly 62 percent of their grant money to local units for education. The 14.5 percent of state grants for welfare is nearly all federal aid that is passed through to local governments in the few states where welfare is still primarily a local function. The states also give nearly 13 percent to local units for general purposes without designation as to how these funds will be spent. Only 4 percent is for highways.

Considering only the "general government" services that are largely funded and/or delivered by state and local governments, the federal government is involved in the delivery of 17 percent of these activities and funds 32 percent, as shown in Table 8.5. The term "general government" includes all public services with the exception of insurance trusts and liquor stores (mostly state) and publicly owned utilities and other market-type activities (mostly local). Federal grants do not fund nongeneral government activities, which constitute 18 percent of state and 13 percent of local direct expenditures. Insurance trusts account for one-third of federal revenues and expenditures.

Federal involvement in public welfare is the highest of any common state and local public service. The central government delivers 24 percent and pays for 70 percent of welfare services. States, on the other hand, deliver 62 percent and pay for 30 percent, with locals delivering 14 percent and the states paying for local service delivery with pass-through federal aid and state funds. As distinguished from national data totals, the average state delivers 69 percent, local units 7 percent. Because small states tend to be more centralized, large states less so, the role of the average state in terms of both funding and delivery is greater than these national data totals indicate for a number of services. While five-eighths of state aid to local governments is for public education, the next largest amount, 13 percent, is for public welfare with nearly all of this money going to county and municipal governments as Table 8.4 indicates. This is, however, somewhat deceptive in that nearly three-fourths, $19 billion of the $26 billion, is accounted for by just two states, New York and California.

Public education is largely a state and local function both in terms of delivery and funding. Higher education is a state function both for funding and service delivery. Local governments deliver 93 percent of elementary and secondary education, K–12, but fund

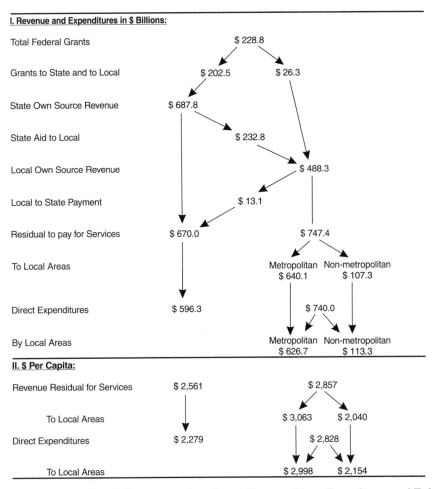

Figure 8.2. State and Local Government Own Source Revenue, Direct Expenditures, and Federal, State, and Local Intergovernmental Transactions, FY 1995. Based on FY 1995 data from the Census web site on the internet (www.census.gov/govs/estimate/95stlus.txt) and trend data for metropolitan areas, 1982 to 1992, from the Governments Division, U.S. Bureau of the Census. The apparent $282 per capita surplus for state governments is almost entirely accounted for by insurance trust funds for employee retirement and unemployment and worker's compensation reserves. The local nonmetropolitan per capita deficit appears to be mostly capital outlay.

only one-fourth of the cost. Hawaii is the only state where the state funds and delivers 100 percent of all public education services. Funding and delivering health and hospital services are more evenly divided between the three levels of government. Police and fire protection, sewers, and other sanitation services are predominantly funded and delivered by local governments (see Table 8.5).

Table 8.3

SERVICE EMPHASIS OF FEDERAL AND STATE GRANTS-IN-AID BY FUNCTION, FY1994

	Percent Distribution ($ Billions)	
	Federal ($218)	**State ($226)**
Public welfare	52.7%	14.5%
Education	12.3	61.6
Housing and community development	9.7	0.5
Highways	8.8	4.2
Health and hospitals	4.3	0.4
Urban mass transit	1.8	0.5
Natural resources and parks	1.3	0.9
District of Columbia	0.3	—
General administration	2.2	0.6
General-purpose assistance	*	12.7
Other	6.6	4.1
Total	100.0%	100.0%

*An item too small to be shown in these terms.

Income Distribution and Taxes

As was pointed out in Chapters 4 and 5, the adoption of metropolitan governmental reform is not a panacea. It has not solved the problem of the distribution of wealth in relation to the central portions of the metropolitan area. The poor tend to be concentrated at the core while state and local taxes are quite regressive in their incidence on persons of lower income for the average state and the average metropolitan area. Recent changes in federal, state, and local taxes have largely given tax relief to people of higher income and corporations. At the same time, newer revenues enacted by state and local governments are predominantly sales taxes and service charges. The justification for this is that taxes are high in the United States. Actually the United States ranks twenty-sixth in taxes as a percentage of gross domestic product (GDP) out of the twenty-eighth developed countries that are members of the OECD (Organization for Economic Cooperation and Development). These data include social security programs of the member nations. Only Turkey and Mexico have lower taxes as a percentage of GDP, and both are far less developed than the United States.[11] Comparatively, taxes are low in the United States, at least for those at the top of the income scale. In fact, at 27.6 percent of GDP, the United States is significantly below the average of 38.8 percent for the other OECD countries.

In addition, neither the federal government nor any but a very few states make any concerted effort to redistribute tax revenues to their poorer political subdivisions. Also, as

Table 8.4
LOCAL INTERGOVERNMENTAL REVENUE FROM STATE GOVERNMENT, FY 1992

I. Distribution Among Local Governments by Function in $ Millions:[1]

Local Governments	Total	Public Education	Public Welfare	Health & Hospitals	Highways	General Support	Other
U.S total	$197,890	$123,565	$25,894	$7,872	$8,514	$16,734	$15,311
Counties	$49,663	$9,911	$18,474	$6,318	$4,536	$5,236	$5,488
Municipalities	37,380	9,265	7,369	1,129	3,448	9,796	6,372
Towns & townships	4,322	1,576	40	16	499	1,701	489
School districts	103,084	103,084	—	—	—	—	—
Special districts	3,442	29	12	408	31	—	—

II. Percentage Distribution Among Local Governments by Function:

Local Governments	Total	Public Education	Public Welfare	Health & Hospitals	Highways	General Support	Other
U.S. total	100.00%	62.44%	13.08%	3.98%	4.30%	8.46%	7.74%
Counties	25.10%	4.86%	9.34%	3.19%	2.29%	2.65%	2.77%
Municipalities	18.89	4.68	3.72	0.57	1.74	4.95	3.22
Towns & townships	2.18	0.80	0.02	0.01	0.25	0.86	0.25
School districts	52.09	52.09	—	—	—	—	—
Special districts	1.74	0.01	0.01	0.21	0.02	—	1.50

[1]There is a certain amount of rounding error in the presentation of these data.
Source: U.S. Bureau of the Census, *1992 Census of Governments*, "Compendium of Government Finances," vol. 4, no. 5, Table 29 (Washington, DC: Government Printing Office, February, 1997).

has been mentioned, with a few exceptions in the case of older suburbs and some rural areas, the central part of our urban regions tends to be the location of poorer residents, ethnic minorities, and the homeless. Personal income is generally higher in suburban areas. In a sample of thirty-two geographically distributed metropolitan areas containing 57 percent of the MSA population, suburban areas averaged 24 percent higher per capita personal income and as much as 50 percent higher in some MSAs.[12] Suburban areas often enact zoning, building, subdivision, and occupancy regulations designed to keep out lower-income residents. RCAs are designed to keep property values above a certain level and have a similar result.

Throughout the period between 1980 and 1993, nationally, constant dollar per capita personal income was almost exactly the same with some ups and downs. Over this time span, constant dollar national income increased by more than one-third. Only the top 20 percent of families increased their share of per family income, up 12.9 percent; the top 5 percent increased their share by 28.2 percent; while the bottom 20 percent witnessed their share decline by 21.8 percent. All families except those in the top 20 percent lost out in terms of their respective shares of family income.[13]

Income Groups	Percentage of Aggregate Family Income		Percentage Change per Family Unit
	1980	1993	
Top 5%	15.3%	19.1%	+28.2%
Top 20%	41.5%	46.2%	+12.9%
4th 20%	24.3%	23.6%	-3.3%
3rd 20%	17.5%	15.9%	-10.4%
2nd 20%	11.5%	10.1%	-13.8%
Bottom 20%	5.2%	4.2%	-21.8%

With 80 percent of the population living in metropolitan areas, it is likely that this situation prevailed in the nation's urban areas as well, and it may have been even more pronounced.[14] This is a massive change in the distribution of family income for such a short time period. A recent article by John W. Sloan documents these changes over a longer period, with rather stark results. He compares the growth of average family income, by quintile, for two periods: 1947 to 1973 and 1973 to 1992, as shown in Figure 8.3. The earlier twenty-six-year period was one of growth between 2.46 percent and 2.99 percent annually for all income groups, whereas the later nineteen-year period was one in which growth for the lowest quintile was a negative –0.69 percent and that for the top quintile a positive +0.93 percent, with graduations shown similar to those in the inset table above for the shorter period between 1980 and 1993.[15]

Again it must be pointed out that the structure of the federal system—federal, state, and local—as well as the underlying cultural norms listed by Greer (Chapter 3), have a direct impact on the financing of local government and the failure of larger governments to redistribute financial resources to poorer states and core cities at the center of our urban regions. With some minor redistribution common for public education, few states give significantly more money to poorer local governments—though Wisconsin and Minnesota are partial exceptions. Federal grants to state and local government do not go to poorer state and local governments in a manner commensurate with their lack of financial resources and need for public services. In fact, more federal money is funneled to rich and small states. Federal grants are distributive, not redistributive, that is, Congress tends to "spread the money around." A 1989 article discusses this situation with reference to the combined ability of state and local governments to finance public services. Most states have also failed to redistribute resources to their poorer local governments.[16]

A perennial problem in federal systems is the maldistribution of taxable resources, which denies some states and many local units the ability to finance a basic level of public services. Federal expenditures in the United States constitute over one-fifth of GNP; defense and grants explain more than four-fifths of the interstate variation in per capita state and local tax capacity and revenue collection. The federal government spends more money in tax-rich states, and this spending is directly related to interstate variation in business tax capacity which, in turn, is a major determinant of differences in overall state tax capacity and revenue collection. Lacking a redistributive grant system that places a floor under the tax capacity

Table 8.5

SERVICE DELIVERY AND FINANCIAL RESPONSIBILITY FOR STATE AND
LOCAL GENERAL GOVERNMENT PUBLIC SERVICES, FY1995

	Percent[1] of Total	Percent of Service Delivery			Percentage of Financial Reponsibility		
		Federal	State	Local	Federal	State	Local
Education	33.5%	6%	25%	69%	14%	57%	29%
Higher education	8.6%	*	84%	16%	5%	87%	8%
K–12 education	24.9%	6%	1%	93%	7%	67%	26%
Public welfare	16.3%	24%	62%	14%	70%	30%	*
Health & hospitals	9.2%	19%	38%	43%	25%	39%	36%
Highways	6.7%	1%	59%	40%	24%	49%	27%
Police & fire protection	3.1%	12%	8%	80%	12%	9%	79%
Sewers and other sanitation	3.5%	7%	3%	90%	15%	3%	82%
All other	27.7%	16%	39%	45%	20%	43%	37%
TOTAL	100.0%	17%	35%	48%	32%	37%	31%

*An item too small to be shown in percentages.
[1]These data include state and local services and those where the federal government also performs or finances a portion of these activities. Services not included are publicly owned public utilities, debt service, liquor stores, and insurance trusts.

of our poorer states, federal spending patterns only exacerbate these differences: *The rich get richer and the poor, poorer.*

Between 1957 and 1993, constant dollar per capita gross national product (GNP), per capita national income, and per capita personal income doubled between 1957 and 1993 as corporate receipts increased by a factor of 3.4 times.[17] Total per capita government revenue increased 57 percent faster than family income, rising from $3,644 to $9,428, 2.6 times the earlier figure (see Table 8.6).

Federal, state, and local taxes that primarily affect personal income increased 3.4 times in constant dollars, while over the same period they rose from 42.7 percent of total government revenue to 55.7 percent. Personal income taxes increased only slightly faster than personal income, but this is deceptive. Income taxes increased significantly for low- and middle-income groups and declined significantly for those at the top of the income scale. In 1993, per capita general sales taxes were 4.6 times the 1957 constant dollar amount. Insurance trust revenue, 97 percent of which is based on wage and salary income, increased 6.3 times over this thirty-six-year period.

Per capita revenues that tend to impact both personal and business income increased at about the same rate as personal and family income, but they declined as a percentage of total government revenue from 33.6 percent to 25.1 percent. Selective sales taxes maintained their 1957 constant dollar amount; property taxes rose at the same rate as personal income, while utility and other service charges increased 44 percent and 82 percent faster than personal

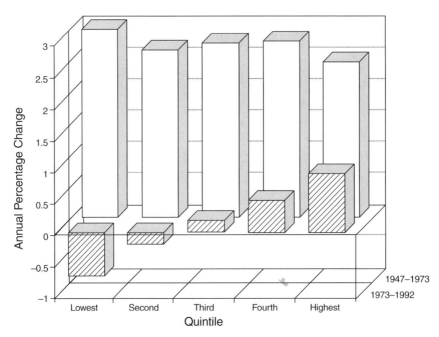

Figure 8.3. Annual Growth of Mean Family Income by Quintile, 1947 to 1973 and 1973 to 1992. This graph illustrates the changes in average annual percentage growth rates before and after 1973. It is adapted from data presented by John W. Sloan in "The Reagan Presidency, Growing Inequality, and the American Dream," *Policy Studies Journal* 25, no. 3 (Fall 1997): 371–86.

and family income. Corporate income taxes declined 13 percent in constant dollars between 1957 and 1993 and dropped from 17.6 percent of total government revenue to 5.9 percent. This would lead one to conclude that relative to income taxes, the business community has shed most of its 1957 tax obligation for the support of governmental services and/or business leaders have been very effective in securing tax concessions from government. Both conclusions seem applicable.

The remaining sources of government revenue cover a miscellany of items that have also been rising much faster than personal income. The remaining sources include things like interest earnings, sale of property, special assessments, severance taxes, death and gift taxes, fines and forfeitures, and the like. Gambling is one of the newer and fastest-growing items in this category and it, too, tends to affect primarily low- and middle-income earners. Miscellaneous revenue increased by a factor of 5.5 times over this period and from 6.2 percent to 13.2 percent of total government revenue.

Conclusion

The mainstream media have devoted very little sporadic attention to these basic changes in our socioeconomic structure and the massive changes in the way we finance government in this nation. They seem primarily interested in what politicians and administrators say they do, not what they actually do—or in the scandals and peccadillos of those in prominent

Table 8.6
1957–1993 CHANGE IN CONSTANT DOLLAR INCOME AND
FEDERAL, STATE, AND LOCAL GOVERNMENT REVENUE

Item	1993 Constant Dollars		1993 as Multiple of 1957
	1957	1993	
Per capita gross national product	$12,920	$25,409	1.98x
Per capita national income	10,625	20,149	1.90x
Median family income	22,469	36,959	1.65x
Per capita personal income	10,175	21,288	2.09x
Total corporate receipts[1] — in $ Billions	3,571	12,270	3.44x

Major Revenue Sources of Federal, State, and Local Governments that are Primarily Incident on:	1993 Per Capita Constant Dollars		1993 as Multiple of 1957	Sources as Percent of Total Revenue	
	1957	1993		1957	1993
1. Personal Income					
Individual income taxes[2]	$1,082	$2,455	2.27x	29.69%	26.04%
General sales taxes	117	538	4.61x	3.21	5.71
Insurance trust revenue[3]	356	2,258	6.34x	9.77	23.95
Subtotal	$1,555	$5,251	3.38x	42.67%	55.70%
2. Both Business and Personal Income					
Selective sales taxes	$458	$463	1.01x	12.57%	4.91%
Property taxes	372	761	1.97x	10.21	7.75
Utility charges	85	238	2.80x	2.33	2.52
Other service charges	306	939	3.07x	8.40	9.96
Subtotal	$1,221	$2,401	1.97x	33.57%	25.14%
3. Business Income					
Corporate income tax	$641	$558	0.87x	17.59%	5.92%
4. Other Sources					
Other revenues	$227	$1,248	5.50x	6.23%	13.24%
Total, all sources	$3,644	$9,428	2.59x	100.00%	100.00%

[1]For 1993 these data understate corporate receipts because of the proliferation of nonprofit and not-for-profit corporations over this time period.

[2]The federal individual income tax as a percent of adjusted gross income (AGI) for the top 1 percent of tax returns dropped from 59 percent in 1950 to 28 percent for the 1993–1995 period. There was no drop in the percentage of AGI paid for the average tax return of the bottom 50 percent of tax returns for tax years 1993–1995.

[3]For 1993, 96.7 percent of insurance trust revenue was derived from or based on wages and salaries and not applicable to other types of income.

government positions. Television news programs are more show than substance. With increasing consolidation of the print media, as well as radio and television, they appear more concerned than ever with the bottom line, advertising revenue, and less with analysis and dissemination of news concerning the basic changes taking place in this country. Perhaps there is even antipathy toward exposing these transformations in government, the social structure, and the economy.

The uploading of personal income to the top 20 percent of families and the downloading of the tax burden on lower income groups is self-reinforcing. Those at the top have more money to spend and more to invest to generate even more income. They also have more resources with which to influence our money-driven electoral system. The reverse is true for those at the lower levels of income. This is particularly deleterious for central cities and older suburban areas, with their lower levels of per capita personal income. Similar statements can be made with reference to rich and poor state and local governments. This changed distribution of income, taxes, and tax burdens is likely to continue and become increasingly inequitable relative to the ability to pay taxes given the current political climate in Washington, D.C. and a significant number of state capitols.

The failure of the U.S. government and the states to deal with the problems caused by the maldistribution of resources; the downward redistribution of tax burdens and the upward concentration of income; and the financial problems of our core cities and inner suburbs as well as those of poorer state and local governments may be the Achilles heel of the federal system over the next several years. The city-suburban-rural distribution of population results in a system of representation that magnifies the influence of suburban and rural areas and makes it difficult, if not impossible, to address the real needs of our central cities and older suburbs. Aside from the normal tendency of the affluent to be more politically active, it also means that more affluent groups and communities are overrepresented in state and national legislatures.

CHAPTER NINE

The Future of Metropolitan Government and Governance

A little more than fifty years ago, the legendary political scientist Charles Merriam wrote in his preface to Victor Jones's classic work, *Metropolitan Government*, that "the adequate organization of modern metropolitan areas is one of the great unsolved problems of modern politics."[1] We believe that the theoretical, empirical, and pragmatic discussion set forth in the preceding chapters provides valuable insights, or lessons, into the nature of metropolitan governance, and allows us, drawing upon this eclectic material, to suggest, in a modest way, the degree to which metropolitan governmental structure and governance should be altered to strengthen its capacity to function more effectively and efficiently and promote the well-being of all citizens dwelling in our metropolitan areas.

In terms of theory, we are of the persuasion that the arguments set forth by the metropolitan government advocates and the public choice scholars each contain a substantial amount of merit; yet neither position is beyond reproach or free of criticism. We are impressed by the metropolitan government argument (notwithstanding L. J. Sharpe's poignant observation that the metro concept seems to be in decline around the world and that no one really loves metro government),[2] and persuaded of the necessity in our metropolitan areas for some sort of regional governmental structure to promote regionwide political leadership, address issues of demonstrable regionwide import on a regional basis, and deliver system-maintenance services. However, we are troubled by the cavalier fashion in which metropolitan government theorists dismiss the political and service advantages that flow from the fractionated, or polycentric, character of local government in the metropolis, including: providing citizens with a sense of community identification and an arena for practicing participatory democratic politics, maximizing consumer choice and sovereignty in regard to public services, responding to the diverse lifestyle policy preferences of the citizenry, and functioning as competitive market mechanisms for the efficient delivery of services. To be sure, the public choice theorists provide a sweeping, grand defense of the polycentric character of government in the metropolis, and its resultant benefits of public sector competition and the maximization of citizen policy preferences, but scholars hewing to this line of thought downplay the fact that each local polity is part of a larger region, and largely dismiss the need for regional political structures and leadership.

In a more empirical and pragmatic sense, our review of the experiences of the metropolitan governments of Baton Rouge, Miami, Nashville, Jacksonville, and Indianapolis, as well as the more limited regional structural innovations of Minneapolis–St. Paul and Portland, allows us to summarize the capabilities and limitations of these institutions. Much to their credit, they have provided the political bedrock for facilitating and maturing regional political leadership, incorporating a healthy dose of regionalism into the local policy process and promoting the more orderly growth and development of their regions. In addition, the metropolitan governments, in particular, have served as a valuable element of a vigorous growth machine, substantially improved the public infrastructure, and delivered a uniform degree of system-maintenance services throughout the region. In a contrary vein, these governments have failed to pass the test or "pass through the hoop" of serving as innovative and effective redistribution structures for improving the well-being of the less fortunate. In this sense, the record strongly underscores that the various metropolitan governments have taken a "rain check" on the matter of social equity. It may well be that, given the many restrictions on local public policy, consolidated local governments simply do not have the authority or scope to make such changes. Perhaps only the federal and state governments are capable of solving these inequities.

Also in an empirical and pragmatic sense, we have underscored the importance and widespread use of incremental governmental strategies in the metropolis. For instance, local governments resort to a variety of intergovernmental contracts with private or public vendors to assist them in meeting their service responsibilities. Councils of governments and other voluntary regional bodies have provided at least a small measure of regional political leadership and policy-making authority. The reorganization of urban county governments, increasing their administrative, financial, and service capacity, has transformed these political entities into better service providers. And over time, the states have gradually assumed an increasing role in the governmental affairs of the metropolis, particularly in regard to regulatory policies, finance, functional activities, and regional planning for growth and development.

Particularly noteworthy is the steady proliferation and growing functional importance of special-purpose governments—including special districts and authorities—in metropolitan areas. As Kathryn A. Foster reported in her recent study: "Although the rise of specialized governance has occurred throughout the nation, it has been most rapid in metropolitan areas. Between 1952 and 1992 the number of special districts in the 785 counties comprising U.S. metropolitan areas grew from 4,943 to 13,343, an increase of 8,400 units, or 170 percent."[3] Foster reports that each metropolitan area has an average of forty-three special purpose governments; however, this figure lacks a significant amount of meaning because of the wide variation in the number and scope of special-purpose governments in each metropolitan area. For example, while the Houston metropolitan area has 665 special districts, the corresponding number for the Lynchburg, Virginia region is three.[4]

A variety of reasons account for the popularity of special-purpose governments in metropolitan areas. First, special-purpose governments provide a politically feasible structure, unlike the comprehensive metropolitan government approach, for providing a variety of services on both a very local and a regional basis, including, most commonly, natural resources (drainage, flood control, soil and water conservation, and irrigation), fire protection, housing and community development, and water and sewer services. Additional services provided by special-purpose governments include mass transportation, parks and recreation, airports, libraries, seaports, highways, and public utilities. Second, compared to general-purpose governments, special-purpose governments are far less subject to state-imposed policy constraints, particularly with regard to selected tax sources, service charges, borrowing money, debt limits, competitive bidding, and financial reporting and procurement procedures. Special districts tend to fill in the service gaps left by the state and general-purpose local governments.

Special-purpose governments have long borne the criticism of scholars for constituting the "bad boys" of American local government for further fragmenting the governmental structure of the metropolis and for being inherently undemocratic and politically captured by the clientele they serve.[5] Whatever the merit of this general line of thought, we share in particular the perspective of James W. Doig and Jerry Mitchell that the predominantly single-function focus of special-purpose government (only about 10 percent are multifunctional in character) constitutes a serious drawback of these governmental entities, since their proliferation makes it that much more difficult to achieve a satisfactory measure of coherence and consistency among state and local priorities and program activities.[6]

The Problem Defined

We do not believe that there is currently a crisis or breakdown in the governmental structure and process of our metropolitan areas; the formal and informal system of metropolitan governance, although it may be assailed as chaotic, confusing, crazy-quilt, or simply incomprehensible to the average citizen, is seemingly viable and far from broken. In a collective sense, the bewildering structural array of general-purpose and special-purpose governments splashed across the usual metropolis are largely responding to and meeting the varied service needs of the citizenry, with the less fortunate, to some extent, falling outside this deft generalization. To be sure, one of the reasons why this somewhat chaotic system still functions reasonably well is the incremental activity of the federal government and particularly the states. The states, over the course of the twentieth century, have significantly increased their role in terms of the funding and delivery of services in metropolitan areas. Nevertheless, we believe, that the time has come to begin the business of "sorting out" the governmental functions in the metropolis, much as we have embarked on this task in the larger federal system. In this regard, moving from an intergovernmental to an interorganizational perspective of governance, we first need to structure a metropolitan governmental process that will ensure the development of what Robert Warren and his colleagues have described as "operational citizens," who have the ability and resources to develop meaningful urban polities, intent on building better communities and improving the lives of all.[7] Second, in this age of "functional cities," with the economic fortunes of the core cities and suburbs heavily intertwined, we require metropolitan political arrangements that facilitate the ability of our metropolitan regions to be competitive players in the global economy. On this point, it serves us to bear in mind the common-sense and keen observation of H. V. Savitch and his colleagues: "Self-sufficiency neither was nor will be a viable modus operandi for cities and suburbs. As time goes by, interdependence, resource synergy, and the ability to interact beyond exclusive spheres become more important for metropolitan success."[8]

The road of scholarly inquiry that we have traveled brings us to this point: We concur with Warren and his colleagues that: "The most basic task of an urban governance agenda, then, is to help identify the cognitive, institutional, and normative restructuring that is needed to move this set of conditions to a *federal* [our emphasis] system in which viable, widespread urban self governance is legitimized and practiced by urban citizens."[9] We are mindful as well that local polities are the foundation of our federal system: They provide an important sense of community and political identification, constitute the most effective and democratic scale for innovating and implementing decisions that bear on the day-to-day affairs of individuals, and serve as valuable arenas for practicing participatory democracy and enriching civic life. In view of all this, we strongly agree that any re-engineering of the formal governmental system of the metropolis must ensure the continued importance and vitality of general-purpose local governments.

On the other hand, a wide consensus is currently found among all quarters of scholars of metropolitan government and politics that system-maintenance services—due to principles involving economies of scale, fiscal equivalence, redistributive effects, the relatively narrow range of consumer preference, capital intensiveness, and spillover effects—would most profitably be delivered at the regional level. As Foster has stated: "Analysts of all ideological cloth agree that certain services, notably criminal investigation, sewerage treatment, and transit, are logically and cost effectively produced at a regional scale."[10] In a more ideal and sweeping sense, Sharpe substantially adds to this listing by including master planning, arterial highways, traffic management, public transport, general utilities, recreation areas, housing, trunk sewers and main drainage, refuse disposal, water supply, police, major cultural institutions, fire, and environmental protection.[11]

We endorse the early statements of Paul Studenski,[12] Victor Jones,[13] and Luther Halsey Gulick,[14] and the more recent appeals of Anthony Downs[15] and David Rusk[16] that the states—long regarded as the "keystones" or the "strategic middle" of our federal system— should exercise their "heavy hand" as responsible legal and political parents and commence the business of sorting out governmental functions in the metropolis. Simply stated, this state action is necessary for streamlining and reinvigorating the urban governance process, ensuring that our metropolitan regions do not fall victim to their economic and social problems, and guaranteeing that our metropolitan areas remain competitive players in the global economy.

It is beyond debate to acknowledge that the states are in the best legal and political position to alter the character of metropolitan governmental structure and governance. As the Council of State Governments underscored almost forty years ago: "Responsibility for providing a workable pattern of local government in metropolitan areas, with variations as circumstances require, is clearly a state responsibility, all the more so because the present complex pattern is its handiwork. . . . There is no doubt that if localities are to function well, the state must provide the proper framework and many of the means to do so."[17] And as Patricia S. Florestano and Vincent L. Marando have written: "It is the states which have the widest range of powers to respond to metropolitanization. States, if they choose, can alter local service delivery, change financing arrangements and formulas, adjust local government boundaries, and grant or withhold local government home rule in light of metropolitanization."[18] We recognize, of course, that whether the states will act decisively with regard to restructuring metropolitan governmental structure is open to some measure of conjecture, especially since, in an overwhelming majority of the states, a majority of the members of the legislature hail from suburban or nonmetropolitan areas.

Recommendations

Although we recognize that it is a tall order to set forth a model of metropolitan governance, and are fully cognizant, as Savitch and Vogel remind us, that one-size solutions do not fit all regions,[19] we believe that the states should give serious consideration to the following set of recommendations concerning metropolitan governance arrangements. These arrangements, collectively, involve a measure of both the centralization and decentralization of political power, policy making, and service delivery. First, in our scheme of things, the general-purpose local governments of the metropolis—cities and counties—should continue to be entrusted with the provision of lifestyle services, such as public education, fire and police protection, and neighborhood parks, and the states should practice some devolution of power, as Warren and his colleagues have so well argued,[20] by granting these local polities a much greater freedom of action or relative autonomy—a degree of autonomy enhancing their power of policy initiation and providing them with more immunity from state supervisory control.

Efforts should be undertaken by the states—perhaps taking the form of cash grants—to supplement these basic institutions of representative democracy with an operative element of strong, or participatory, democracy, structured by a citywide network of neighborhood associations, a concept first propounded by Milton Kotler[21] and Alan Altshuler[22] some thirty years ago, and more recently given greater currency and refined by Jeffrey M. Berry, Kent E. Portney, and Ken Thomson in their work *The Rebirth of Urban Democracy*.[23] These neighborhood associations, which would be granted a limited degree of financial and policy powers, would serve to shrink the distance between policy making and the citizenry, reduce political alienation, and provide ordinary citizens with the opportunity to make face-to-face collective decisions concerning the allocation of goods and services in their neighborhoods. We believe that providing local governments with greater autonomy, coupled with a citywide network of neighborhood associations (inclusive of residential community associations), would reinvigorate democracy on the local level and a reinvigorated sense of democracy would facilitate politically empowered citizens to develop policies that would serve to improve the quality of their lives.

Second, in an effort to curtail the continuing proliferation of minor, localized special districts, which are often established merely to provide street lighting to a small area or to fund a special project, we believe that the states should take immediate stopgap action to provide counties and large special districts with the authority to establish localized service and taxing areas, with the power to impose additional property taxes, sales taxes, and/or service charges, and to issue revenue bonds or incur general obligation debt for the provision of additional service or infrastructure needs. In the smaller states, the state governments themselves could, perhaps, directly provide for infrastructure and service needs and arrange for appropriate financing.

Third, we believe that all states should establish structures similar to the Ontario (Canada) Municipal Board, the Minnesota Municipal Board, and the Virginia Commission on Local Government, with the authority to review and approve the incorporation of new local governments, particularly municipalities and special districts, and efforts by municipalities to annex land. Such a board would have the ability to prevent, or play a significant role in preventing, municipal incorporation or the creation of new units, and direct these efforts toward annexation by adjacent municipalities or special districts, with appropriate financial arrangements involving the creation of special taxing or service charge areas.

Fourth, we are of the persuasion that the states should exercise their heavy legal and political hand and establish in their metropolitan area(s), *without* the approval of the voters, a multifunctional service authority. Some members of the governing board of this authority would be appointed by the governor; the remainder would be selected in some fashion by the local governments of the area served. The authority would be able to levy a property or sales tax, and/or service charges (or a combination of these revenue sources), and would be responsible for the provision of system-maintenance services, such as water, sewer, mass transportation, refuse collection and disposal, environmental protection, and the administration and operation of major cultural, recreational, and sports facilities. We envision that these service responsibilities could be directly provided by the authority, or through a contract with a city or county government or private vendor. This course of action by the states would result in the virtual elimination of all single-function special-purpose governments and the transfer of system-maintenance functions from the general-purpose governments to the authority. Such a regional structure would be able to provide a comprehensive, coherent, and "seamless" package of infrastructure services. We recognize, of course, that in the geographically smaller states, such as Connecticut, Delaware, Massachusetts, and Rhode Island, the establishment of multifunctional service authorities could be circumvented by having the states assume further system maintenance services.

On the face of it, our recommendation that the states should establish metropolitan multifunctional agencies does not represent, unlike schemes involving comprehensive metropolitan governments, a radical departure concerning the way we think about or practice government in our metropolitan areas. Somewhat more than fifty years ago, the Council of State Governments, in its report *The States and the Metropolitan Problem*, acknowledged the substantial merit of creating a multifunctional service district in a metropolitan area.[24] In 1961, the United States Advisory Commission on Intergovernmental Relations weighed in with its endorsement of the creation of these bodies, subject to areawide approval by the citizenry.[25] Multifunctional metropolitan governmental agencies have been established in various metropolitan areas. These include the Port Authority of New York and New Jersey (originally the New York Port Authority, established in 1921), which oversees an array of economic development, port, and transportation activities. Another example is the Hartford Metropolitan District, established in 1929, which has considerable powers involving regional planning, highways, storm drainage and flood control, refuse collection and disposal, recreation, and sewer and water services. For a variety of reasons, it has largely confined its operations to the provision of sewer and water services.[26] As a result of legislation passed by the state of Washington in 1957 authorizing the establishment, by local initiative, of metropolitan municipal corporations for the delivery of sewage disposal, water supply, mass transportation, garbage disposal, parks and recreation, and planning services, a multifunctional agency was established in the Seattle metropolitan area in 1958 to provide regional sewerage and mass transportation services.[27] As previously reported, Portland's multifunctional metropolitan district, known as "Metro," provides regional planning, transportation planning, solid waste collection and disposal, recycling, air and water control services, and operates a convention center and a zoo, while the Metropolitan Council of Minneapolis–St. Paul has recently assumed responsibility for the provision of mass transportation and sewer services.

We do not view our recommendation that the states act decisively by establishing multifunctional service agencies in their metropolitan area(s) as politically naïve, hopeless, or beyond the parameters of the current state policy agenda. This is simply because, when considered over time, such action by the states would constitute a logical progression or extension of their role in the governmental affairs of the metropolis, which has led first, to the creation of a department of urban affairs; second, to the enactment of legislation encouraging local intergovernmental cooperation and common policy making through the use of contracts, compacts, and joint service agreements, and the establishment of regional councils; third, to increased state fiscal aid to local governments; and, fourth, in some instances, to the assumption of local governmental functions. It should be further stressed that many states have land-use programs and exercise review and control authority over local planning involving coastal zones, wetlands, flood plains, surface mining, power plant sites, pollution and environmental problems, open space, and even, in some instances, housing. And, of course, as previously elaborated, the states of Indiana and Minnesota imposed by legislative fiat an areawide governmental structure on the metropolitan areas of Indianapolis and Minneapolis–St. Paul, respectively. Given this record of increasing involvement by the states in the governmental affairs of metropolitan areas, we believe that the perspective of Florestano and Marando, advanced two decades ago, has even greater currency today: "We are optimistic about what states will do. . . . We see some basic trends in (1) an awakening awareness on the part of the state official as to the needs and concerns of metropolitan areas; (2) an increased level of expenditure for urban and local needs, with some special attention to governments in metropolitan areas; (3) more competency among state level officials, and with that more of a tendency to experiment with innovative answers to metropolitan area questions; and (4) finally, some initial attempts at formulating strategies to deal with urban and metropolitan areas."[28]

Despite the generally hostile political attitude of local elected officials toward comprehensive metropolitan governmental reform proposals, due to their perceived loss of political power, we may well conjecture that their support for single-purpose government might translate into their equal political support for metropolitan multifunctional agencies that improve system-maintenance services. Over time, it might be desirable for the states to provide optional forms of government for large multipurpose special districts. Concerning all this, Foster noted that local officials find special-purpose governments attractive because of their geographical and functional specialization and their financial ability to construct facilities and provide expensive capital-intensive services. In sum, Foster concludes that local officials look with favor on special-purpose governments because:

> The combination of district attributes and local government constraints indeed provides sufficient reasons for local officials to surrender service control to independent special districts. . . . Districts' low visibility presents local government officials with unmistakable opportunities for political gain. By transferring service responsibilities to districts, local officials may evade politically perilous decisions to raise taxes or incur large amounts of debt. In a similar vein, local officials can dispose of politically difficult decisions about growth by consigning control over development-oriented services to nominally neutral, politically insulated authorities. . . . This enables local officials to simultaneously keep taxes in line, indulge private investors' progrowth interests, and disclaim responsibility for unpopular development projects. Low visibility also enhances districts' potential as abundant sources of political patronage posts, which elected officials may find appealing despite the additional scrutiny it brings.[29]

In addition, we believe that the business community of a metropolitan area (and of the state generally) would view with favor and provide political support for the creation of a multifunctional service agency, believing that it would provide the metropolitan area with a modern and efficient public infrastructure, a necessary component to compete in the global economy. As Weiping Wu has noted: "One of the most important functions performed by the public sector is the provision of efficient infrastructure, both physical and economic. . . . By permitting smooth flows of goods and services, it enables modern, competitive industries to develop. It can reduce the cost of and time necessary for the transport of goods and services, and in turn raise overall productivity. By relieving the private sector of the need to develop infrastructure in-house, it saves resources for more productive investments. Cities with aging infrastructure may bear a substantial amount of risk as the deterioration of roads, bridges, sewer systems, waste treatment facilities, and telephone systems will diminish their attractiveness for economic expansion."[30]

We realize, of course, that our proposal that the states should establish metropolitan multifunctional service agencies without the acquiescence of the citizens will be greeted with a curious sense of alarm by many scholars, public officials, and citizens, who believe that the citizens, acting in their sovereign capacity, should constitute the judge and jury and decide by referendum on any major change in metropolitan governmental arrangements. However, we remain somewhat puzzled by, and obviously unsympathetic to, the notion that citizens, practicing the fine art of participatory democracy, should exercise a veto on matters involving regional governmental structure, while the vast majority of state policy issues are resolved through the process of representative democracy. We are cognizant, as well, that our proposal to establish metropolitan multiservice agencies is a somewhat speculative venture, given the fact that in most state legislatures a majority of the members represent suburban or nonmetropolitan areas. Nevertheless, we believe that the time has come for the states to act decisively in matters pertaining to metropolitan governance, as Indiana and Minnesota have already done, and return to the practice of the nineteenth century, when state legislatures routinely approved new metropolitan governmental arrangements without the involvement and approval of the citizenry.

We are also aware that our proposal will be criticized for promoting and forcing on the metropolitan citizenry a governmental structure that has long been criticized by scholars as essentially being insular, undemocratic, and not accountable to the public. However, we feel that this criticism may be rendered less valid if the following measures are adopted. First, the governor would be required to appoint governing board members representing a broad spectrum of the metropolitan community, not only with regard to residential location, but also in terms of socioeconomic attributes. Second, public accountability and control of these bodies could be facilitated by having board members serve relatively short terms, perhaps no more than four years. And, finally, metropolitan multifunctional agencies would be required to hold monthly public meetings and make extensive use of citizen advisory committees.

Conclusion

We share the perspective of Florestano and Marando concerning the critical role of the states in shaping the governmental structure of the metropolis: "Metropolitan areas have problems that cannot be ignored indefinitely. Such problems can reach a crisis level before a state takes action. The major question to be addressed is whether states will be able to provide the necessary leadership. The way states handle the problems of metropolitan areas in the next decade will probably determine both the future development of metropolitan areas and the future of state government."[31] In the final analysis, the future of our metropolitan areas is critically dependent on appropriate action and policies by the states.

NOTES

Preface

1. In this regard, see Paula C. Baker, Elinor Ostrom, and Robert Goehlert, *Metropolitan Reform: An Annotated Bibliography* (Bloomington: Workshop in Political Theory and Policy Analysis, Indiana University, 1979) for an excellent, although somewhat dated, bibliography on the government and politics of metropolitan areas.
2. Paul Studenski, *The Government of Metropolitan Areas in the United States* (New York: National Municipal League, 1930).
3. For a nice summary statement of this position see Robert L. Bish and Vincent Ostrom, *Understanding Urban Government: Metropolitan Reform Reconsidered* (Washington, DC: American Institute for Public Policy Research, 1973).

Chapter 1

1. Lewis Mumford, *The City in History: Its Origins, Its Transformations, and Its Prospects* (New York: Harcourt, Brace, and World, 1961), 3.
2. Most of the data presented in this chapter comes from or is derived from publications of the U.S. Bureau of the Census. Additional sources include publications of the U.S. Advisory Commission on Intergovernmental Relations (ACIR), 1960 to 1996. As of 1998, only some of the tabulations of the number of local governments by type and by state were available from the 1997 *Census of Governments*. The Governments Division of the Census Bureau is delayed in publishing this information and a number of its reports are no longer being issued due to cutbacks in personnel and funding at the Commerce Department. As a result, many of the analyses of change over time are brought forward only as far as the 1992 *Census of Governments*, with some further updates from the various annual series that the Census publishes. Though not in any significant order, Census publications of particular importance include: 1930 to 1990 *Census of Population* and annual updates since 1990; 1952 to 1997 *Census of Governments*; 1948 to 1997 *Special Reports* of the Governments Division of the Census Bureau including *Historical Statistics of the United States: Colonial Times to 1957* and later updates; 1953–1997 *Statistical Abstract of the United States*; 1982 to 1997 *Consolidated Federal Funds Reports*; 1957 to 1995 annual series of the Governments Division on *Government Finances, Public Employment,* as well as the finances of county governments, municipalities and townships, school districts, and the like; 1983 and 1994 *County and City Data Book*; *State and Metropolitan Area Data Book 1991*; and 1997–1998 preliminary reports and diskettes from the Governments Division of the Census Bureau.
3. www.census.gov/ftp/pub/Press-Release/cb97-194.html
4. The measure used is a simple correlation coefficient (r). It is a measure of association that ranges from -1.00 to $+1.00$ for negative and positive relationships. The closer it is to 1 the higher the

association between these variables. A minus sign (–) means that as one variable increases the other declines. A plus sign (+) indicates that the two variables move in the same direction at the same time. The coefficient squared gives the theoretical percentage of association. For the relationship between each state's metropolitan population and gross state product (GSP), $r = +.75$. If Rhode Island, as an outlier, is deleted, $r = +.79$ and both relationships are curvilinear. Theoretically, MSA population explains over half the variation in gross state product. Most of the relationships shown in this book have an N of 50 because they are looking at the relationship of variables for the fifty states. With an N of 50, the simple correlation coefficient is significant at the .05 level if it is plus or minus .27.

5. U.S. Advisory Commission on Intergovernmental Relations (ACIR), *Residential Community Associations*, A-112 (Washington, DC: 1989).

6. G. Ross Stephens, "The Least Glorious, Most Local, Most Trivial, Homely, Provincial, and Most Ignored Form of Local Government," *Urban Affairs Quarterly* 24, no. 4 (June 1989): 504.

7. G. Ross Stephens, "State Systems of Local Government and the Census Typology." Grant research report to the University of Missouri Research Board, 1995.

8. G. Ross Stephens and Gerald W. Olson, *Pass-through Federal Aid, 1957–1977*, Report to the National Science Foundation, vol. 1, 1979, 73–93; and updates to 1992. 1997 data were not yet available.

9. G. Ross Stephens, "State Centralization and the Erosion of Local Autonomy," *Journal of Politics* 36, no. 1 (February 1974): 44–76, and later updates through 1992.

10. Ibid.

11. Forty-odd years ago schools were a state function in North Carolina. After the 1954 school desegregation decision, public education was devolved to large cities and county governments in a failed effort to thwart desegregation, but the state still pays for over three-fourths of the cost of public schools.

12. New York could be classified as a combined system. In what is probably the most complex system of local government in the nation, it has all types of local governments: classified townships, some of which exercise municipal powers; classified municipalities; special districts ranging from very minor to major operations; mostly noncoterminous school districts, though there are twenty-seven dependent school systems operated by county governments and the City of New York. County governments now have municipal authority. New York is classified as conventional even though it has a more complex system of local government than other states classified as combined systems.

13. Henry J. Schmandt and John Goldbach, "The Urban Paradox," in Henry J. Schmandt and Warner Bloomberg, eds., *The Quality of Urban Life*, Urban Affairs Annual Reviews (Beverly Hills, CA: Sage Publications, 1969), 473–98.

14. ACIR, *Residential Community Associations*.

15. These data use Stephens's typology and updates as well as the typology adapted to show the federal-state relationship, 1974 and updates through 1992.

16. ACIR, *RTS 1991: State Revenue Capacity and Effort* M-187 (Washington, DC: September 1993) 20.

17. Thomas H. Reed, *Municipal Government in the United States*, (New York: Appleton-Century, 1934) 351.

18. From the Internet, urdef.est at www.census.gov. For more technical information used in defining metropolitan area standards, the following documents are available from the Office of Management and Budget, Washington, D.C. 20503: *Summary of Standards Followed for Establishing Metropolitan Statistical Areas (MSAs), Official Standards for Establishing Metropolitan Statistical Areas, General Procedures and Definitions, Detailed Procedures*, and *Background and Rationale for Official Standards.*

19. See the documents listed in the previous endnote.

20. *1997 State and Metro Area Data Book* (Washington, DC: office of John Russ, HUD), 172–77.

21. As with metropolitan areas, the definition of coastal areas has changed somewhat over time, but the variation is not sufficiently different to materially alter the information presented.

22. Census projections and estimates for 1992, 1994, and 1996 are used here for estimating the 1996 distribution.

23. G. Ross Stephens, "Urban Underrepresentation in the U.S. Senate," *Urban Affairs Review* 31, no. 3 (January 1996): 404–18.

24. Gerrymandering as used herein means adjusting the electoral system, process, or district boundaries to give advantage to one political party or faction. Overt gerrymandering is drawing electoral district lines in a manner that gives political advantage. Silent gerrymandering is failure to redraw district boundaries when conditions change or the population changes, when that gives advantage to one party or faction. Procedural gerrymandering is selecting an electoral process, such as a particular type of primary, when that gives advantage to one party or faction.

25. G. Ross Stephens, "Special Districts," a paper delivered to the March 1990 conference of the Southwestern Political Science Association, Austin, TX.

26. The simple correlation is +.67.

27. 1992 *Census of Governments*, "Finances of Special Districts," vol. 4, no. 2 (Washington, DC: Government Printing Office, 1997).

28. The relationship for state centralization is $r = -.54$; that for the state special district activity index is $r = +.47$.

29. Paul Studenski, *The Government of Metropolitan Areas* (New York: National Municipal League, 1930) and Victor Jones, *Metropolitan Government* (Chicago: University of Chicago Press, 1942).

30. Oliver Williams, *Metropolitan Political Analysis* (Philadelphia: University of Pennsylvania Press, 1971).

31. This is from a 1933 article reprinted in the *Public Administration Review* 46, no. 2 (March-April 1986): 209.

32. In addition to the Defense Department, defense-related agencies include personnel from the Coast Guard (Treasury Department), the military portions of the National Aeronautics and Space Agency (NASA), the atomic weapons portions of the Energy Department, and FTE estimates for the military reserves, since they have become an important part of the defense structure. In terms of contracting out, many of the things the military agencies once did with their own personnel are now provided by private contractors, such as major maintenance and training, housekeeping and food service activities, recreational facilities (officers and non-com clubs, golf courses, etc.), as well as the purchase of virtually all supplies and equipment. These data are from an article, "The Ballooning Federal Bureaucracy Is a Myth—Most Growth is State and Local," in the *Public Affairs Report* 38, no. 5 (September 1997) (Berkeley, CA: Institute of Governmental Studies), 7–8.

33. County area aggregate data include all local governments within each county area. For most central counties this means that suburban governments are often included within the central county data.

34. Stephens and Olson, *Pass-through Federal Aid.*

35. Partly because of federal regulations and grants, most states, and some larger local governments, have created their own agencies concerned with housing and urban development; more integrated departments of transportation; and agencies concerned with environmental protection, though many use a variety of names to designate these entities. Most have some agency concerned with local government and most have devised their own version of ACIR, even though it went out of existence at the federal level in 1996. Having units with comparable activities and administrative structures makes it easier for state and local governments to interact with federal agencies.

36. *Kansas City Star*, April 2, 1997, 1, 16.

37. Nelson Wikstrom, *Councils of Governments: A Study of Political Incrementalism* (Chicago: Nelson-Hall, 1977), 16–18.
38. Scott Greer, *The Emerging City* (New York: The Free Press, 1962), 198, 201.
39. Williams, *Metropolitan Political Analysis*.

Chapter 2

1. For an excellent bibliography, see Paula C. Baker, Elinor Ostrom, and Robert Goehlert, *Metropolitan Reform: An Annotated Bibliography* (Bloomington, IN: Workshop in Political Theory and Policy Analysis, Indiana University, 1979).
2. Thomas H. Reed, "Progress in Metropolitan Integration," *Public Administration Review* 9 (Winter 1949): 1–10.
3. I have borrowed the terminology of "system maintenance" and "lifestyle" services from Oliver Williams, *Metropolitan Political Analysis* (Philadelphia: University of Pennsylvania Press, 1971).
4. Williams, *Metropolitan Political Analysis*.
5. Material in this paragraph is drawn from Paul Studenski, *The Government of Metropolitan Areas in the United States* (New York: National Municipal League, 1930), 65–85 and 170–204.
6. Woodrow Wilson, *Congressional Government: A Study in American Politics* (Boston: Houghton-Mifflin, 1885), 255.
7. Woodrow Wilson, "The Study of Administration," *Political Science Quarterly* 2 (June 1887): 197.
8. Wilson, "The Study of Administration," 210.
9. Wilson, "The Study of Administration," 209.
10. Frank J. Goodnow, *Politics and Administration* (New York: Macmillan, 1900).
11. Frederick W. Taylor, *Shop Management* (New York: Harper & Row, 1911).
12. Ernest W. Burgess, "The Growth of the City: An Introduction to a Research Project," in Robert E. Park, ed., *The City* (Chicago: University of Chicago Press, 1925), 49–50.
13. President's Research Committee on Social Trends, *Recent Social Trends in the United States* (Washington, DC: Government Printing Office, 1932).
14. Roderick D. McKenzie, *The Metropolitan Community* (New York: McGraw-Hill, 1933), 98–110.
15. Morris Janowitz, *The Community Press in an Urban Setting* (Glencoe, IL: The Free Press, 1952).
16. See Jack Gibbs, *Urban Research Methods* (New York: D. Van Nostrand, 1961), 74.
17. See Stuart A. Queen and David B. Carpenter, *The American City* (New York: McGraw-Hill, 1953), 84.
18. Amos H. Hawley and Basil G. Zimmer, "Resistance to Unification in a Metropolitan Community," in Morris Janowitz, ed., *Community Political Systems* (New York: The Free Press, 1961), 146.
19. For an extended discussion of the norms and principles of the scientific management movement, see Martin J. Schiesl, *The Politics of Efficiency* (Berkeley: University of California Press, 1977), especially 111–32.
20. Schiesl, *The Politics of Efficiency*, 43–45.
21. John Nolen, "General Planning Board for Metropolitan Boston, " *National Municipal Review* 1 (April 1912): 231.
22. George E. Hooker, "City Planning and Political Areas," *National Municipal Review* 6 (May 1917): 337–345.
23. George C. Sikes, "Consolidation Problems in California," *National Municipal Review* 7 (March 1918): 166.
24. Chester C. Maxey, "The Political Integration of Metropolitan Communities," *National Municipal Review* 11 (August 1922): 229–53.
25. Ibid., 229.

26. Ibid.
27. Ibid., 253.
28. Ibid., 230–40.
29. Ibid., 252–53.
30. Ibid., 252.
31. Thomas H. Reed, "The Region, a New Governmental Unit," *National Municipal Review* 14 (July 1925): 417–423.
32. Shelby M. Harrison, "Some Regional Problems and Methods of Their Study," *American Political Science Review* 20 (February 1926): 156–63.
33. Rowland A. Egger, "City-County Consolidation in Allegheny County, Pennsylvania," *American Political Science Review* 23 (February 1929): 121–23.
34. William Anderson, *American City Government* (New York: Henry Holt, 1925).
35. A. Chester Hanford, *Problems in Municipal Government* (Chicago: A.W. Shaw, 1926).
36. Joseph Wright, ed., *Selected Readings in Municipal Problems* (Boston: Ginn, 1925).
37. William Bennett Munro, *Municipal Government and Administration* (New York: MacMillan, 1923).
38. Chester Maxey, *Urban Democracy* (Boston: Heath, 1929).
39. Thomas H. Reed, *Municipal Government in the United States* (New York: Century, 1926).
40. Studenski, *The Government of Metropolitan Areas in the United States.*
41. Ibid., 3.
42. Ibid., 23.
43. Ibid., 29.
44. Ibid., 30.
45. Ibid., 64.
46. Ibid.
47. Ibid., 210–11.
48. Ibid., 215.
49. Ibid., 216.
50. Ibid., 255.
51. Ibid., 367.
52. Ibid., 389.
53. Ibid., 386–87.
54. Ibid., 341.
55. Ibid., 389.
56. Charles E. Merriam, Spencer D. Parratt, and Albert Lepawsky, *The Government of the Metropolitan Region of Chicago* (Chicago: University of Chicago Press, 1933), 189.
57. Ibid., 79.
58. Ibid., 191.
59. William Anderson, *The Units of Government in the United States* (Chicago: Public Administration Service, 1934), 35–37.
60. McKenzie, *The Metropolitan Community.*
61. National Resources Committee, *Our Cities: Their Role in the National Economy* (Washington DC: The Committee, 1937), 68.
62. Victor Jones, *Metropolitan Government* (Chicago: University of Chicago Press, 1942). It should be noted that in his later writings Jones disavowed his belief in the metropolitan government approach. See, for example, Victor Jones, "From Metropolitan Government to Metropolitan Governance," in K. G. Denike, ed., *Managing Urban Settlements: Can Our Governmental Structures Cope?* (Vancouver: The Centre for Human Settlements, 1979), 24–39.
63. Jones, *Metropolitan Government*, 52.
64. Ibid., 87.

65. Ibid., 121.

66. Ibid., 90–91.

67. Ibid., 99.

68. Ibid., 154.

69. Ibid., 108–10.

70. Ibid., 110–21.

71. Ibid., 337.

72. Ibid., 319.

73. Ibid., 341–342.

74. Victor Jones, "Local Government Organization in Metropolitan Areas: Its Relation to Urban Redevelopment," in Coleman Woodbury, ed., *The Future of Cities and Urban Redevelopment* (Chicago: University of Chicago Press, 1953), 477–606.

75. Jones, "Local Government Organization in Metropolitan Areas: Its Relation to Urban Development," 604–5.

76. John C. Bollens, *The States and the Metropolitan Problem* (Chicago: Council of State Governments, 1956).

77. Betty Tableman, *Governmental Organization in Metropolitan Areas*, Institute of Government Study, no. 21 (Ann Arbor: University of Michigan Press, 1951).

78. Robert C. Wood, *1400 Governments* (Cambridge: Harvard University Press, 1961).

79. Luther Halsey Gulick, *The Metropolitan Problem and American Ideas* (New York: Alfred A. Knopf, 1962).

80. Ibid., 123.

81. Ibid., 125.

82. Ibid.

83. Ibid., 127–28.

84. Ibid., 129.

85. Ibid., 133.

86. Ibid., 135.

87. Ibid., 129.

88. Ibid., 152.

89. Ibid., 140.

90. Ibid., 163.

91. National Research Council, *Toward an Understanding of Metropolitan America* (Washington, DC: National Academy of Sciences, 1975), 105.

92. *Modernizing Local Government* (New York: Committee for Economic Development, 1966), 44.

93. *Reshaping Government in Metropolitan Areas* (New York: The Committee for Economic Development, 1970), 45.

94. Advisory Commission on Intergovernmental Relations, *Regional Decision Making: New Strategies for Substate Districts* (A-43) (Washington, DC: U.S. Government Printing Office, 1973), 347–74.

95. Kent Mathewson, ed., *The Regionalist Papers* (Detroit: The Metropolitan Fund, 1974).

96. Kent Mathewson, ed., *The Regionalist Papers*. 2nd ed. (Detroit: The Metropolitan Fund, 1978).

97. Material in this paragraph and the following is drawn from John C. Bollens and Henry J. Schmandt, *The Metropolis: Its People, Politics, and Economic Life*. 4th ed. (New York: Harper & Row, 1982), 304–9.

98. Bollens and Schmandt, *The Metropolis*, 311–22 and 324–32.

99. See Nelson Wikstrom, *Councils of Governments: A Study of Political Incrementalism* (Chicago: Nelson-Hall, 1977).

100. Bollens and Schmandt, *The Metropolis*, 366–67 and 373–75.

101. Vincent Ostrom, Robert Bish, and Elinor Ostrom, *Local Government in the United States* (San Francisco: Institute for Contemporary Studies, 1988), 212.

102. David Rusk, *Cities Without Suburbs* (Washington, DC: Woodrow Wilson Press, 1993).
103. Ibid., 35.
104. Neal R. Pierce, *Citistates: How Urban America Can Prosper in a Competitive World* (Washington, DC: Seven Locks Press, 1993).
105. Ibid., 32.
106. Ibid., 34.
107. Anthony Downs, *New Visions for Metropolitan America* (Washington, DC: The Brookings Institution, 1994).
108. Henry G. Cisneros, ed., *Interwoven Destinies: Cities and the Nation* (Washington, DC: (New York: Norton, 1993).
109. William R. Dodge, *Regional Excellence: Governing Together to Compete Globally and Flourish Locally* (Washington, DC: National League of Cities, 1996).
110. Charles Lindblom, *The Intelligence of Democracy* (New York: Free Press, 1965), 3.
111. Vincent Ostrom, Charles M. Tiebout, and Robert Warren, "The Organization of Government in Metropolitan Areas: A Theoretical Inquiry," *American Political Science Review* 55 (December 1961): 831–42.
112. H. Paul Friesema, *Metropolitan Political Structure: Intergovernmental Relations and Political Integration in the Quad-Cities* (Iowa City: University of Iowa Press, 1971).
113. Wikstrom, *Councils of Governments*.
114. Robert L. Bish, *The Public Economy of Metropolitan Areas* (Chicago: Markham, 1971), 153.
115. Brett Hawkins and Thomas R. Dye, "Metropolitan 'Fragmentation': A Research Note," *Midwest Review of Public Administration* 4 (February 1970): 24.
116. Alan Campbell and Seymour Sacks, *Metropolitan America: Fiscal Patterns and Governmental Systems* (New York: Free Press, 1967), 179.
117. Werner Z. Hirsch, "The Supply of Urban Public Services," in Harvey S. Perloff and Lowdon Wingo, Jr., eds., *Issues in Urban Economics* (Baltimore: John Hopkins Press, 1968), 508.
118. For citizen attitudes toward metropolitan government, see Amos H. Hawley and Basil G. Zimmer, *The Metropolitan Community: Its People and Government* (Beverly Hills, CA: Sage Publications, 1970), especially 90–125.
119. Vincent Marando, "The Politics of City-County Consolidation," *National Civic Review* 64 (February 1975): 76.
120. Milton Kotler, *Neighborhood Government: The Local Foundations of Political Life* (New York: Bobbs-Merrill, 1969), xiii.
121. See, for example, Kotler, *Neighborhood Government: The Local Foundations of Political Life*, and Alan A. Altshuler, *Community Control: The Black Demand for Participation in Large American Cities* (New York: Pegasus, 1970).

Chapter 3

1. Scott Greer, *Governing the Metropolis* (New York: John Wiley and Sons, 1962), 124.
2. Robert C. Wood, *Suburbia: Its People and Their Politics* (Boston: Houghton Mifflin Company, 1958), 18.
3. John C. Bollens and Henry J. Schmandt, *The Metropolis: Its People, Politics, and Economic Life*, 4th ed. (New York: Harper & Row, 1982) 380.
4. In 1997 the Ohio Supreme Court declared the state's system for funding public education unconstitutional.
5. This was a part of the research carried out by Metropolitan Community Studies, Inc., from 1957 to 1960 for *Metropolitan Challenge* (Dayton, OH: Otterbein Press, 1959) and *County Governmental Reorganization*, Sunday supplement of the *Dayton Journal Herald*, January 16, 1960.

6. *Metropolitan Organization: The St. Louis Case*, M-158, (Washington, DC: U.S. Advisory Commission on Intergovernmental Relations, September 1988).

7. Vincent L. Marando and Carl R. Whitely, "City-County Consolidation: An Overview of Voter Response," *Urban Affairs Quarterly* vol. 7, no. 2 (December 1972): 181–203.

8. These include the County Land Trust, the Regional Cultural and Performing Arts Development District, the Regional Convention and Visitors Commission, the St. Louis Regional Convention Center and Sports Authority, and the Metropolitan Zoological Park and Museum District (1992 *Census of Governments*, vol. 1, no. 1 and vol. 4, no. 2). See also ACIR, *Metropolitan Organization: The St. Louis Case*, M-158, September 1988.

9. *Kansas City Star*, November 19, 1997: A-1, A-13; U.S. Bureau of the Census, *State and Metropolitan Area Data Book 1991* (Washington, DC: Government Printing Office) 124.

10. Information concerning the newly created city-county was obtained from the mayor's office, September 30, 1997; the city attorney, October 1, 1997; from the city's public relations officer, October 1, 1997; and from reports in the *Kansas City Star*, January 9, 1997, A-1, A-11; September 10, 1997, A-1, A-10; October 1, 1997, C-1, C-8; October 2, 1997, C-2; and October 13, 1997, A-1, A-17. The new government went into operation October 1, 1997 with the swearing in of the new legislative commission and elected executive. The first meeting of the new Board of Commissioners was held October 2, 1997. At this meeting the newly installed mayor/chief executive appointed the former city administrator as administrator of the consolidated city-county government (*Kansas City Star*, October 3, 1997, C-2).

11. Marando and Whitely, "City-County Consolidation." These statements also appear to apply to attempts at city-county reorganization proposals that have been attempted since 1972.

12. Vincent L. Marando, "The Politics of City-County Consolidation," *National Civic Review* (February 1975): 77.

13. Tobe Johnson, "Metropolitan Government: A Black Analytical Perspective," pamphlet. (Washington, DC: Joint Center for Political Studies, 1972).

14. Wood, *Suburbia*, 299.

15. Kansas City *Star*, October 13, 1997, A-1 and A-17.

16. Kansas City *Star*, February 26, 1998, A-1.

17. Henry J. Schmandt, "The City and the Ring," *American Behavioral Scientist* 4, no. 3 (1960): 17–19; G. Ross Stephens, "The Power Grid of the Metropolis," in Frederick M. Wirt, ed., *Future Directions in Community Power Research: A Colloquium* (Berkeley, CA: Institute of Governmental Studies, University of California, 1971), 125–45.

18. Oliver P. Williams, Harold Herman, Charles S. Leibman, and Thomas R. Dye, "Suburban Attitudes, Opinions, and Local Policies," in Bryon T. Downs, ed., *Cities and Suburbs: Selected Readings in Local Politics and Public Policy*. (Belmont, CA: Wadsworth, 1971), 160.

19. The measure used to compare the role played by the federal government is an adaptation of Stephens's index of state centralization applied to the federal government vis-à-vis the average state in terms of state and local activities, and the state centralization index vis-à-vis local government for the average state. It uses a series of three subindices that measure financial responsibility, services delivered, and FTE personnel adjusted for the federal versus state and local differences in labor versus cash and capital inputs for public services performed by federal versus state and local governments. Local services are more labor intensive than those delivered by states, and state and local services are more labor intensive than those performed by the federal government.

20. *Factors Affecting Voter Reaction to Governmental Reorganization in Metropolitan Areas*, M-15, (Washington, DC: U.S. Advisory Commission on Intergovernmental Relations, 1962), 13.

21. Ibid., 13.

22. Bollens and Schmandt, *The Metropolis*, 478–88.

23. Wood, *Suburbia*, 19.

Chapter 4

1. For an excellent, although somewhat dated, overview of the sorry record of metropolitan governmental reform in the United States, see Joseph F. Zimmerman, "Metropolitan Reform in the U.S.: An Overview," *Public Administration Review* 30 (September/October 1970): 531–43.

2. Material describing the circumstances and developments culminating in the city-parish merger of Baton Rouge and East Baton Rouge Parish is largely drawn from William C. Havard, Jr. and Floyd L. Corty, *Rural-Urban Consolidation: The Merger of Governments in the Baton Rouge Area* (Baton Rouge: Louisiana State University Press, 1954), 3–44. See also Charles G. Whitwell, "The New Parish-City Government of Baton Rouge," *Southwestern Social Science Quarterly* (December 1948): 227–31, and R. Gordon Kean, Jr., "Consolidation That Works," *National Municipal Review* 45 (November 1956): 478–85.

3. William C. Havard, "Baton Rouge Committee Reports on City-Parish," *National Civic Review* 49 (September 1960): 439.

4. R. Gordon Kean, Jr., "Consolidation That Works," *National Municipal Review* 45 (November 1956): 478–85.

5. John C. Bollens and Henry J. Schmandt, *Metropolis: Its People, Politics, and Economic Life*. 2nd ed. (New York: Harper & Row, 1970), 304–5.

6. Material describing the circumstances and developments culminating in the city-county consolidation of Nashville and Davidson County is largely drawn from David A. Booth, *Metropolitics: The Nashville Consolidation* (East Lansing, MI: Institute for Community Development and Services, Michigan State University, 1963), particularly 11–23 and 71–93. See also Robert E. McArthur, "The Metropolitan Government of Nashville and Davidson County," in *Regional Governance: Promise and Performance: Substate Regionalism and the Federal System*. vol. II. (Washington, DC: United States Advisory Commission on Intergovernmental Relations, 1973), 26–35.

7. Booth, *Metropolitics*, 87.

8. Daniel R. Grant, "Opinions Surveyed on Nashville Metro," *National Civic Review* 54 (July 1965): 375.

9. Daniel R. Grant, "A Comparison of Predictions and Experience with Nashville's Metro," *Urban Affairs Quarterly* 1 (September 1965): 34–54.

10. T. Scott Fillebrown, "The Nashville Story," *National Civic Review* 58 (May 1969): 197–200, 210.

11. Bruce D. Rogers and C. McCurdy Lipsey, "Metropolitan Reform: Citizen Evaluations of Performances in Nashville–Davidson County, Tennessee," *Publius* 4 (Fall 1974): 19–34.

12. "Nashville Seeks to Enliven Its Downtown," *New York Times*, November 2, 1997, 44.

13. Material describing the circumstances and developments culminating in the city-county consolidation of Jacksonville and Duval County is largely drawn from Richard Martin, *A Quiet Revolution: The Consolidation of Jacksonville–Duval County and the Dynamics of Urban Political Reform*. (Jacksonville, FL: White Publishing Company, 1993), especially 1–272. See also John M. DeGrove, "The City of Jacksonville: Consolidation in Action," in *Regional Governance*, vol. II, 17–25.

14. Martin, *A Quiet Revolution*, 15.

15. Lee Sloan and Robert French, "Race and Governmental Consolidation in Jacksonville," *Negro Educational Review* (April–July 1970): 78.

16. See Martin, *A Quiet Revolution*, 279–321, and John Fischer, "Jacksonville: So Different You Can Hardly Believe It," *Harper's* 243 (July 1971): 21.

17. Richard A. Martin, "Jacksonville Area Highlights Activity," *National Civic Review* 59 (June 1970): 326.

18. Martin, *A Quiet Revolution*, 323–334.

19. Bert Swanson, "Jacksonville: Consolidation and Regional Governance," in H. V. Savitch and

Ronald K. Vogel, eds., *Regional Politics: America in a Post-City Age* (Thousand Oaks, CA: Sage Publications, 1996), 239–43.

20. Richard Feiock, "The Impacts of City/County Consolidation in Florida," *Governing Florida* 2 (Fall 1992): 5.

21. J. Edwin Benton and Darwin Gamble, "City/County Consolidation and Economies of Scale: Evidence from a Time-Series Analysis in Jacksonville, Florida," *Social Science Quarterly* 65 (March 1984): 195.

22. Swanson, "Jacksonville: Consolidation and Regional Governance," 249.

23. Ibid.

24. Material describing the circumstances and developments culminating in the consolidation of Indianapolis and Marion County is largely drawn from C. James Owen and York Willbern, *Governing Metropolitan Indianapolis: The Politics of Unigov* (Berkeley: University of California Press, 1985), especially 28–136. See also York Willbern, "Unigov: Local Government Reorganization in Indianapolis," in *Regional Governance*, vol. II, 47–73.

25. William Blomquist and Roger B. Parks, "Unigov: Local Government in Indianapolis and Marion County, Indiana," in L. J. Sharpe, ed., *The Government of World Cities: The Future of the Metro Model* (New York: John Wiley & Sons, 1995), 80.

26. "In Privatizing City Services, It's Now 'Indy-a-First Place,'" *New York Times*, March 2, 1995, A-14. See also Rob Gurwitt, "Indianapolis and the Republican Future," *Governing* 7 (February 1994): 24–28.

27. Blomquist and Parks, "Unigov: Local Government in Indianapolis and Marion County, Indiana," 83.

28. Willbern, "Unigov: Local Government Reorganization in Indianapolis," 67.

29. Indianapolis–Marion County Central Committee, "The Record Speaks for Itself," (mimeographed), 2–5.

30. Blomquist and Parks, "Unigov: Local Government in Indianapolis and Marion County, Indiana," 84–85. See also Wendy Wagner, "A Visit to Indianapolis," *Richmond Times Dispatch*, May 12, 1997, A1, A5.

31. Willbern, "Unigov: Local Government Reorganization in Indianapolis," 71.

32. Blomquist and Parks, "Unigov: Local Government in Indianapolis and Marion County, Indiana," 86.

33. Ibid.

Chapter 5

1. Material describing the circumstances and developments leading to the establishment of the federative, or two-tier, governmental structure of Miami–Dade County is largely drawn from Edward Sofen, *The Miami Metropolitan Experiment* (Garden City, NY: Anchor Books, 1966), especially 1–91. For more recent information we have drawn upon Genie Stowers, "Miami: Experiences in Regional Government," in H. V. Savitch and Ronald K. Vogel, eds., *Regional Politics in a Post-City Age* (Thousand Oaks, CA: Sage Publications, 1966), 185–205.

2. Sofen, *The Miami Metropolitan Experiment*, 102.

3. Sofen, *The Miami Metropolitan Experiment*, 176–197.

4. Stowers, "Miami: Experiences in Regional Government," 200.

5. See, "Rich Areas in Miami Talk Secession," *New York Times*, December 12, 1996, A12, and "By Wide Margin, Miami Voters Preserve City," *New York Times*, September 5, 1997, A30.

6. "Another Crisis of Metro: Resignation Under Fire of the Chief Officer of Dade County Raises New Questions About the Workings of His Metropolitan Government," *Business Week* (February 18, 1961): 102.

7. Office of the County Manager, Dade County, *Metro Government: Model for Action*, 5.
8. Juanita Greene, "Dade Metro: Turbulent History, Uncertain Future," *Planning* 45 (February, 1979): 14–16.
9. Melvin B. Mogulof, *Five Metropolitan Governments* (Washington, DC: The Urban Institute, 1972), 82–83.
10. Ibid., 48.
11. Stowers, "Miami: Experiences in Regional Government," 204.
12. Sofen, *The Miami Metropolitan Experiment*, 239.
13. Ibid., 245.
14. Stowers, "Miami: Experiences in Regional Government," 196.
15. Sheila L. Croucher, *Imagining Miami: Ethnic Politics in a Postmodern World* (Charlottesville: University of Virginia Press, 1997), 38.
16. Material describing the circumstances and developments leading to the establishment of the Twin Cities Metropolitan Council is drawn from John H. Harrigan and William C. Johnson, *Governing the Twin Cities Region: The Metropolitan Council in Comparative Perspective* (Minneapolis: University of Minnesota Press, 1978), 22–38, and Ted Kolderie, "Governance in the Twin Cities Area of Minnesota," in *Regional Governance: Promise and Performance: Substate Regionalism and the Federal System.* vol. II. (Washington, DC: United States Advisory Commission on Intergovernmental Relations, 1973), 113–38. See also Arthur Naftalin and John Brandl, *The Twin Cities Strategy* (St. Paul: Metropolitan Council of the Twin Cities Area, 1980).
17. John J. Harrigan, "Minneapolis–St. Paul: Structuring Metropolitan Government," in H. V. Savitch and Ronald K. Vogel, eds., *Regional Politics: America in a Post-City Age*, 213.
18. Ibid., 217.
19. Ibid., 217–22.
20. Myron Orfield, *Metropolitics: A Regional Agenda for Community and Stability* (Washington, DC: Brookings Institution Press, 1997), 121.
21. Harrigan, "Minneapolis–St. Paul: Structuring Metropolitan Government," 225–226.
22. Orfield, *Metropolitics*, 121–122.
23. Harrigan, "Minneapolis–St. Paul: Structuring Metropolitan Government," 225–226.
24. Material describing the circumstances and developments leading to the establishment of Metro is largely drawn from Carl Abbott, *Portland: Planning, Politics, and Growth in a Twentieth-Century City* (Lincoln: University of Nebraska Press, 1983), 229–66. See also Arthur C. Nelson, "Portland: The Metropolitan Umbrella," in H. V. Savitch and Ronald K. Vogel, eds., *Regional Politics: America in a Post-City Age*, 253–271.
25. Alan Ehrenhalt, "The Great Wall of Portland," *Governing* 11 (May 1997): 24.
26. Ibid., 20.
27. Nelson, "Portland: The Metropolitan Umbrella," 267–268.
28. Ehrenhalt, "The Great Wall of Portland," 21.
29. Mogulof, *Five Metropolitan Governments*, 52.
30. Ibid., 54–55.
31. Paul Peterson, *City Limits* (Chicago: University of Chicago Press, 1981).
32. Edward C. Banfield and Morton Grodzins, *Government and Housing in Metropolitan Areas* (New York: McGraw-Hill, 1958).

Chapter 6

1. Vincent Ostrom, Charles M. Tiebout, and Robert Warren, "The Organization of Government in Metropolitan Areas: A Theoretical Inquiry," *American Political Science Review* 60 (December 1961): 831–842.

2. Vincent Ostrom, *The Intellectual Crisis in American Public Administration* (Tuscaloosa: The University of Alabama Press, 1973).
3. Ibid., 81–91.
4. Ibid., 91–98.
5. Robert Dahl and Charles E. Lindblom, *Politics, Economics, and Welfare* (New York: Harper & Row, 1953).
6. William J. Baumol, *Welfare Economics and the Theory of the State* (Cambridge: Harvard University Press, 1965).
7. Anthony Downs, *An Economic Theory of Democracy* (New York: Harper & Row, 1957).
8. James M. Buchanan and Gordon Tullock, *The Calculus of Consent* (Ann Arbor: University of Michigan Press, 1962).
9. Mancur Olson, *The Logic of Collective Action* (Cambridge: Harvard University Press, 1965).
10. Gordon Tullock, *The Politics of Bureaucracy* (Washington, DC: Public Affairs Press, 1965).
11. William H. Ricker, *The Theory of Political Coalitions* (New Haven and London: Yale University Press, 1962).
12. Charles E. Lindblom, *The Intelligence of Democracy* (New York: Free Press, 1965).
13. R. L. Curry and L. L. Wade, *A Theory of Political Exchange: Economic Reasoning in Political Analysis* (Englewood Cliffs, New Jersey: Prentice-Hall, 1968).
14. Charles M. Tiebout, "A Pure Theory of Local Expenditures," *Journal of Political Economy* 44 (October 1956): 416–424.
15. Ibid., 420.
16. Ibid., 418.
17. Ibid., 423.
18. Ibid.
19. Ibid.
20. Ibid.
21. Ostrom, Tiebout, and Warren, "The Organization of Government in Metropolitan Areas."
22. Ibid., 831.
23. Ibid.
24. Ibid., 833.
25. Ibid., 842.
26. Werner Z. Hirsch, "Local Versus Areawide Urban Government Services," *National Tax Journal* 17 (December 1964): 331–39.
27. Ibid., 332.
28. Ibid., 333.
29. Ibid., 334.
30. Ibid.
31. Ibid.
32. Ibid.
33. Ibid., 335.
34. Ibid.
35. Ibid., 339.
36. Robert Warren, "A Municipal Services Market Model of Metropolitan Organization," *Journal of the American Institute of Planners* 30 (August 1964): 199.
37. Ibid., 196.
38. Ibid.
39. Ibid.
40. Ibid.
41. Ibid.
42. Ibid.

43. Ibid., 198.
44. Ibid., 199.
45. Ibid.
46. Ibid., 200.
47. Ibid.
48. Ibid.
49. Vincent Ostrom and Elinor Ostrom, "A Behavioral Approach to the Study of Intergovernmental Relations," *The Annals of the American Academy of Political and Social Science* 359 (May 1965): 138.
50. Ibid., 138.
51. Ibid., 142.
52. Vincent Ostrom and Elinor Ostrom, "Public Choice: A Different Approach to the Study of Public Administration," *Public Administration Review* 31 (March/April 1971): 211.
53. Robert L. Bish and Robert Warren, "Scale and Monopoly Problems in Urban Government Services," *Urban Affairs Quarterly* 8 (September 1972): 99.
54. Ibid., 101–2.
55. Ibid., 99.
56. Ibid., 102.
57. Ibid., 105.
58. Ibid., 105–6.
59. Ibid., 117.
60. Ostrom, *The Intellectual Crisis in American Public Administration*, 116.
61. Ibid.
62. Ibid., 117.
63. Ibid., 118.
64. Robert L. Bish, *The Public Economy of Metropolitan Areas* (Chicago: Rand McNally, 1971).
65. Ibid., 148–58.
66. Elinor Ostrom and Roger B. Parks, "Suburban Police Departments: Too Many and Too Small?" in Louis H. Masotti and Jeffrey K. Hadden, eds., *The Urbanization of the Suburbs* (Beverly Hills, CA: Sage Publications, 1973), 397.
67. Robert L. Bish and Vincent Ostrom, *Understanding Urban Government: Metropolitan Reform Reconsidered* (Washington, DC: American Enterprise Institute for Public Policy Research, 1973).
68. Ibid., 24.
69. Ibid.
70. Ibid., 30.
71. Ibid., 1–2.
72. Ibid., 2.
73. Vincent Ostrom and Elinor Ostrom, "Public Goods and Public Choices," in E. S. Saves, ed., *Delivering Public Services: Toward Improved Performance* (Boulder, CO: Westview Press, 1977), 7–49.
74. Gordon P. Whitaker, "Coproduction: Citizen Participation in Service Delivery," *Public Administration Review* 40 (May/June 1980): 242.
75. Gina Davis and Elinor Ostrom, "A Public Economy Approach to Education," *International Political Science Review* 40 (May/June 1980): 242.
76. Ostrom and Ostrom, "Public Goods and Public Choices," 34.
77. Ibid.
78. Stephen L. Percy, "Citizen Participation in the Coproduction of Urban Services," *Urban Affairs Quarterly* 19 (June 1984): 435–38.
79. Ronald J. Oakerson and Roger B. Parks, "Local Government Constitutions: A Different View of Metropolitan Governance," *American Review of Public Administration* 19 (December 1989): 279–94.

80. Ibid., 280.

81. Ibid., 284.

82. Ibid., 281.

83. Ibid.

84. *The Organization of Local Public Economies* (Washington, DC: U.S. Advisory Commission on Intergovernmental Relations, 1987).

85. *Metropolitan Organization: The St. Louis Case* (Washington, DC: U.S. Advisory Commission on Intergovernmental Relations, 1988).

86. *Metropolitan Organization: The Allegheny County Case* (Washington, DC: U.S. Advisory Commission on Intergovernmental Relations, 1992).

87. *Modernizing Local Government* (New York: Committee for Economic Development, 1966).

88. *Reshaping Government in Metropolitan Areas* (New York: Committee for Economic Development, 1970).

89. Victor Jones, "From Metropolitan Government to Metropolitan Governance," in K. G. Denike, ed., *Managing Urban Settlements: Can Our Governmental Structures Cope?* (Vancouver: The Centre for Human Settlements, University of British Columbia, 1979), 24–39.

90. Milton Kotler, *Neighborhood Government: The Local Foundations of Political Life* (New York: Bobbs-Merrill, 1969).

91. Alan A. Altshuler, *Community Control: The Black Demand for Participation in Large American Cities* (New York: Pegasus, 1970).

92. Michael Keating, "Size, Efficiency, and Democracy: Consolidation, Fragmentation, and Public Choice," in David Judge, Gerry Stoker, and Harold Wolman, eds., *Theories of Urban Politics* (Thousand Oaks, CA: Sage Publications, 1995), 124.

93. Ibid.

94. Mark Sproule-Jones and Kenneth D. Hart, "A Public-Choice Model of Political Participation," *Canadian Journal of Political Science* 6 (June/July, 1973): 193–94.

95. Keating, "Size, Efficiency, and Democracy: Consolidation, Fragmentation, and Public Choice," 123.

96. Ibid.

97. Ibid., 125.

98. Ibid., 126.

99. Percy, "Citizen Participation in the Coproduction of Urban Services," 443.

Chapter 7

1. David B. Walker, "Snow White and the 17 Dwarfs: From Metro Cooperation to Governance," *National Civic Review* 76, no. 1 (January–February 1987): 14.

2. Ibid., 14–28.

3. G. Ross Stephens, "Twentieth Century Institutional Change in the American Federal System," unpublished paper, 1997.

4. Stephen S. Jenks and Deil S. Wright, "An Agency-Level Approach to Change in the Administrative Functions of American State Governments," *State and Local Government Review* 25, no. 2 (Spring 1993): 77–86.

5. Rosaline Levenson, *County Government in Connecticut* (Storrs, CT: Institute of Public Service, 1966).

6. G. Ross Stephens, "The Metropolitan Power Matrix," *Connecticut Government* 23, no. 4 (Summer 1970): 4, 8.

7. Using Stephens's index of state centralization.

8. U.S. Bureau of the Census, 1992 *Compendium of Public Employment*, vol. 3, no. 2, Table 19 (Washington, DC: Government Printing Office, 1997).

9. The data and findings shown for special districts are from an article by the authors, titled "Trends in Special Districts," *State and Local Government Review* 30, no. 2 (Spring 1998): 29–38.

10. Population data are not available for special districts so, of necessity, this analysis uses state population. All special districts are less than statewide, though a few cover portions of two states.

11. At one point the Census says there are 1,800 large districts (Table 3, p. 4); at another they say there are 1,495 (p. x); and Table 14, p. 72 lists 2,071 such entities (*1992 Census of Governments*, vol. 4, no. 2.) The data shown are from Table 14. (Washington, DC: Government Printing Office, 1997).

12. The simple correlation (r) is +.80.

13. The partial correlation coefficients are county percentage of direct expenditures, −.71; state centralization, −.47; and SSLG, +.24.

14. Nancy Burns, *The Formation of American Local Government: Private Values in Public Institutions*, (New York: Oxford University Press, 1994), 12.

15. Laura Kaifez, et. al., "Counties in the National Context," *County Government in Arizona: Challenges of the 1980s* (Phoenix: Arizona Academy, 1984), 2.

16. Tanis J. Salant, "County Governments: An Overview," *Intergovernmental Perspective* 17, no. 1 (Winter 1991): 5–9.

17. Counties in Connecticut exist as historical artifacts and Census areas; in Rhode Island they remain as judicial districts and Census areas.

18. Taken from a thirty-page research report to the University of Missouri Research Board by G. Ross Stephens, "State Systems of Local Government and the Census Typology," June 19, 1995.

19. Braxton Apperson III, and Nelson Wikstrom, "The Professionalization of Virginia County Government: An Application of Diffusion Theory," *Public Administration Quarterly* (Spring 1997): 28–53.

20. Thomas P. Murphy, *Metropolitics and the Urban County* (Washington, DC: Washington National Press, Inc., 1970). Missouri uses the so-called "Missouri Plan" for judicial selection, which involves appointment and later approval or rejection by the voters.

21. Henry J. Schmandt, John C. Goldbach, and Donald B. Vogel, *Milwaukee: A Contemporary Profile* (New York: Praeger Publishers, 1971), 31–66.

22. Special legislation is an act of the state legislature that applies to only one local government. Most states no longer allow special legislation, though many achieve the same result by detailed classification of local governments. Today states often require approval by the voters in the area concerned when they enact special legislation.

23. Tanis J. Salant, "County Governments: An Overview," *Intergovernmental Perspective* 17, no. 1 (Winter 1991): 5–9. This entire issue of ACIR's *Intergovernmental Perspective* is devoted to an updating of information concerning contemporary county government.

24. G. Ross Stephens, "The Least Glorious, Most Local, Most Trivial, Homely, Provincial, and Most Ignored Form of Local Government," *Urban Affairs Quarterly* 24, no. 4 (June 1989): 501–512.

25. U.S. Bureau of the Census, *State and Metropolitan Area Data Book 1991*, Table A; 1996 *Statistical Abstract of the United States* (Washington, DC: Government Printing Office, 1996).

26. As was pointed out earlier, there is no legal difference between municipalities and towns (townships). Both are incorporated entities. There are a few "regional school districts" in southern New England, but the authors do not consider them separate local governments, as each member town must annually appropriate money for the continued operation of the school district.

27. Wallace S. Sayre and Herbert Kaufman, *Governing New York City: Politics in the Metropolis* (New York: W.W. Norton and Company, 1960).

28. Robert M. Stein, "Alternative Means of Delivering Municipal Services: 1982–1988," *Intergovernmental Perspective* 19, no. 1 (Winter 1993): 27–30.

29. Ibid.
30. U.S. Bureau of the Census, 1992 *Census of Governments*, "Finances of County Governments," vol. 4, no. 3 (Washington, DC: Government Printing Office, 1992), Appendix B.
31. Norman Beckman, "Alternative Approaches for Metropolitan Reorganization," *Public Management* 46 (June 1964): 130.
32. John M. DeGrove, "Land-use Planning: State-Local Roles," *National Civic Review* 63, no. 2 (February 1974): 72–76.
33. Walker, "Snow White and the 17 Dwarfs": 18.

Chapter 8

1. These data are for 1991, the last year for which all the measures shown in the inset table are available. They were published by the U.S. Advisory Commission on Intergovernmental Relations (ACIR), which terminated its activities in 1996 as a result of continually declining support from Congress. *RTS: State Revenue Capacity and Effort*, M-187 (Washington, DC: ACIR, September 1993). The range for PCI, where the average state is given a rating of 100, has not changed significantly since 1991. U.S. Bureau of the Census, *Statistical Abstract of the United States* (Washington, DC: Government Printing Office, 1997). The section of the Treasury Department that calculated the total taxable resources (TTR) measure has also been eliminated.
2. G. Ross Stephens and Karen Toombs Parsons, "Rich States, Poor States: An Addendum," *State and Local Government Review* 21, no. 2 (Spring 1989): 50–59.
3. Ibid., 57–58.
4. Taken from the Internet at www.census.gov and other Census publications.
5. This simplified regression line index was developed by one of the authors to analyze the degree of regressivity or progressivity of a tax or revenue structure. In this instance, it measures the calculated slope of the regression line across six categories of adjusted gross income (numbered 1, 2, 3, . . . n) as shown in Figure 8.1. The calculated average tax for the top category is divided by the calculated average tax for the bottom classification ($Y = a + bX$). This is a linear measure that smooths out the perturbations across income groups. See G. Ross Stephens, "New Federalism by Default, Little OPEC States, and Fiscal Darwinism," in Dennis R. Judd, ed., *Public Policy Across States and Communities* (Greenwich, CT: JAI Press, 1985), 49–71. Using these and other measures, all three levels of government have been becoming more regressive since the 1950s. Data are obtained from www.census.gov on the Internet and the latest usable information on the structure of government revenue systems from *Significant Features of Fiscal Federalism*, vols. I and II, M-185 and 190 (Washington, DC: ACIR, 1993, and 1994). Unfortunately ACIR is no longer an operating agency due to budget cuts and the Census Bureau now publishes much less information than in earlier years due to the loss of half the personnel of the Commerce Department between 1990 and 1996.
6. Kevin Phillips, *Boiling Point: Democrats, Republicans, and the Decline of Middle-Class Prosperity* (New York: Harper Perennial, 1993), 110.
7. U.S. Bureau of the Census, *Statistical Abstract of the United States* (Washington, DC: Government Printing Office, 1953), 360; *1982 Census of Governments*, "Historical Statistics," 6, no. 4, (Washington, DC: Government Printing Office, 1985).
8. Tax Foundation, *Tax Features* 41, no. 8 (October 1997): 2, and the Internet, www.census.gov.
9. *Kansas City Star*, October 10, 1997, A-2.
10. U.S. Bureau of the Census, *Federal Expenditures by State for Fiscal Year 1996*, Table 7 (Washington, DC: Government Printing Office, 1996).
11. U.S. Bureau of the Census, *Statistical Abstract of the United States*, (Washington, DC: Government Printing Office, 1997), 844.

12. U.S. Bureau of the Census, *State and Metropolitan Area Data Book 1991* (Washington, DC: Government Printing Office, 1991).

13. These constant dollar figures use implicit price deflators and chain-type price indices for personal consumption. Council of Economic Advisors, 1991–1996, *Economic Report of the President*, and *Statistical Abstract of the United States* (Washington, DC: Government Printing Office, 1995–1997).

14. There is a research problem in trying to delineate some of the characteristics of MSAs. The Census Bureau no longer publishes as much data for metropolitan areas as was the case for earlier Census of Governments years due to cutbacks in funding and personnel. Failure to publish this type of information may, in part at least, be blamed on the fact that our representative system overrepresents suburban and rural areas. It may mean that state and federal policy makers see little need to document the differences that exist between central cities, suburban and fringe areas, and the more rural parts of the nation.

15. John W. Sloan, "The Reagan Presidency, Growing Inequality, and the American Dream," *Policy Studies Journal* 25, no. 3 (Fall 1997): 376.

16. Stephens and Parsons, "Rich States, Poor States."

17. This increase for corporate receipts probably understates the real increase because of the rapid rise in the number of nonprofit and not-for-profit corporations over this time span and the ability of multinational corporations to shift corporate receipts overseas.

Chapter 9

1. Charles E. Merriam, preface to Victor Jones, *Metropolitan Government* (Chicago: University of Chicago Press, 1942), ix.

2. L. J. Sharpe, "The Future of Metropolitan Government," in L. J. Sharpe, ed., *The Government of World Cities: The Future of the Metro Model* (New York: John Wiley & Sons, 1955), 27.

3. Kathryn A. Foster, *The Political Economy of Special Purpose Government* (Washington, DC: Georgetown University Press, 1997), 2.

4. Foster, *The Political Economy of Special Purpose Government*, 3.

5. For one example of this perspective, see, *The Problem of Special Districts in American Government* (Washington, DC: The United States Advisory Commission on Intergovernmental Relations, 1964).

6. James W. Doig and Jerry Mitchell, "Expertise, Democracy, and the Public Authority," in Jerry Mitchell, ed., *Public Authorities and Public Policy: The Business of Government* (Westport, CT: Greenwood Press, 1992), 23.

7. Robert Warren, Mark S. Rosentraub, and Louis F. Weschler, "Building Urban Governance: An Agenda for the 1990s," *Journal of Urban Affairs* 14, no. 3/4 (1992): 399–422.

8. H. V. Savitch, David Collins, Daniel Sanders, and John P. Markham, "Ties That Bind: Central Cities, Suburbs, and the New Metropolitan Region," *Economic Development Quarterly* 7 (November 1993): 342.

9. Warren et. al., "Building Urban Governance": 402.

10. Foster, *The Political Economy of Special Purpose Government*, 33.

11. Sharpe, "The Future of Metropolitan Government," 19.

12. Paul Studenski, *The Government of Metropolitan Areas in the United States* (New York: National Municipal League, 1930).

13. Victor Jones, *Metropolitan Government* (Chicago: University of Chicago Press, 1942).

14. Luther Halsey Gulick, *The Metropolitan Problem and American Ideas* (New York: Alfred A. Knopf, 1962).

15. Anthony Downs, *New Visions for Metropolitan America* (Washington, DC: Brookings Institution, 1994).

16. David Rusk, *Cities Without Suburbs* (Washington, DC: Woodrow Wilson Press, 1993).

17. *State Responsibility in Urban Regional Development: A Report to the Governors' Conference* (Chicago: Council of State Governments, 1962), 17.

18. Patricia S. Florestano and Vincent L. Marando, *The States and the Metropolis* (New York: Marcel Dekker, 1981), 16.

19. H. V. Savitch and Ronald K. Vogel, "Perspectives for the Present and Lessons for the Future," in H. V. Savitch and Ronald K. Vogel, eds., *Regional Politics: America in a Post-City Age* (Thousand Oaks, CA: Sage Publications, 1996), 294.

20. Warren et al., "Building Urban Governance: An Agenda for the 1990s," 403–5.

21. Milton Kotler, *Neighborhood Government: The Local Foundations of Political Life* (New York: Bobbs-Merrill, 1969).

22. Alan A. Altshuler, *Community Control: The Black Demand for Participation in Large American Cities* (New York: Pegasus, 1970).

23. Jeffrey M. Berry, Kent E. Portney, and Ken Thomson, *The Rebirth of Urban Democracy* (Washington, DC: Brookings Institution, 1993).

24. *The States and the Metropolitan Problem* (Chicago: Council of State Governments, 1956), 121–23.

25. *Governmental Structure, Organization, and Planning in Metropolitan Areas* (Washington, DC: United States Advisory Commission on Intergovernmental Relations, 1961), 26–30.

26. G. Ross Stephens, "Hartford's Metropolitan Experience," *Connecticut Government* 18 (October 1964): 1–4, 8.

27. *State Responsibility in Urban Regional Development*, 87.

28. Florestano and Marando, *The States and the Metropolis*, 160.

29. Foster, *The Political Economy of Special Purpose Government*, 102.

30. Weiping Wu, "Economic Competition and Resource Mobilization," in Michael A. Cohen, Blair A. Ruble, Joseph S. Tulchin, and Allison M. Garland, eds., *Preparing for the Urban Future: Global Pressures and Local Forces* (Washington, DC: Woodrow Wilson Center Press, 1996), 146–47.

31. Florestano and Marando, *The States and the Metropolis*, 46.

NAME INDEX

Abbott, C., 185n.24
Altshuler, A. A., 118, 171, 181n.121, 188n.91, 192n.22
Anderson, W., 35, 179n.34
Apperson, B., 189n.19

Baker, P. C., 175n.1, 178n.1
Banfield, E. C., 104, 148, 185n.32
Baumol, W., 107, 186n.6
Beard, C. A., 21
Beard, W., 21
Beckman, N., 190n.31
Benton, J. E., 80, 184n.21
Berry, J. M., 171, 192n.23
Bish, R. L., 47, 50, 112–114, 175n.3, 180n.101, 181n.114, 187n.53, 187n.64, 187n.66
Blomquist, W., 84–86, 184n.25, 184n.27, 184n.32
Bollens, J. C., 42, 51, 59, 180n.76, 180n.97, 180n.98, 180n.100, 181n.3, 182n.22, 183n.5
Booth, D., 73, 183n.6, 183n.7
Brandl, J., 185n.16
Buchanan, J. M., 107, 186n.8
Burgess, E. W., 32, 178n.12
Burns, N., 133, 189n.14

Campbell, A., 50, 181n.116
Carpenter, D. B., 178n.17
Cisneros, H. G., 48, 181n.108
Cohen, M. A., 192n.30
Collins, D., 191n.8
Cook, W. C., 42
Corty, F. L., 183n.2
Croucher, S. L., 95, 185n.15
Curry, R. L., 107, 186n.13

Dahl, R., 107, 186n.5
Davis, G., 115, 187n.75
de Tocqueville, A., 105–106
DeGrove, J. M., 183n.13, 190n.32
Dodge, W. R, 48, 181n.109

Doig, J. W., 169, 191n.6
Downs, A., 48, 107, 170, 181n.107, 185n.7, 192n.15
Downs, B. T., 182n.18
Dye, T. R., 50, 62, 181n.115

Egger, R. A., 35, 179n.33
Ehrenhalt, A., 101, 185n.25, 185n.28

Feiock, R., 80, 184n.20
Fillebrown, T. S., 75, 183n.10
Florestano, P. S., 170, 173–174, 192n.18, 192n.28, 192n.31
Foster, K. A., 168, 170, 173, 191n.3, 191n.4, 191n.10, 192n.29
French, R., 78, 183n.15
Friesema, H. P., 49, 181n.112

Gamble, D., 80, 184n.21
Garland, A. M., 192n.30
Gibbs, J., 178n.16
Goehlert, R., 175n.1, 178n.1
Goldbach, J., 11, 176n.13, 189n.21
Goodnow, F. J., 31, 178n.10
Grant, D. R., 74–75, 183n.8, 183n.9
Graves, B., 54
Graves, W. B., 8
Greene, J., 185n.8
Greer, S., 26, 51, 64, 178n.38, 181n.1
Grodzins, M., 104, 148, 185n.32
Gulick, L. H., 42–44, 170, 180n.79, 191n.13
Gurwitt, R., 184n.26

Hamilton, A., 105–106
Hanford, A. C., 35, 179n.35
Harrigan, J. L., 95, 98–99, 185n.16, 185n.17, 185n.21, 185n.23
Harrison, S. M., 35, 179n.32
Hart, K. D., 119, 188n.94
Havard, W., 70, 183n.2, 183n.3
Hawkins, B., 50, 181n.115

Hawley, A. H., 32, 178n18, 181n.118
Herman, H., 62
Hirsch, W. Z., 50, 109–110, 181n.117, 186n.26
Hooker, G. E., 33, 178n.22
Hoover, H., 32, 35

Jacobi, M., 54, 60
Janowitz, M., 178n.15
Jefferson, T., 51
Jenks, S. S., 125, 188n.4
Johnson, T., 182n.13
Johnson, W. C., 185n.16
Jones, V., vii, 39–42, 118, 167, 170, 179n.62, 179n.63, 180n.74, 180n.75, 188n.89, 191n.1, 191n.13

Kaifez, L., 189n.15
Kaufman, H., 143, 189n.27
Kean, R. G., 70, 183n.2, 183n.4
Keating, M., 119–120, 188n.92, 188n.95
Kelly, K. 54, 60
Kolderie, T., 185n.16
Kotler, M., 50, 118, 171, 181n.120, 180n.121, 188n.90, 192n.21

Leibman, C. S., 62
Lepawsky, A., 39, 179n.56
Levenson, R., 188n.5
Lindblom, C. E., 49, 107, 181n.110, 185n.3, 185n.12
Lipsey, C. M., 75, 183n.11
Lugar, R., 81–82

Madison, J., 105–106
Marando, V., vii, 50–52, 56, 59, 170, 173–174, 181n.119, 182n.7, 182n.11, 182n.12, 192n.18, 192n.31
Marinovich, C., 54, 58, 61
Markham, J. P., 191n.8
Martin, R., 76, 183n.13, 183n.14, 183n.16, 183n.17, 183n.18
Mathewson, K., 45, 180n.95, 180n.96
Maxey, C. C., 33–35, 178n.24, 179n.38
McArthur, R. E., 183n.6
McKenzie, R. D., 32, 39, 178n.14, 179n.60
Mencken, H. L., 155
Merriam, C. E., 39–40, 167, 179n.56, 191n.1
Mitchell, J., 169, 191n.6
Mogulof, M. B., 94, 104, 185n.9, 185n.29
Mumford, L., 3, 175n.1
Munro, W. B., 35, 179n.37
Murphy, T. P., 189n.20

Naftalin, A., 185n.16
Nelson, A. C., 185n.24, 185n.27

Nolen, J., 33, 35, 178n.21

Oakerson, R. J., 115–116, 187n.79
Olson, G. W., 176n.8, 177n.34
Olson, M., 107, 186n.9
Orfield, M., 185n.20, 185n.22
Ostrom, E., vi, 47, 49, 111, 113, 115, 175n.1, 178n.1, 180n.101, 187n.49, 187n.52, 187n.66, 187n.73, 187n.75, 187n.76
Ostrom, V., vi, 47, 105–106, 108–115, 175n.3, 180n.100, 181n.111, 185n.1, 186n.2, 186n.21, 187n.49, 187n.52, 187n.60, 187n.66, 187n.73, 187n.76
Owens, C. J., 184n.24

Park, R. E., 178n.12
Parks, R. B., 84–86, 116, 184n.25, 184n.27, 184n.32, 187n.66, 187n.79
Parratt, S. D., 39, 179n.56
Parsons, K. T., 190n.2, 191n.16
Percy, S. L., 115, 187n.78, 188n.99
Peterson, P., 185n.31
Phillips, K., 154, 190n.6
Pierce, N. R., 181n.104
Portney, K. E., 171, 192n.23

Queen, S. A., 178n.17

Reed, T. H., 14, 29, 34–35, 176n.17, 178n.2, 179n.31, 179n.31
Ricker, W. H., 107, 186n.11
Rogers, B. D., 75, 183n.11
Rosentraub, M. S., 191n.7
Ruble, B. A., 192n.30
Rusk, D., 47, 170, 181n.102, 192n.16

Sacks, S., 50, 181n.116
Salant, T. J., 189n.16, 189n.23
Sanders, D., 191n.8
Savitch, H. V., 169–170, 183n.19, 184n.1, 185n.17, 185n.24, 191n.8, 192n.19
Sayre, W. S., 143, 189n.27
Schiesl, M. J., 178n.19, 178n.20
Schmandt, H. J., 11, 51, 59, 176n.13, 180n.97, 180n.98, 180n.100, 181n.3, 182n.17, 182n.22, 183n.5, 189n.21
Sharpe, L. J., 167, 170, 191n.2, 191n.11
Sikes, G. C., 33,35, 178n.23
Sloan, J. W., 162, 191n.15
Sloan, L., 78, 183n.15
Sofen, E., 94, 184n.1, 184n.2, 184n.3, 185n.12
Sproule-Jones, M., 119, 188n.94
Stein, R., 145, 189n.28
Steineger, J., 54, 60

Stephens, G. R., 176n.6, 176n.7, 176n.8, 176n.9, 177n.23, 177n.25, 177n.34, 182n.17, 188n.3, 188n.5, 189n.24, 190n.2, 191n.16, 192n.26
Stowers, G., 94, 184n.1, 184n.4, 184n.11, 185n.14
Studenski, P., vi, 29, 35–40, 170, 175n.2, 177n.29, 178n.5, 179n.40, 191n.12
Swanson, B., 80–81, 183n.19, 184n.22

Tableman, B., 180n.77
Taylor, F. W., 31, 178n.11
Thomson, K., 171, 192n.23
Tiebout, C. M., 49, 105, 107–109, 119, 186n.14, 186n.21
Tulchin, J. S., 192n.30
Tullock, G., 107, 185n.10, 186n.8

Vogel, R. K., 170, 183n.19, 184n.1, 185n.17, 185n.24, 189n.21, 192n.19

Wade, L. L., 107, 186n.13
Walker, D. B., 122, 147–148, 188n.1, 190n.33
Warren, R., 49, 105, 108–112, 169, 171, 185n.1, 186n.21, 186n.26, 187n.53, 191n.7, 191n.9, 192n.20
Weschler, L. F., 191n.7
West, B., 73
Whitaker, G. P., 115, 187n.74
Whitely, C. R., 51–52, 56, 59, 182n.7, 182n.11
Whitwell, C. G., 183n.2
Wikstrom, N., 178n.37, 180n.99, 181n.113, 189n.19
Willbern, Y., 86, 184n.24, 184n.28
Williams, O., 26, 62, 177n.30, 178n.39, 178n.3, 178n.4, 182n.18
Wilson, W., 31, 178n.6, 178n.7, 178n.8, 178n.9
Wirt, F. M., 182n.17
Wisdom, B., 60
Wood, R. C., 42, 51, 59, 67, 180n.79, 181n.2, 182n.14, 182n.23
Woodbury, C., 41
Wright, D. S., 125, 188n.4
Wright, J., 35, 179n.36
Wu, Weiping, 173, 192n.30

Zimmer, B. G., 32, 178n.18, 181n.118
Zimmerman, J. F., 183n.1

SUBJECT INDEX

Administrative city, 11–14
Advisory Commission on Intergovernmental
   Relations (ACIR), 11–13, 45, 53, 66,
   175n.2, 190n.1
   public choice, 117
   recommendations for metropolitan
      government, 172
African Americans, 56
Annexation, 24, 29, 46
Association of Bay Area Governments, 49
Atlanta, Georgia
   annexation, 25, 102, 167
Attitudes about metropolitan government
   citizens, 62
   public officials, 62

Baton Rouge–East Baton Rouge Parish
   consolidated government, 30, 68
   annexation, 25
   assessment of, 70, 87
   city-county consolidation, 46, 104
   structure, service delivery, and funding, 68–70
Bureaucracy, 21–24, 58–59

Canadian provinces, 127–129
Census of Governments, 6, 7, 19, 129, 175n.2,
   191n.14
Central cities, 16, 18, 30
   extraterritorial powers, 40
   dominance of, 58
Centralization/decentralization, 125, 127–128,
   182n.19
Chicago, Illinois, 39
   fragmentation, 39
Citistates, 47–48
City-county consolidation, 24, 30, 135, 137, 140
City-county separation, 24, 30, 37, 40, 52
Coastal county areas, 3–4, 17
Committee for Economic Development, 44–45,
   113, 117–118
Contract city, 11–14

Contracting, 145–146
Council of State Governments, 170, 172
Councils of governments (COGs), 25, 147, 168
County government, 6, 8–10, 19, 129
   county home rule charters, 136
   functions of, 133–136
   Hawaii, 134
   number of, 133
   optional forms, 136
   origins of, 133
Crisis situations, 59–60

Democracy, 105–107
Department of Housing and Urban
      Development (HUD), 147
Department of Transportation (DOT), 147
Dependent city, 11–14
District of Columbia, 150
   tax capacity, 150
Dynamic model of city, 141–144

Ecology of local government, 57, 67
Elected officials, 58, 173
Enabling rules, 116–117

Factors influencing structural reform, 56–62
Family income, 161–163
Federal government, 41, 43
   federal aid to state and local government,
      64–66
   urban planning, 146
Federal system, 5–6, 122, 149, 162, 169–170
Ford Foundation, 44
Functional triads (iron triangles), 143

Gerrymandering, 18
Government employees, 21–23
Government reform
   opposition, 66–67
   support, 66–67
Grants-in-aid, 22, 125, 150, 156

federal aid to state and local government,
64–66
state grants to local government, 22–23
Grass-roots government, 51

Hartford Metropolitan District, 172

Incrementalism, 168
Indianapolis–Marion County consolidated
government, 68, 192
assessment of, 85–86, 87
city-county consolidation, 46, 81–86, 104
structure, service delivery, and funding, 83–85
Intergovernmental transfers, 155–158, 161
contracts, 157
grants-in-aid, 22–23, 64–66
services-in-aid, 160
shared taxes, 157
Interstate and international metropolitan areas,
17

Jacksonville–Duval County consolidated
government, 30, 68, 102, 167
assessment of, 87
city-county consolidation, 46, 75–81, 104
structure, service delivery, and funding, 78–81

Kansas City, Kansas–Wyandotte County
consolidated government, 53–61, 135
central city dominance, 58
organization, 54–55
patronage, 58–59
white flight, 56
Kansas City, Missouri, 20
annexation, 25, 46
Jackson County, Missouri reorganization, 135
metropolitan population, 20
Union Station, 53

Lifestyle services, 26, 29, 61
Local role in the federal system, 14, 116–117,
124–129

Metropolis, 14–15
Metropolitan areas, problems of, 36, 38–39, 42,
48–49, 174
Metropolitan fund, 45–46
Metropolitan government
intellectual underpinnings, 31
unitary approach, 29
Metropolitan St. Louis Survey, 53
Metropolitan statistical areas (MSAs), 3–4,
15–18, 122, 149, 176n.18
consolidated metropolitan statistical areas
(CMSAs), 16–18, 20

New England county metropolitan areas
(NECMAs), 15–16
primary metropolitan statistical areas
(PMSAs), 16
urbanized areas (UAs), 16
Metropolitan Washington Council of
Governments, 49
Miami–Dade County consolidated government,
88, 113, 167
assessment of, 91
establishment of Metro, 88–89
federative government, 91, 94
structure, service delivery, and funding,
83–85, 103
Municipal corporations, 172
Municipalities, 6, 8–9, 19–20, 127, 129
activity of, 136–137
annexation, 29
number of, 136

Nashville–Davidson County consolidated
government, 30, 68, 102, 167
assessment of, 74–75, 87
city-county consolidation, 46, 52, 70–75, 104
structure, service delivery and funding, 73, 74,
103
National Municipal League, 32–33
New England county metropolitan areas
(NECMAs), 16–17

Organization for Economic Cooperation and
Development (OECD), 160

Philadelphia metropolitan area, 62
Planning, 147
Political city, 11–14
Political leadership, 60, 107
Politics-administration dichotomy, 31
Port Authority of New York and New Jersey,
172
Portland, Oregon Metro, 68, 99–102, 122, 167,
172
assessment of, 101
structure, responsibilities, and revenues,
100–101, 103
Urban Growth Boundary (UGB), 101
Public administration, 105–107
Public choice, vii, 49, 167
philosophical basis, 105–107
political economy studies, 107;
Public education, 138–141, 158–159
expenditures, 141, 158–159
Public goods, 108–110, 112–113, 145
Public interest groups, 143

Regression line index, 151–152, 190n.5
Representation, 57
Residential Community Associations
    (RCAs), also known as homeowners
    and condominium associations, 5–6,
    11–12, 20, 63, 145

Schmandt and Goldbach conceptual model,
    11–13
  administrative city, 11
  contract city, 11, 13
  dependent city, 11–13
  political city, 11, 13
School districts, 6–7, 10–11, 18–20, 129
  activity of, 142
  number of, 140–141
  voter approval of taxes, 52
Service delivery, 155, 163
  regional approaches, 123–124
Single and dual majorities, 61
Southeast Michigan Council of Governments,
    49
Special districts, 6, 8, 18–20, 40, 129
  disestablishment of, 34
  numbers of, 129–132, 168
Special legislation, 133
St. Louis County, 136
State and local taxes
  tax revenue capacity, 149–150, 165
  tax structures, 152
State governments, 26
  metropolis, 43
  relationship to localities, 41, 124–125
State planning and development districts
    (SPDDs), 147
State role vis-a-vis local governments, 127–129
State systems of local government (SSLG), 6, 8

combined systems, 10
conventional systems, 10
New England towns, 10
southern system, 9
state-county type, 9
state-municipal type, 9
Suburban areas, 16–17, 103, 126, 161
  suburban ideology, 51
  opposition to metro government, 41
Suburban municipalities, 58
System-maintaining services, 26, 29, 61, 122

Taxing areas, 61–62
Towns and townships, 6–8, 10, 19–20, 129,
    136–138
  functions of, 138
  Midwestern, weak type townships, 137–138
  New England townships, 136
  number of, 128
  personnel, 140
Toy governments, 129
Twin Cities Metropolitan Council, 95–99
  assessment of, 98–99
  Minneapolis-St.Paul, 68, 95, 102, 122, 167,
    172
  moralistic political culture, 95
  structure, responsibilities, and funding,
    96–98, 103

Urbanized areas, 4, 16

Virginia's independent cities, 62
Voters, 59
  voting with feet, 108

White flight, 56